Workers' participation
in decisions within undertakings

Workers' participation in decisions within undertakings

International Labour Office   Geneva

ISBN 92-2-101988-8 (limp cover)
ISBN 92-2-101987-X (hard cover)

First published 1981

Photoconposed in India
Printed in Switzerland

The International Labour Office has long kept track of the question of workers' participation in decisions within undertakings, and has regularly published information on the measures taken in that regard in countries belonging to the Organisation. The International Labour Conference, for its part, has adopted several instruments dealing with particularly important aspects of such participation. A first group included the Right to Organise and Collective Bargaining Convention, 1949, the Collective Agreements Recommendation, 1951, and the Co-operation at the Level of the Undertaking Recommendation, 1952. At that time the word "participation" was not widely used and the then customary terms "negotiation" and "collaboration" were preferred. More recently the Conference adopted the Communications within the Undertaking Recommendation and the Examination of Grievances Recommendation in 1967, and the Workers' Representatives Convention and Recommendation in 1971.[1]

Over the past 15 years the ILO has held three meetings (Geneva, 1967; Belgrade, 1969; Oslo, 1974) on the subject of workers' participation in decisions within undertakings from a world point of view; another such meeting is to be held in the Netherlands in 1981. For the first of those meetings a comparative study was prepared, and published, with extracts from the report on the meeting, in the Labour-Management Relations Series.[2] The present work is a new, updated and consequently rearranged version of that study.

This study must not be regarded as expressing the views of the International Labour Organisation: it is published for information only, with the intention of giving readers an up-to-date picture of the various systems of workers' participation in decision-making.

Three observations need to be made with regard to the scope of the subject. First, as the title indicates, the subject does not include participation at the industrial or national level, in spite of the possible connection between such arrangements and participation at the level of the undertaking.[3] Secondly, the subject of this study is participation in decisions within undertakings, whether they belong to the private, the mixed or the public sector, whereas the public service is not included. Thirdly, the present study concentrates on institutional machinery for participation, and does not deal with new forms of work organisation that tend to associate the workers with the programming and organisation of their own tasks in factories and offices; this latter kind of participation, which is discussed in other publications,[4] has objectives and characteristics of its own and gives rise in the circles concerned to problems and reactions which are not always identical with those mentioned in the present volume.

This new version has been prepared by Mr. Jacques Monat, of the Labour Law and Labour Relations Branch of the International Labour Office. The above-mentioned three meetings have provided valuable information,[5] as have studies on workers' participation in management by the International Institute for Labour Studies.[6] Lastly, the present work is also based on the steady stream of information reaching the Office through the publications it receives and meetings or missions in which its officials take part.[7] Since, in the field of participation, change is constant and often rapid, readers wishing to be regularly informed of new developments and of measures taken or proposed in various countries are advised to consult the ILO's quarterly *Social and Labour Bulletin*, in which articles on this subject are regularly published.

Notes

[1] These instruments can conveniently be consulted in ILO: *International standards and guiding principles, 1944–1973*, Labour-Management Relations Series, No. 44 (Geneva, 1975).

[2] idem: *Participation of workers in decisions within undertakings*, Documents of a technical meeting, Geneva, 20–29 November 1967, Labour-Management Relations Series, No. 33 (Geneva, 1969).

[3] In this connection see idem: *Participation by employers' and workers' organisations in economic and social planning* (Geneva, 1971). It will be recalled that in 1960 the International Labour Conference had adopted the Consultation (Industrial and National Levels) Recommendation (No. 113). See idem: *Consultation at the industrial and national levels*, General survey by the Committee of Experts on the Application of Conventions and Recommendations, Report III (Part 4B), International Labour Conference, 61st Session, 1976.

[4] idem: *New forms of work organisation*, Vol. 1: *Denmark, Norway and Sweden, France, Federal Republic of Germany, United Kingdom, United States*; Vol. 2: *German Democratic Republic, India, Italy, USSR, Economic costs and benefits* (Geneva, 1979); idem: *Managing and developing new forms of work organisation*, edited by G. Kanawaty, Management Development Series, No. 16 (Geneva, 1980); also International Institute for Labour Studies, Research Series: No. 4: *Alternative forms of work organisation: Improvements of labour conditions and productivity in Western Europe*, by Reinhold Weil (Geneva, 1976); No. 6: *The French approach to the humanisation of work*, by Yves Delamotte (Geneva, 1976); No. 8: *Democracy at work and perspectives on the quality of working life in Scandinavia*, by E. Thorsrud (Geneva, 1976); No. 10: *Group production methods and humanisation of*

work: The evidence in industrialised countries, by John L. Burbidge (Geneva, 1976); No. 11: *The quality of working life: Trends in Japan,* by Shin-ichi Takezawa (Geneva, 1976); No. 14: *The attitudes of French and Italian trade unions to the "humanisation of work",* by Yves Delamotte (Geneva, 1976); No. 15: *Assessing the quality of working life: The US experience,* by Stanley E. Seashore (Geneva, 1976); No. 18: *The organisation of work and industrial relations in the Italian engineering industry,* by Matteo Rollier (Geneva, 1976); No. 33: *Social aspects of work organisation: Implications for social policy and labour relations,* Selected papers and proceedings of an international symposium, Moscow, 15–18 February 1977 (Geneva, 1978); No. 50: *Les aspects sociaux de l'organisation du travail: Un bilan provisoire,* by Yves Delamotte (Geneva, 1979).

[5] See ILO and United Nations Development Programme: *Report on the international seminar on workers' participation in decisions within undertakings,* Belgrade, 2–11 December 1969 (Geneva, ILO, 1970), and ILO: *Workers' participation in decisions within undertakings, Oslo symposium,* Summary of discussions of a symposium on workers' participation in decisions within undertakings, Oslo, 20–30 August 1974, Labour-Management Relations Series, No. 48 (Geneva, 1976).

[6] See in particular, International Institute for Labour Studies, Research Series: Workers' participation in management: No. 29: *Workers' participation in management in Israel: Successes and failures,* by Amira Galin and Jay Y. Tabb (Geneva, 1978); No. 30: *Workers' participation in management in Poland,* by Z. Rybicki, M. Blazejczyck, A. Kowalik, M. Trzeciak and J. Waclawek (Geneva, 1978); No. 32: *Workers' participation in management in the Federal Republic of Germany,* by F. Fürstenberg (Geneva, 1978); No. 34: *Workers' participation in management in France,* by L. Greyfié de Bellecombe (Geneva, 1978); No. 35: *Workers' participation in management in Spain,* by Juan N. Garcia-Nieto (Geneva, 1978); No. 58: *Workers' participation in management in Great Britain,* by O. Clarke (Geneva, 1980).

[7] Most of the works, reports and articles consulted are listed in the bibliographies issued by the International Institute for Labour Studies: *Workers' participation in management, Selected bibliography, 1950–1970,* by Annette Marclay (Geneva, 1971); idem, *1970–1974,* by Roland van Holle and Maryse Gaudier (Geneva, 1975); idem, *1974–1976,* by Maryse Gaudier (Geneva, 1977); idem, *1977–1979,* by Maryse Gaudier (Geneva, to be published in 1981).

CONTENTS

PART I

GENERAL INTRODUCTION

The object of these introductory chapters is to provide the reader with a brief general review of the subject of workers' participation in decisions within undertakings: it is important to convey some impression of the breadth, diversity and complexity of the subject before proceeding to a detailed description of the various procedures for such participation, the several fields in which they may apply and the problems which they raise.

AN INCREASINGLY TOPICAL SUBJECT

1

The idea that the workforce should have a share in decisions which affect the operation of the undertaking was variously expressed in some of the social doctrines that emerged in the nineteenth century; but only towards the end of the First World War did it take broad practical shape (apart from collective bargaining and the growth of co-operative enterprises) with the establishment of joint committees, councils, etc., in a number of countries. In Great Britain joint committees were advocated by the Whitley Report of 1916 and set up in municipal undertakings two years later; legislation on works councils was promulgated in Austria (1919), Czechoslovakia (1920) and Germany (1920); factory committees were recognised in Russia by decree of 23 April 1917.

After prospering for some years the movement for institutional forms of participation, except collective bargaining, lost much of its impetus, and the question dropped into the background for a whole decade. Efforts were indeed made in some parts of the world to induce employers to recognise trade unions and negotiate with them,[1] so that they might share in handling problems of immediate concern to the workers; yet in accordance with the ideas of the time, those efforts tended in fact to emphasise the clash of interests between workers and employers rather than the desirability of associating the workforce in settlement of the problems raised by an industrial operation.

However, during and after the Second World War the subject of workers' participation in decisions within undertakings rose to prominence once again. That was the time at which works councils or committees were established or re-established, by law or by agreement, in several European countries.[2] It was also the time when systematic arrangements for joint representation on supervisory boards[3] were introduced in the big West German coal and steel companies.

In the past 15 years or so this renewal of interest in institutions for workers' participation in decisions within undertakings (apart from collective bargaining) has been particularly pronounced in Europe and in some developing countries.

In Western Europe interest in the subject has been reflected in various ways: the Commission of the European Communities has organised research and made proposals; special committees have been set up to consider various aspects of participation in, for instance, Finland, France, the Federal Republic of Germany, the Netherlands, Norway, Sweden and the United Kingdom; in Denmark and Norway the national agreements on co-operation in the undertaking have been revised. The legislation on works committees or councils has been amended or supplemented in Austria, Belgium, France, the Federal Republic of Germany, Luxembourg, the Netherlands and Spain; workforce representation on the supervisory boards of companies has been developed by way of legislation in Austria and the Federal Republic of Germany, and such representation has been introduced, also by legislation, on boards of directors in the private sector in Denmark, Luxembourg, Norway and Sweden; important Bills have been brought before parliament, or have been prepared, in Denmark, the Netherlands and the United Kingdom. In Greece the Constitution which came into force in 1975 expressly states that general statutory conditions of employment may be supplemented by collective agreements freely entered into. In Norway the right of participation was the subject of a constitutional amendment in 1980. In Portugal the Constitution of 1976 proclaims the right to bargain collectively and the workers' right to set up workers' committees and co-ordinating committees for the defence of their interests in undertakings: these bodies, which have power to supervise management, are now governed by a law issued in September 1979. In Spain the Constitution adopted in 1978 provides that the right to bargain collectively shall be guaranteed by law and that the public authorities shall effectively promote the various kinds of participation within the undertaking.

In Yugoslavia, which has established since 1950 an elaborate system of self-management, worker participation in the solution of problems at the level of the undertaking is a major objective of the system and a series of constitutional and legislative reforms were introduced in the latter part of the 1970s.

In the USSR and other planned economy countries of Eastern Europe the economic reforms introduced since 1965 have contributed to the development of participation by workers and their representatives in management and to a broadening of the scope of works agreements. (Previously, apart from a few tasks which were left to the works trade union committees, it had been management policy to insist on the sole responsibility of the manager of the undertaking.) This development was expressed particularly in the new labour codes that were adopted in several of the countries in question; and the right of participation is embodied today in the constitutions of Czechoslovakia, the German Democratic Republic, Poland and Romania, as well as in the basic principles of labour legislation in the USSR and its federated republics.

In Australia the Federal Government set up in June 1978 a tripartite committee of experts to advise on participation because it wished workers and employers to work out their own arrangements. A few months before, the congress of the Australian Council of Trade Unions had adopted a detailed industrial democracy policy. The committee's work has already led to the publication of a tripartite statement on participation.[4]

In Japan various publications, studies and experiments bear witness to the interest aroused by the question of worker participation in decisions within the undertaking.

In Canada and the United States observers of the system of collective bargaining at company or plant level which is generally practised in those countries have often emphasised the degree of participation and industrial democracy which the system engenders.[5] Collective bargaining at the level of the undertaking or establishment has developed in several other industrial market economy countries, particularly Italy, Japan, the United Kingdom and Sweden, where a law adopted in 1976 confers special importance upon it.

In the developing countries collective bargaining, usually and mainly at the level of the undertaking or establishment, has in most cases been developed and improved as the unions have grown stronger and the workers' level of education has risen. Decisions have been taken, requiring workers to be represented in various ways on management bodies, in Africa (Algeria, Angola, Benin, the Congo, Egypt, Madagascar, Mali, Mozambique, Somalia and Tanzania), Latin America (Peru and Venezuela), Southern Asia (India, Pakistan and Sri Lanka) and the Middle East (Iraq, Syria and Democratic Yemen). This representation is mostly in public undertakings. It often stems from a more or less far-reaching policy of socialisation or self-management (particularly in Algeria and Peru). Moreover, various measures—mostly legislative—have been taken to establish, provide for or recommend the establishment of works committees or councils in Africa (Burundi, Gabon, Mauritania, Mauritius, Somalia, the Sudan, Swaziland, Tanzania, Tunisia and Zambia), in Southern and Eastern Asia (Burma, India, the Republic of Korea, Nepal, Pakistan, Sri Lanka and Thailand), in the Middle East (Bahrain, Iraq, Oman, the Syrian Arab Republic), and also in Jamaica, Panama and Uruguay in the Americas. High-level committees have recently considered the problems and prospects of workers' participation in India and Jamaica. In the Philippines the President of the Republic wrote to the Secretary of Labour and to the presidents of the employers' and workers' confederations on 1 May 1978, instructing them "to devise machinery to promote systematically and on a sustained basis improved labour-management co-operation within undertakings". This machinery "should focus on matters of common interest to employers and workers which are not usually dealt with through collective bargaining". In Ecuador the Constitution which was adopted by referendum in 1978 stated that workers' participation in management through share ownership would be promoted by the State. In India a recent constitutional amendment requires measures—legislative or other—to be taken with a view to ensuring workers' participation in management.

The introduction or development of some institutional arrangements for participation (particularly workers' representation on the boards of directors or supervisory boards of private companies) has generally been opposed in management circles, and does not have the support of all the world's trade union movements (see Chapter 3). However, the above instances suffice to indicate the extent of the interest presently taken in the problem of workers' participation in many countries. They show also that the term "participation" may cover very different situations, and it is therefore necessary to state the meaning or meanings of the term as clearly as possible. In that connection reference may be made to the report of a technical meeting on rights of trade union representatives and participation of workers in decisions within undertakings, which was held in Geneva in 1967:

> . . . The meeting considered . . . whether it was possible to arrive at an internationally agreed definition of the term "participation", in order to elucidate what was meant by "participation of workers in decisions within undertakings". It found that it was not possible to arrive at such a definition, as the term "participation" was interpreted differently by different categories of people in different countries and at different times . . . However, . . . the expression "participation of workers in decisions within undertakings" allowed a comparison of the influence of workers on the preparation, making and follow-up of decisions taken at the undertaking level in various matters (such as . . . wages and conditions of work, . . . discipline and employment, vocational training, . . . technological change and organisation of production, as well as their social consequences, investment and planning, etc.) [by] methods as different as joint consultation and communications, collective bargaining, representation of workers [on] managerial [bodies] and workers' self-management. . . The meeting emphasised that the expression "participation of workers in decisions within undertakings" was distinct from and therefore wider than the concept of workers' participation in management.[6]

It should also be borne in mind throughout perusal of the present study that the same or similar terms may cover widely different realities, according to the place. For instance, a "works council"[7] in Austria or the Federal Republic of Germany is not identical with a "works council"[8] in Belgium or a "works committee"[9] in France, for one thing because in Austria and the Federal Republic of Germany the council is composed of workforce representatives only. Joint consultation committees in Japan are different too, since there the personnel are generally represented only by trade union delegates and the committee's functions may vary from one establishment to another. Nor does the term "collective bargaining" necessarily imply an identical process in different countries, for example it may take place at various levels.

Notes

[1] The Wagner Act in the United States (1935), the Matignon Agreements in France (1936), the Saltsjöbaden Agreement in Sweden (1938).

[2] Joint production committees were set up during the war in several English-speaking countries. In addition, relevant legislation was adopted in Western Germany in 1946 and 1952, as well as in Austria in 1947, Belgium in 1948, Bulgaria in 1947, Czechoslovakia in 1945, Finland in 1946, France in 1945, Poland in 1945 and Spain in 1947; and national agreements were concluded in Denmark in 1947, Norway in 1945 and Sweden in 1946. See ILO: *Co-operation in industry*, Studies and reports, New series, No. 26 (Geneva, 1951).

[3] The supervisory board of a company is responsible for appointing, supervising and if necessary dismissing the members of the board of management, and in addition must give its approval before decisions of major importance to the company can be taken.

[4] National Employee Participation Steering Committee: *Employee participation: A broad view* (Canberra, Australian Government Publishing Service, 1979).

[5] See, for instance, John P. Windmuller (ed.): "Industrial democracy and industrial relations", in *Annals of the American Academy of Political and Social Sciences* (Philadelphia), May 1977.

[6] ILO: *Participation of workers in decisions within undertakings*, Documents of a technical meeting (Geneva, 20–29 November 1967), Labour-Management Relations Series, No. 33, op. cit., p. 153, paras. 40–43.

[7] *Betriebsrat.*

[8] *Conseil d'entreprise.*

[9] *Comité d'entreprise.*

VARIETIES OF PARTICIPATION

2

The variety of conceptions of workers' participation in decisions within undertakings can best be appreciated by considering the objectives sought by such participation, the means used to bring it about, and the areas in which the participation is applied.

It should be borne in mind that in addition to participation by workers in decisions within undertakings there are other, sometimes to some extent related forms of participation such as the following:

(1) Popular participation in development. This is essentially a way of mobilising the people of a country so as to associate them as much as possible in the development effort (it may of course be extended to the kind of workers' participation at issue here).

(2) Profit-sharing. Admittedly this aims at fuller identification of the workforce with the undertaking, but in practice it is seldom combined with greater participation in decisions, and is most often just a form of bonus payment.

(3) Workers' participation in company capital, as through employees' shareholding. This too is aimed at fuller identification with the undertaking, but it occurs only exceptionally on a scale such as to bring about any significantly greater participation in decisions.

OBJECTIVES

The various objectives claimed for more or less pronounced participation of workers in decisions within undertakings are often closely linked: but for the sake of clarity an attempt will be made to classify them in three main groups, depending on whether the chief emphasis is placed on ethical, on socio-political or on economic considerations.

Ethical or moral objectives

In an ethical or moral context, participation in decision-making is designed to promote individual development or fulfilment, in accordance with a conception of human rights and dignity to which the Universal Declaration of Human Rights (1948) probably gives the most widely publicised expression:

> All human beings are born free and equal in dignity and rights. They are endowed with reason and conscience and should act towards one another in a spirit of brotherhood. (Article 1)
> Everyone, as a member of society, . . . is entitled to realisation . . . of the economic, social and cultural rights indispensable for his dignity and the free development of his personality. (Article 22)

This general proposition, that all workers, as human beings, must be enabled to seek full development of their personality, has been elaborated in various doctrinal statements—papal encyclicals,[1] national constitutions, the programmes of trade union movements, management statements and the recent reports of bodies commissioned by the governments of a number of countries to study and encourage institutional participation.

For instance, the special Advisory Committee set up by the Government of Jamaica defined "worker participation" as "the extension of the individual's human rights at the work place" and stressed that the "procedures, institutions, rules and styles of management" should bring the worker "recognition, treatment and attention as a human being rather than as a mere statistical unit of production".[2]

In support of this ethical approach it has been pointed out that the workers, who contribute to the production of goods and services—sometimes at the risk of their health and even their lives—and in any case pass most of the day in the undertaking and depend upon it for their livelihood and that of their families, are entitled to have their point of view taken into account as regards its operation.

The above humanitarian ideas are reinforced by the notions of equity and social justice now current in both the industrialised and the developing countries although such notions have often been neglected during the process of industrialisation and in proposed models of industrial organisation and management.

Lastly, it has become clear that in most countries nowadays the younger generations are increasingly unwilling to accept authority in which they have no share and are also determined to participate in decisions. This is no doubt due to more education and to the development of the pupils' critical faculties in post-primary schooling, and also to new methods of education ("pupil participation") which encourage initiative, creativity and readiness for the collective responsibility required in small work groups even among the very young.

Socio-political objectives

Socio-political objectives vary widely, and are often presented under the label of "industrial democracy". It is often pointed out that at election time the most eminent participants in radio or television broadcasts emphasise the importance of every citizen's vote for the conduct of public affairs. Since in a democratic system workers have the same political rights as other citizens, it seems odd that they should not be entitled to a say, within the undertakings where they are employed, in decisions which directly concern them. A Swiss trade union writer states that political democracy is incompatible with the absence of democracy in economic life: a citizen cannot be regarded as sufficiently mature for political democracy and simultaneously denied democratic rights in economic life.[3]

Accordingly, those who wish to have the workers participate in decisions within undertakings, and to strengthen political democracy by applying its principles in the economic field, have often declared their intention of changing the state of affairs described above. A study carried out in South Australia, for instance, emphasised that the support given to democratic government institutions is stronger among people who have experienced democracy in other situations, for instance at school or at the workplace.[4]

A "Green Book" published by the Commission of the European Communities in 1975,[5] refers to "the increasing recognition being given to the democratic imperative that those who will be substantially affected by decisions made by social and political institutions must be involved in the making of those decisions":

In particular, employees are increasingly seen to have interests in the functioning oı enterprises which can be as substantial as those of shareholders, and sometimes more so. Employees not only derive their income from enterprises which employ them, but they devote a large proportion of their daily lives to the enterprise. Decisions taken by or in the enterprise can have a substantial effect on their economic circumstances, both immediately and in the longer term; the satisfaction which they derive from work; their health and physical condition; the time and energy which they can devote to their families and to activities other than work; and even their sense of dignity and autonomy as human beings. Accordingly, continuing consideration is being given to the problem of how and to what extent employees should be able to influence the decisions of enterprises which employ them.[5]

This general objective of making the undertaking more democratic may lead to the introduction of quite widely differing arrangements according to the particular purpose in each case, which may be to give the workers (i.e. their representatives) the right to negotiate conditions of employment at the level of the undertaking and to protect themselves against the consequences of managerial decisions which may be unfavourable to them; or to associate the workers on an advisory footing in the discussion of questions of common interest raised by the operation of the undertaking: or again to change the rules governing the operation of the undertaking or certain parts of it.

Sometimes, indeed, the objective of making the workplace more democratic by way of worker participation in decisions at that level is part of a broader objective, namely to transform the whole economy.

In Belgium, for instance, works councils were introduced as part of a more general "Economic Organisation Act", which also established joint councils for particular industries and a central economic council.

The industrial democracy programme adopted by the Swedish Trade Union Confederation (LO) at its 1971 Congress emphasised that—

> Industrial democracy is part of the effort made by the labour movement to extend democracy throughout society. . . . Life away from the workplace has developed in one way and life at the workplace in another. The difference constantly grows and is at the root of the increasing need which employees feel to exert an influence on conditions of work and on management. . . . If arbitrary situations are allowed to persist in one sector of society, they are an obstacle to the progress of democracy in the other sectors. . . . Industrial democracy should be regarded as part of the general process of democratisation.[6]

However, the programme indicates that "in this effort to democratise the whole of society, the methods of political democracy need not be transmitted to other levels of society. Democratic values should rather be allowed to impregnate the whole social order and relations between individuals".[7]

The possible transforming effect of participation on the economy and society has also been mentioned, for instance, in the United Kingdom, in the report of a committee of inquiry on industrial democracy (the "Bullock Report"),[8] and, in the Federal Republic of Germany, in the report of the committee on participation set up by the Federal Government to survey the situation and make proposals (the "Biedenkopf Committee")[9] as well as in the programme of the German Confederation of Trade Unions (DGB). Similarly, an extensive study published by the European Trade Union Institute establishes a link between the notion of a "participative economy" and the workers' growing aspiration to participate not only in political life but also in economic life and decision-making.[10]

In India the Second Five-Year Plan, which was directed to the establishment of a socialist society, stated that a socialist society was based not only on cash incentives but also on the idea of serving the community and its willingness to recognise such service; so individual workers must be induced to feel that in their own way they were helping to build a State directed towards progress. Consequently the introduction of industrial democracy was a prerequisite for the establishment of a socialist society.

The report of a committee set up by the Government of Jamaica states that the introduction of worker participation in a mixed economy can be called "a logical and organic development on the road to social equality, social justice and the total democratisation of power".[11]

In many developing countries growing interest in worker participation in decisions within undertakings seems to be regarded as a by no means minor element in the participation of the people in development which is mentioned in the United Nations international strategy for the Second Development Decade in connection with the attainment of the objectives of national development plans.

The programme of action adopted by the tripartite world conference on employment, income distribution and social progress and the international division of labour, which was held in Geneva in June 1976, recalls in this connection that "a basic-needs-oriented policy implies the participation of the people in making the decisions which affect them through organisations of their own choice":

Government must try to involve employers' organisations, trade unions and rural workers' and producers' organisations in decision-making procedures and in the process of implementation at all levels. . . . Employers' and producers' organisations, trade unions and other workers' organisations such as rural workers' organisations have an important role to play in the design and implementation of successful development strategies. . . . [12]

For its part, the "ICFTU Development Charter" adopted by the Executive Committee of the International Confederation of Free Trade Unions in May 1978 states in paragraph 24 that collective bargaining in particular and industrial democracy in general lead to a more equitable distribution of income and the satisfaction of basic needs.

In various countries the participation of workers' organisations in economic and social planning and programming is often used as an argument to obtain similar participation at the level of the undertaking. As pointed out by some of the experts at the technical meeting held in Geneva in 1967, decisions to be taken at the level of the undertaking might be influenced by decisions already taken at the national level, particularly those of joint or tripartite committees on which employers and trade unions were represented.[13] The links between workers' participation at the level of the undertaking and the possibility of having them participate in economic organisation at the national level were among the subjects chosen for discussion by the members of the symposium on workers' participation in decisions within undertakings that was held by the ILO in Oslo in August 1974.[14]

As was emphasised by the author of the summary of the discussion at Oslo—

Workers' participation is an eminently political issue. This does not only mean that in a pluralistic society legislation introducing some form of workers' participation will be the outcome of the interplay between political parties and other forces exercising political power and influence, and hence may become a central issue in parliamentary elections. What is more important is that if the term "political" refers in general to any action aimed at shaping or changing the society in which we live, then workers' participation has a vital political dimension. This is least visible in those countries where workers' participation is looked upon merely as a management technique aimed at improving either work organisation at the shop-floor level or employer-employee communications. It is clearest in schemes that aim at redefining the respective roles of owners, managers and workers in the enterprise, and at radically changing the power relationships between them.[15]

Often, indeed, the issue of workers' participation is stated nowadays in terms of the distribution—or redistribution—of power in the under-taking:

Among those who favour the principle of associating workers with the decision-making process at the enterprise level there are two broad schools of thought. There are first those who argue that decision-making power derives from ownership and that therefore the logical way of involving workers in decision-making is to give them access to property rights in the undertaking or a share in company ownership. . . . There are others—and they seem to be in the majority—who argue that workers are entitled to have a say in the management of their enterprise irrespective of ownership and simply because they work there. . . . As was pointed out by the participant from the Government of Jamaica at the Oslo Symposium, "employees who invest their lives in a company, [like] shareholders who invest their capital, have a right to influence decisions". The Norwegian Minister of Labour, Mr. Leif Aune, said in his opening speech at the Oslo Symposium that "workers' participation is based on fundamental concepts of justice" and that "the ordinary worker invests his labour and ties his fate to his place of work. For this reason he has a legitimate claim to have a share in influencing various aspects of company policy."[16]

With regard to the relationship between ownership and the right of decision, it may be observed that in the socialist countries of Eastern Europe collective ownership of the means of production is one of the foundations of the workers' right to participate in decisions. For instance, according to a comparative study which appeared in a Czechoslovak publication, "participation by workers in the management of the work unit is the inseparable counterpart of collective ownership and represents the social relationship which integrates that economic relationship".[17]

In a number of market economy countries governments and employers have turned to profit sharing for the workers and to workers' shareholding. However, it is exceptional for such schemes themselves to have provided the basis for a real extension of workers' participation in decisions within undertakings: the workers concerned do generally have no more power than small stockholders at general meetings.

In the "industrial communities" of Peru (see Chapter 6) an attempt has been made to bring about gradual co-ownership by the workers: part of the profits is transferred annually to a community comprising the workforce of the undertaking, which is represented on the board of directors on a scale that rises until equality with the shareholders is reached. Other systems, as will be seen in Chapter 6, are being studied in Denmark and Sweden with a view to establishing a degree of co-ownership by the workers thanks to payment of part of profits into a special fund and correspondingly increasing participation by the workers' representatives (or their unions) in management. Interest in such schemes is also emerging in certain West European countries.

This trend reflects the concept of economic democracy, which, in those countries, supplements and indeed goes together with industrial democracy, particularly in trade union circles. In a sense this concept constitutes a challenge to the existing distribution of economic power, being as a rule originally based on an analysis of the concentration of property or of the control of capital in the hands of a minority. Attention has been drawn in the same connection to the importance assumed by the banks and the other financial institutions that invest the savings of depositors and the large sums belonging to certain unemployment insurance or pension funds (particularly those that supplement benefits payable under the general social security scheme). Reference has also been made, in the United Kingdom[18] and Sweden[19] for instance, to the extent to which profits are ploughed back in most undertakings. A French leader-writer has stated the problem as follows: "By their labour the workers secrete capital, i.e. property, over which they have rights: so it would be perfectly proper for the system itself to open the way to co-management for them."[20]

It is sometimes argued that there should not be too close a link between property and the power of decision. According to this doctrine, in big undertakings today—and those are the ones in which the problem of participation is no doubt the most acute, because of the remoteness of those who take the big decisions from those who carry them out or bear the consequences—it is usual for the power of decision to be exercised in fact, to a large extent, not by the owners or shareholders but by professional managers who are themselves salaried employees and seldom own much of the company's equity. This point was also made in a publication of the European Communities in connection with the role played within firms by the representatives of capital and of labour: "Over the years, there has been a tendency in public companies towards concentration of real power in the hands of a few top men, whilst shareholders and, often, directors are no longer in a position to exercise supervision."[21] A similar statement can be found in the report of the British committee of inquiry on industrial democracy: " . . . To regard the company as solely the property of shareholders is to be out of touch

15

with the reality of the present-day company as a complex social and economic entity, subject to a variety of internal and external pressures, in which the powers of control have passed from the legal owners to professional management."[22]

In any case, many people seem to consider that the interests both of the suppliers of labour and the suppliers of capital should be taken into account in the constitution and operation of the undertaking.

In Switzerland, during the big public discussion of participation which has taken place in recent years, a trade unionist pointed out that—

Over the years a wide range of developments in labour and social law, a series of fiscal measures, the new role of the State in the regulation of cyclical trends and the promotion of economic growth have emphasised the social function of capital and obliged it to serve the community by restricting in various ways the exercise of the power which it confers. . . . Those in charge must no longer pursue the interest of the owners alone, they must pursue the collective interest, i.e. the interest—objectively perceived—of the undertaking as such, including that of the workers which is an integral part thereof. . . . There ought to be a general charter for undertakings, under which capital and labour as well as management would have their respective powers and functions harmoniously distributed and supervised.[23]

Another problem which, it is hoped, can be solved by workers' participation is the distance intervening—particularly in holding companies, groups of companies, undertakings which have widely separated establishments and, *a fortiori*, multinational corporations— between the central point where the most important decisions are taken and the places where goods and services are produced or provided.[24] Reference will subsequently be made, for example, to the action taken in certain countries to establish central joint committees for whole large undertakings, and the rules proposed by the European Communities for a "European limited company" will be described. In resolutions adopted at its Tenth Ordinary Congress, in 1975, the German Confederation of Trade Unions (DGB) affirmed that the unions concerned "must have rights of information, consultation, supervision and co-determination . . . institutionalised on an international scale" in relation to the operations of the parent companies of multinationals.[25] The same question arises as regards collective bargaining; but although there has been research and discussion on the subject, it is still exceptional for such bargaining to take place at a transnational level.

In the past few years several international trade union organisations have adopted formal statements which refer to worker participation in multinational undertakings. They include the "Charter of trade union rights and the economic, social and cultural demands of the workers in capitalist countries" adopted by the World Federation of Trade Unions at its Eighth World Congress, in October 1973; the "Charter of trade union demands for the legislative control of multinational companies" adopted by the International Confederation of Free Trade Unions at its Eleventh World Congress, in October 1975; a resolution entitled "For renewed trade union action regarding the multinationals" adopted by the World Confederation of Labour at its Nineteenth Congress, in October 1977; and a "Resolution on the workers' right of participation in multinational companies" adopted by the Executive Council of the European Trade Union Confederation in February 1975.

On 16 November 1977 the Governing Body of the International Labour Office adopted a tripartite declaration of principles concerning multinational enterprises and social policy, several paragraphs of which—in the part on labour-management relations—deal with collective bargaining and consultation.[26]

In other cases the social objectives adduced to advocate workers' participation in decisions are mostly confined to improving the atmosphere in the undertaking and promoting better relations between management and personnel. There is less emphasis on workplace democratisation than on fuller integration of the workers into the operation of the undertaking.

Economic objectives

Economic objectives relate directly or indirectly to increasing the efficiency of the undertaking. By associating the workers with the decisions taken, it is hoped to improve the quantity and quality of output and the utilisation of labour, raw materials and equipment, as well as the introduction of new techniques. There is growing awareness of the fact that the knowledge, experience and intelligence of those who actually do the work is not sufficiently used with a view to improving industrial organisation and methods. It is also hoped, through participation, to reduce the areas of conflict of interest between management and labour and to improve labour relations. As indicated in a publication of the International Institute for Labour Studies—

. . . possible contributions to efficient use of human resources may come about for the following reasons:

(i) workers have ideas which can be useful;

(ii) effective communications upwards are essential to sound decision-making at the top;

(iii) workers may accept decisions better if they participate in them;

(iv) workers may work harder if they share in decisions that affect them;

(v) workers may work more intelligently if, through participation in decision-making, they are better informed about the reasons for and the intention of decisions;

(vi) workers' participation may foster a more co-operative attitude amongst workers and management, thus raising efficiency by improving team work and reducing the loss of efficiency arising from industrial disputes;

(vii) workers' participation may act as a spur to managerial efficiency.[27]

17

Conversely, it has been pointed out, the alternatives to participation in the shape of misunderstanding, resistance, low morale and suspicion are all too prevalent.

Numerous experiments with workers' participation in decisions have been made with the above objectives, for example through the establishment of joint production committees or conferences or the adoption of collective incentive schemes.

In general, public authorities regard the development of workers' participation as a means of improving efficiency and preventing labour unrest.

In the United Kingdom the report of the committee of inquiry on industrial democracy emphasised that in order to improve the productivity and efficiency of industry, and so the living standards of the nation, a new approach was required, and that the willingness of the trade unions to accept a share of responsibility for the increased efficiency and prosperity of British companies offered an opportunity to create a new basis for relations in industry which should not be allowed to pass:

For if we look beyond our immediate problems it appears to us certain that the criterion of efficiency in the world of tomorrow, even more than in that of today, will be the capacity of industry to adapt to an increasing rate of economic and social change. We are convinced that this in turn will depend upon the extent to which the measures of adaptation that are necessary are recognised and adopted with the assent of a workforce whose representatives are involved equally and from the beginning in the processes of decision-making.[28]

It was pointed out in a study of workers' participation in management in Poland that the old traditions which affect workers' attitudes and reactions must be eliminated so that the personnel is equally concerned with the director in ensuring the best possible operation of the undertaking. Socialisation of the means of production or nationalisation of industry do not automatically change the attitudes and behaviour of the workers. The same study emphasises that labour democracy is regarded as a powerful factor for improving the productivity of undertakings, because it can stimulate a spirit of initiative and responsibility among the workers, enable the management to benefit from the practical experience of the rank and file, and improve co-operation between the two levels.[29]

The record of decisions of the Eleventh Congress of the Hungarian Socialist Workers' Party states that in addition to its importance as a means of creating socialist relations between managers and subordinates, "democracy in offices and workshops helps to promote the creative character of work . . . and increases the sense of responsibility and the activity of the personnel".[30]

It will be observed also that in the developing countries efforts are often made in public undertakings—generally an important sector in the economy—to associate the workers more fully in decisions with the object of making management more flexible and obtaining better economic results.

Technical development on the one hand and a difficult economic situation on the other, such as that which has prevailed for some years in many countries, often lead to shut-downs, short-time working and reorganisations (mergers, concentration of production in particular units, etc.) involving the transfer or redundancy of personnel. Such developments seem to have often led to the growth of workers' participation, including representation on managerial bodies, even in countries where the unions had long been opposed to participation in this particular form. In the opinion of many observers the introduction of co-determination in the coal and steel companies of the Federal Republic of Germany made it possible to solve some of the serious problems raised by technical and economic change and reorganisation with a minimum of social difficulty and tension; but other observers, particularly among employers, stress the relative ease with which workers could be resettled in that period of high economic activity.

Inflation itself seems to have contributed directly or indirectly to the spread of participation: directly by increasing the demand for information and negotiation at the level of the undertaking in order to restore the purchasing power of wages as soon and as much as the employer's capacity to pay permits; indirectly, because greater participation in decisions is perhaps regarded, according to some observers, as partial compensation for the restricted ability of the unions to obtain wage increases.

Apart from such problems it must be added, in the words of the above-mentioned European Green Book, that—

... The current economic situation, with its reduced possibilities for growth, has emphasized the need for mechanisms which will adequately ensure the pursuit of goals other than economic growth, such as the improvement of the quality of life and working conditions [and] the protection of the environment and the interests of the consumer. The pursuit of such goals can probably be secured only by the existence of decision-making processes in enterprises which have a broader, more democratic base than such processes often have at present.[31]

Observations

An attempt has been made in the preceding pages to indicate the objectives that are often advanced to promote workers' participation in decisions within undertakings; because these objectives, when clearly and vigorously expressed, cannot fail to affect the action that is taken. But a number of observations must be made.

First, the objectives need not be mutually exclusive—indeed, at the origin of many experiments in participation, various considerations must have played their part.

Secondly, some kinds of participation have been developed rather pragmatically, to solve problems that actually arose, without any pronounced ideological or doctrinal attitudes.

Moreover, although some participation schemes rely on areas of common interest between workers and their employers, such as effective management and successful operation of the undertaking (conditions which will enable it to make a profit, to develop and therefore to offer stable employment—even additional employment—good pay and satisfactory conditions of work), it is considered in some countries and occupational groups that the interests of the two parties, on fundamental issues at least, are naturally divergent. So, in the latter case, participation is regarded essentially as an effort to reconcile the contradictory interests of management and labour by frankly admitted confrontation in the shape of bargaining aimed at a mutually acceptable compromise. So it is that collective bargaining at the level of the undertaking, which enables agreement to be reached on many matters of direct concern to management and labour, is often regarded as a procedure for participation in decisions and is in fact almost the only kind of participation to be accepted by both employers and workers in a good many countries where bargaining at that level is a current practice.

Apart from ideological considerations, certain modern methods of management, based on criteria of efficiency and influenced both by experience of industrial life and by social psychology or occupational sociology (particularly in respect of motivation) also contribute in their way to the growth of participation by promoting the decentralisation of authority and of responsibility as well as more thorough consultation.

The notion of participation marks a break (such as has already affected labour law in general for several decades) with former conceptions of the employment relationship like the "master and servant" concept and that of mere hire of services and payment of wages under a contract between parties who were regarded as legally equal. Besides a fair wage, a worker nowadays expects security, job satisfaction and personal fulfilment through his work.

So it seems that hardly anyone asks nowadays whether or not there ought to be participation by workers in decisions within undertakings. The question, rather, is how to achieve such participation and what forms it should take.[32] On this last point the measures taken or intended diverge, sometimes considerably, according to the country and the position of the persons concerned.

METHODS

The belief that workers' participation in decisions within undertakings ought to be promoted for some reason does not in itself imply acceptance of a particular means of bringing it about. The diversity of methods is as great as the diversity of aims.

First of all, participation may be individual. Inevitably if a worker is employed in an undertaking he takes part in its operations. He can also influence some of the decisions to be reached by making suggestions about them or drawing attention to the disadvantages of a particular course. However, "workers' participation in decisions within undertakings" usually and mainly refers to collective participation (even where this is direct—i.e., not through representatives—for instance, in decisions regarding the organisation or performance of the work in a shop or service).

Methods of ensuring this collective participation will depend on political, economic, social and cultural conditions and also on the objectives envisaged by the legislator or the parties concerned. Participation machinery will be described later in the present study. At this point it will suffice to recall in general terms the major features of participation, which can take place under a managerial policy of information and consultation, or through collective bargaining, or through a works council or similar body, or by representation of the personnel on a managerial body, or under the principle of workers' self-management.

Information and consultation

One of the outstanding trends in industrial relations in the past 30 years has certainly been the development of personnel information and consultation procedures, either on a voluntary basis or in accordance with legislative or agreed rules.

In the Communications within the Undertaking Recommendation, 1967, the International Labour Conference advised that "management should, after consultation with workers' representatives, adopt appropriate measures to apply an effective policy of communication with the workers and their representatives" and in particular that information should be given and consultation take place between the parties concerned "before decisions on matters of major interest are taken by management, in so far as disclosure of the information will not cause damage to either party". In other words, "an effective policy of communication" means that the management informs and consults the workers or their representatives, asking for their opinion before a decision is reached; but it is management which takes the decision.

21

Collective bargaining

In industrial relations theory there is sometimes a tendency to discriminate, or at least to distinguish, between "negotiation" or "bargaining"—on matters in which the interests of employers and workers are supposed to diverge—and "participation" or "consultation" in matters of "common interest". The Co-operation at the Level of the Undertaking Recommendation adopted by the International Labour Conference in 1952 recognised this distinction, implicitly at least, when it stated that "appropriate steps should be taken to promote consultation and co-operation between employers and workers at the level of the undertaking on matters of mutual concern not within the scope of collective bargaining machinery, or not normally dealt with by other machinery concerned with the determination of terms and conditions of employment".

In a study like the present one, participation in all kinds of decisions within undertakings must necessarily be covered, whatever the conditions or procedures under which they are taken. Thus it would be improper to disregard a class of decisions which are extremely important for the worker, namely those that arise out of collective bargaining when it occurs at plant or company level. However, collective bargaining as such will be discussed no more than briefly at a later stage in this study since other recent ILO publications have dealt especially with it.[33]

Co-decision in works councils or similar bodies

In the past few years, particularly in some Western European countries, a right of co-decision has been given to bodies of the works-committee type which were at first entitled only to be informed and consulted. This right of co-decision relates to specific matters, generally affecting personnel policy or welfare. The decision has to be a joint one, and this condition sometimes amounts to a power of veto. In practice such a procedure frequently gives rise to negotiation, to bargaining, or even to a compromise in the form of an agreement—in effect, a collective agreement. A kind of informal negotiation, distinct from collective bargaining in the ordinary sense, is tending to emerge in various types of participation machinery. So, in the opinion of some observers, discussions between representatives of the workers and of shareholders, within a body such as the board of directors or the supervisory board of a company, often constitute a kind of bargaining.[34] Similarly, in some countries consultation also may come close to negotiation. A recent French report, for instance, states that it is increasingly difficult to distinguish negotiation from consultation; indeed a hybrid creature has gradually emerged which does more than consult but less than bargain in the English sense of that term.[35]

Membership of management bodies

Under some systems the workers are represented on management bodies such as the board of directors or the supervisory board of a joint stock company or a nationalised undertaking. This sort of participation amounts to co-management, since the powers of such bodies extend to all the problems raised by an industrial operation, although the degree or even the character of the co-management vary, as will be seen below, according to the level at which it takes place (supervisory board, board of directors or other management body) and to whether the workers' representatives are in the minority or not.

Sometimes they are indeed in the minority. This is the case with the personnel representatives in many public undertakings and also under the statutory schemes which apply—either generally or in the private sector only—in Austria, Denmark, Luxembourg, Norway, Peru and Sweden, for example.

Elsewhere, there may be as many representatives of the workers as of the shareholders. This is the system called "parity co-determination": it applies (under an Act going back to 1951) in the big coal and steel companies of the Federal Republic of Germany, where the workers' representatives, mostly appointed by the appropriate trade union, have half the seats on the supervisory board, the other half belonging to the shareholders, with an independent chairman (usually known as the "eleventh man") who is elected by all the members jointly. Under such a system, according to the International Organisation of Employers, worker participation affects the very essence of private enterprise: "The aim in the final analysis is to place on the same footing as source of authority those enjoying the rights of ownership and those whose work has been hired for the purpose of operating the undertaking—in other words a necessarily unstable community of persons bound at one given time to the undertaking by a contract of employment."[36] Still in the Federal Republic, equality of representation on supervisory boards is now also the rule (under an Act of 1976) as regards joint-stock companies in industries other than coal and steel if they employ more than 2,000 persons each; but, as is pointed out below, this new system seems—to the trade unions anyway—to ensure the predominance of the shareholders, if only because one of the representatives of the latter is usually chairman and has a casting vote.

Self-management

Under a system of self-management the workers alone sometimes designate the members of the managerial body. The most well known example is the system introduced in Yugoslavia by a law of 1950 under which the management of public undertakings was handed over to the workers concerned.

AREAS OF PARTICIPATION

In order to appreciate the scope of participation in decision-making, which can be more or less extensive, regard should be had to the areas in which it applies.

On that basis, four main classes of decisions are to be distinguished:

(a) those relating to technical matters (production, organisation, equipment, methods) and the performance of the work;

(b) those relating to employment and personnel questions, i.e., to the worker on the job and sometimes outside it also (selection, recruitment, allocation and distribution of work, job classification and evaluation, remuneration, fringe benefits, promotion, career policy, conditions of work, time-tables and holidays, safety and health, welfare services and institutions—sometimes highly extensive, for they include the works medical service or dispensary, canteens, low-price supplies, housing, nurseries, rest homes, children's holiday camps, sports and many kinds of social and cultural activities—as well as training at various levels, further training and retraining where appropriate, discipline, individual and collective lay-offs and dismissals, and relations with shop stewards);

(c) decisions relating to the economic and financial policy of the undertaking (projections, programmes, investments, price policy, distribution of profits); and

(d) lastly, general policy decisions, relating to the very existence of the undertaking and to its structure (appointment of top managers, total or partial shutdowns, mergers and other structural changes such as the relocation of establishments).

In practice, however, the various classes of decisions cannot be completely separated but tend to overlap. It has been pointed out, for instance, that the scope of discussions on how to give the personnel a share in the results of higher productivity soon tends to widen from remuneration schemes to the management of the undertaking in general.[37]

Some decisions are taken at the highest levels—by the managing director, the board of directors, the supervisory board, or even the general meeting of shareholders—whereas others are taken at various lower echelons.

The degree of participation may vary with the particular class of decisions, i.e. in one and the same undertaking there may be co-decision by collective bargaining as regards terms and conditions of employment, consultation on questions of organisation of work, information on business policy and administration of welfare schemes by the workers directly.

Some decisions at the highest level, relating for instance to a change of programme, may have considerable repercussions in personnel matters (such as job security or hours of work)—hence the importance of knowing at what level the participation occurs in order to assess its real importance. In some countries even collective bargaining deals merely with the consequences for the personnel of certain general policy decisions which remain prerogatives of the management. On the other hand even grievance procedures and the like, which would be expected to have no direct influence on policy decisions, are in some cases—particularly in the United States—so extensively used that in practice they have a profound effect on the general policy of the undertaking, or even the industry, in such matters as the introduction of new techniques and the closing of factories.

It must also be borne in mind that in many public undertakings, in particular, some decisions are in effect taken outside the undertaking, for instance, those relating to rates of pay that only apply the terms of collective agreements concluded at higher levels. Of course, in such cases representatives of management and even of the personnel may have been present at the negotiations, but they did not decide on their own. In some other kinds of decisions also the margin of independence is reduced by such external factors as the immediate economic or market situation or by legislation, public fiscal policy, arbitration awards or a state plan. However, in such cases the workers' representatives within a particular undertaking are often empowered to discuss and negotiate the particular conditions which are to apply there.

On the whole, the area of welfare, which varies in extent from country to country, is one of those in which workers' participation in decisions meets with the least resistance and where the workers are particularly active under most participation systems. In many cases the works council or local trade union branch thus has occasion for continuous activity which is of direct and tangible importance to the workers, although not as a rule closely linked to industrial claims. Such activity is often the first and the chief means of bringing home to newly recruited workers the advantages of working together, and may therefore help to facilitate their adjustment to the industry and their integration in the undertaking. Frequently also welfare schemes provide the institution representing the workers most of its financial and administrative resources—which may serve as a base for extending participation to other fields.

Advocates of the gradual spread of participation often emphasise that

25

consultation or decision-making in a particular area, even a small one, provides experience for the workers (and workers' representatives) and is at the same time a first stage from which workers' participation can develop in other fields. Inversely, it is feared in some trade union circles, in particular, that the special importance sometimes attributed to welfare is mostly a sign of paternalism and may blunt the willingness of workers and their representatives to demand improved conditions. Although employers and management often agree that workers could or should participate in the solution of particular kinds of problems, they generally seek to keep participation within certain limits.

Notes

[1] Particularly *Mater et Magistra*, and *Gaudium et Spes*, pastoral constitution on the Church in the modern world. See J. Joblin, SJ: "The papal encyclical 'Mater et Magistra'", in *International Labour Review* (Geneva, ILO), Sep. 1961, pp. 127–143, and idem: "The Church in the world: A contribution to pluralism", ibid., May 1966, pp. 459–476.

[2] *Report of the Advisory Committee on Worker Participation* (Kingston, multigraphed, no date), Part I, pp. 14 and 17.

[3] B. Hardmeier: "Gewerkschaften und Mitbestimmung", in *Participation dans la profession et l'entreprise*, Annuaire de la Nouvelle Société helvétique (Bern, 1973), p. 58.

[4] *Worker participation in management (private sector)*, Report of the Committee (Adelaide, 1973), p. 3.

[5] "Employee participation and company structure in the European Community", *Bulletin of the European Communities* (Luxembourg, Office for Official Publications of the European Communities), Supplement 8/75, p. 9.

[6] *Företagsdemokrati*, Program antaget av 1971 års LO-Kongress (Stockholm, LO, 1972).

[7] ibid.

[8] *Report of the Committee of Inquiry on Industrial Democracy* (Chairman: Lord Bullock), Cmnd. 6706 (London, HM Stationery Office, 1977); see below, Chapter 6.

[9] *Mitbestimmung im Unternehmen*, Bericht der Sachverständigenkommission zur Auswertung der bisherigen Erfahrungen bei der Mitbestimmung (Mitbestimmungskommission), Deutscher Bundestag, 6. Wahlperiode, Drucksache VI/334 (Bonn, 1970).

[10] Institut syndical européen: *Au-delà de Keynes: une économie de participation* (Brussels, 1979).

[11] *Report of the Advisory Committee on Worker Participation*, op. cit., p. VI.

[12] See the *Official Bulletin* of the International Labour Office, 1977, Series A, No. 2, pp. 84 and 87.

[13] ILO: *Participation of workers in decisions within undertakings*, op. cit., p. 153.

[14] idem: *Workers' participation in decisions within undertakings, Oslo symposium*, op. cit., pp. 59–60.

[15] Johannes Schregle: "Workers' participation in decisions within undertakings", in *International Labour Review* (Geneva, ILO), Jan.–Feb. 1976, pp. 2–3.

[16] Schregle, op. cit., pp. 3–4.

[17] Marie Kalenska: "Účast pracovníků na řizeni podniku v socialistickych zemich", in *Acta Universitatis Carolinae*, Juridica 2–3 (Prague, Univerzita Karlova), Vol. XXIII, 1977, p. 130.

[18] *Report of the Committee of Inquiry on Industrial Democracy*, op. cit.

[19] See R. Meidner, A. Hedborg and E. Fond: *Löntagarfonder* (Stockholm, Tidens Förlag, 1975), commonly known as "the Meidner report".

[20] Pierre Drouin in *Le Monde* (Paris), 11 Sep. 1973, p. 37.

[21] "Worker participation in the European Community", in *European Documentation* (Luxembourg), No. 1977/3, p. 4.

[22] *Report of the Committee of Inquiry on Industrial Democracy*, op. cit., p. 41.

[23] Guido Casetti: "La participation des travailleurs dans l'entreprise", in Confédération des syndicats chrétiens: *La participation des travailleurs dans les entreprises* (Bern, 1973), pp. 52–54.

[24] On this subject, see ILO: *Multinationals in Western Europe: The industrial relations experience* (Geneva, 1976); also International Institute for Labour Studies: *Relations between management of transnational enterprises and employee representatives in certain countries of the European Communities*, A pilot study, by Roger Blanpain, Tom Etty, Alan Gladstone, Hans Günter, Research Series, Transnational Enterprises and Labour, No. 51 (Geneva, 1979).

[25] ILO: *Multinationals in Western Europe: The industrial relations experience*, op. cit., p. 49.

[26] See idem: *Tripartite declaration of principles concerning multinational enterprises and social policy* (Geneva, 1977), particularly paras. 48–56. See also Organisation for Economic Cooperation and Development: *International investment and multinational enterprises* (revised edition, Paris, 1979).

[27] Kenneth F. Walker: "Workers' participation in management: Problems, practice and prospect", in *IILS Bulletin* (Geneva, International Institute of Labour Studies), No. 12, p. 6.

[28] *Report of the Committee of Inquiry on Industrial Democracy*, op. cit., pp. 160 and 161.

[29] International Institute for Labour Studies: *Workers' participation in management in Poland*, op. cit., pp. 19 and 3.

[30] *Az MSZMP XI. Kongresszusanak jegyzökönyve* (Budapest, Kossuth, 1975), p. 467.

[31] "Employee participation and company structure in the European Community", op. cit., p. 11.

[32] Schregle, op. cit., p. 16.

[33] See note 1, Chapter 8. "Promotion of collective bargaining" was included in the agenda of the 66th (1980) Session of the International Labour Conference with a view to the possible adoption of new standards; see ILO: *Promotion of collective bargaining*, Report V (1), International Labour Conference, 66th Session, 1980.

[34] See, for instance, Johannes Schregle: "Co-determination in the Federal Republic of Germany: A comparative view", in *International Labour Review*, Jan.–Feb. 1978, pp. 90–92.

[35] Gérard Adam: "La négociation collective en France: Eléments de diagnostic", in *Droit social* (Paris), Dec. 1978, p. 443; see also ibid., p. 448.

[36] International Organisation of Employers: *Co-determination and private enterprise: Problems arising from the participation of workers in management decisions in undertakings*, Document prepared by the IOE Secretariat for submission to the General Council at its 44th Annual Meeting, 5 June 1967 (new edition, Geneva, 1969), p. 4.

[37] The same holds good in practice as regards most of the committees which have to monitor application of Scanlon plans (see Chapter 7, note 22) in undertakings having adopted that system.

OBJECTIONS

3

After this summary of the aims of workers' participation (in its broadest sense), the methods used to bring it about and the fields in which it can operate, it will be easier to understand the objections raised to certain of its forms. Mostly, such objections relate not so much to the general idea of allowing workers to participate in decisions—particularly where these may directly affect their conditions of employment or other interests—as to some of the reasons adduced in favour of participation or, more often, to the methods proposed for putting it into effect. (The objections covered here are mainly ones based on general principles, though often with practical considerations in mind, whereas practical difficulties and problems as such will be dealt with later.)

Depending on the extent of participation introduced, changes are likely to follow sooner or later in relations between employers and workers, between the latter and their unions, between unions and management, and between management and public authorities. This often accounts for controversy, and for apprehensions as to the political ideology sometimes thought to underlie the establishment of participation arrangements. Even at the level of the undertaking, participation may, in extreme cases, constitute a threat to property rights, the exercise of authority and the chain of command; and, for the country as a whole, it may imply a new conception of the roles of employers and workers in labour-management relations and a more or less generalised trend towards the delegation of powers.

There is no doubt that it is the politico-social aim of applying the concepts of political democracy to the individual undertaking which gives rise to the strongest objections. A leading French employer who has followed participation problems particularly closely wrote:

The analogy between government and business management does not stand up to examination. A government has the power to make laws, the right to raise taxes, a police force and other ways of imposing obedience on its citizens. A commercial undertaking—

thank heavens—does not have these powers; however, for it to operate effectively, its managers must be independent of those to whom they have to give orders. . . . What would be the authority of the head of a business whose decisions were approved of by one category of personnel and disapproved of by another?[1]

Some years ago the President of the Confederation of German Employers' Associations also asserted that it was not possible to manage an industrial undertaking effectively by applying democratic principles. He added that he failed to see how the manager's personal qualification and efficient management could be improved or maintained if the clear and direct responsibilities of management and owners were superseded by some sort of quasi-parliamentary control which would force the manager to manoeuvre to reconcile different interests.[2]

Conversely, trade union leaders are just as strong in their objections when the purpose of participation is to promote the integration of workers in the undertaking. As one French observer has said: "If there is one expression which the trade unions are united in condemning, it is that of 'integration', that is to say, any measure, procedure or institution in the undertaking, occupation or country which tends to involve trade unions too closely with management."[3]

A number of other objections relate to the economic aims, for instance when the purpose is to improve the efficiency of the undertaking through workers' participation.

Some critics, though admitting that scope for workers' initiative may be a good thing, have questioned whether there is any place for it on the production line or in factories with a high degree of automation:

After all, autocratic, work-centred bosses frequently do get out high production; on occasion their subordinates develop high morale and cohesive work groups. True, without participation the worker may never exercise creativity or imagination or put out an outstanding job. But on many jobs, management has no use for outstanding performance. What is outstanding performance on the part of the assembly-line workers? That he works faster than the line? That he shows creativity and imagination on the job? Management wants none of these. Adequate performance is all that is needed on the assembly line and probably on a large number of other jobs in our society. . . . The case for participation . . . is not as strong as some have suggested. Participation is useful in a great many fields. But it is not a sovereign remedy for all management's ills.[4]

Most of the arguments against participation in decision-making are connected with the methods proposed for its operation. The more far-reaching the effects which these may have on the structure of the undertaking, the more basic the objections are.

The main theme of these objections is the need for management to maintain the maximum unity, authority and freedom of manoeuvre to respond to changes in the economic situation; the distinctive role of the businessman, it is considered, is to innovate and take risks, on the successful outcome of which all the workers in the undertaking ultimately depend. His authority is derived not from legal, political or economic factors external to the undertaking but from the very nature and purpose of the undertaking;[5] it is said in some quarters that authority can be delegated but cannot be shared. In this connection, a British employers' representative on the Social and Economic Committee of the European Communities, speaking in his personal capacity, recently declared that what had to be avoided in a free enterprise economy was a situation in which the general managers of undertakings ceased to assume final responsibility for industrial, commercial, structural and economic decisions. No general manager should have to share this final responsibility, which should be restricted only by law or by collective agreement; nor should he be able to offload it onto others or to refer matters to a joint committee for decision.[6]

It is against proposals for workers' representation on management bodies, and especially their parity representation (or any method whereby shareholders' representatives cease to be in a majority on boards of directors or supervisory boards) that objections have been most firmly and clearly stated.

The confederation of German Employers' Associations considered that extension to other industries in the Federal Republic of Germany of the co-determination system operating in the mining and iron and steel industries "would increase trade unions' power and immediately raise the question of their role and functions in a free economy". It would also "entail a fundamental change" in the country's property structure and would thereby jeopardise the basis of the free socio-economic order and its future development. In support of this view, the President of the Confederation observed that the management of a company had to be responsible to the owners; it could not be effective if important decisions could be subject to compromises between groups which had very different interests and, in some cases, even political beliefs. Nor did the employers think that in the absence of an agreement between the two groups on a supervisory board, it would be appropriate to make one person—and one person only—responsible for taking a final decision which might very frequently have far-reaching repercussions for the company. Decisions of that kind needed to be taken according to economic necessities and should not be subject to the decision of one man acting as an arbitrator.[7]

In reply to the argument that participation in management is necessary to put a check on economic power, the same critic retorted that, in a market economy, such a check is exercised by the functioning of the market itself and that, if additional checks are considered necessary, "these should only be exercised by the State and in the public interest. Trade unions are the representatives of private interests and it is not their job to perform functions on behalf of the public. They should be the first to recognise that acceptance of their demands would lead to changing their character as private representatives of workers' interests. They would become public institutions, and it is difficult to see how far independent collective bargaining could be maintained".[8] In relation to the latter point, it is also sometimes claimed that there is a risk that collective bargaining may be distorted by the presence on the employers' side of the bargaining table of directors who are trade unionists[9] or by the influence of staff representatives who are members of supervisory or management boards on the appointment and re-election of members of the latter. It may be noted in this connection that in the Federal Republic of Germany the council of the employers' association for the steel industry consists of equal numbers of commercial, technical and labour directors, the last, appointed with the agreement of workers' representatives on the supervisory board, coming in practice from trade union circles; the association was not admitted to membership of the Confederation of Employers' Associations, which considered that the association was not entirely independent of the workers. This problem did not arise in the coal industry, where labour directors appointed in the same way are not members of the negotiating committee of the employers' association.

Some observers express the view that in very big concerns ownership is no longer sufficient to give legitimacy to management powers (since these may lead to decisions affecting not only the owners but also the workers and the public in general), and that the equity is in the hands of thousands of individual shareholders, none of whom really exercises ownership rights. The retort has been made that recognition of such rights is the very basis of a free economy and that each shareholder takes a financial risk which is and must remain an individual risk.[9]

The International Organisation of Employers has opposed any proposals for co-determination on a priority basis or proposals under which shareholders would not be in a majority in private undertakings and has observed that, in its opinion, there is—

. . . a breaking up of the rights of ownership when worker representatives enjoy in management bodies the same rights as the providers of capital since, enjoying the same rights, the workers ipso facto enjoy also the right of disposal of the firm's capital assets. . . . Any limitation of the powers which are given to those who are mandated by the shareholders to act on their behalf can only lead to a corresponding diminution of the sense of property ownership that unites the shareholder with the company. Ultimately, lacking any single driving force, open to every varying outside influence, the company is no longer able to command sufficient confidence to attract the further capital it needs.[10]

In lengthy discussions which have taken place in recent years in the United Kingdom, the Confederation of British Industry, although in general agreement with extension of workers' participation by voluntary agreement, took up the following position in regard to any system which would impose trade union delegates as members of boards of directors:

The CBI does not accept that there is a need for imposed change in the control of companies. Companies in the private sector are, and should continue to be, controlled by boards of directors appointed by and legally responsible to shareholders. To change that situation by giving control to trade union representatives would not only damage the efficiency of companies, it would have the most serious consequences on international confidence on Britain's ability to improve her situation, would deter badly needed foreign investment in the UK and it would destroy private enterprise as we know it. . . . Too little has been said about the effects that delegate directors with no responsibility to shareholders might have on directors, managers, investors and consumers. Will investors be ready to advance their savings for investment if they believe that power lies in the hands of people who may be inimical to their interests? Will consumers accept such representatives as the best safeguards of their interest in quality, competitive pricing and choice?

A highly dangerous situation would arise if middle management, in particular, were to feel that their authority and their ability to take decisions was being threatened by union pressure exerted simultaneously from the shop floor and from the boardroom. . . .

It is of the utmost importance to emphasise that where employee representatives become directors—and under the CBI proposals this can only come about voluntarily— they will not be "delegates" representing a sectional interest. They will be directors of the company with precisely the same legal and collective responsibilities as other directors for the over-all well-being and prosperity of that company.[11]

Similar reservations exist in other industrialised market economies; concern in relation to the confidence of potential foreign investors also extends to developing countries, and has led some of the latter to provide for exemption from the strict participation system applied nationally in cases where an undertaking relies on the supply of external capital (this is the case in Tanzania, as will be seen subsequently).

Other arguments are based on the finding of studies, generally carried out a number of years ago, which suggest that workers may attach less importance to participation in management than do their unions. As one observer remarked, "it seems to be a factor of social life in all spheres that a minority take a lively interest and participate actively, while the majority remain relatively passive".[12]

Criticisms of the idea of workers' participation in the management of undertakings are also expressed by many trade unionists who stress the need to preserve the independence of the trade union movement.

In fact, many trade unionists think that, though they must have the opportunity of being consulted before management establishes its policy and of fighting the effects of this policy (if necessary by industrial action) whenever the interests of their members are not respected, it is not their job to share responsibility for decisions which belong to the management.[13] The role of trade unions, they say, is to exert pressure on management to obtain the maximum benefits for workers and not to take its place, or to be associated with decisions that might adversely affect their independence.

One of the great problems is that of the "shared responsibility" implied by participation in management, in particular in the case of decisions that may have unfavourable consequences for workers. As underlined by a French writer already quoted—

> ... After all, we must look at the other side of the medal. At certain stages good management (not only supervised but actually carried out with the participation of the workers) involves the taking of decisions which run counter to the traditional claims of trade union representatives. For instance, in order to win new markets or to attract essential investments, it may be necessary to oppose wage increases. To get over a bad spot, redundancies may be unavoidable. Or even more seriously, technological development may make a particular form of production obsolete and it may be necessary to consider switching into other products or in some cases closing the undertaking down.[14]

Even the minority representation of workers on boards of directors or supervisory boards is criticised: "In some boards of directors we have had the experience of workers' representatives being in a very marked minority, even though they have the right to vote. In most cases they are reduced to the role of stage props. Worse still, they have sometimes become hostages. At the very best they have only been able to act as observers or reporters for their colleagues and their unions."[15] Similar fears have sometimes been expressed in developing countries.[16]

The views of United States trade unionists are well reflected in the following statement:

> ... Equality is established through the collective bargaining process, a conflict relationship, where equals talk to equals. And because American unions have won equality at the bargaining table, we have not sought it in corporate board rooms.
> We do not seek to be a partner in management—to be, most likely, the junior partner in success and the senior partner in failure.
> We do not want to blur in any way the distinctions between the respective roles of management and labor in the plant.
> We guard our independence fiercely—independent of government, independent of any political party and independent of management.
> Similarly, we guard our strength and our militance and when we bargain, we bargain on all issues—whether they are mandatory subjects for bargaining under our laws or not—because realistically, they are all on the table.
> And we probably bargain on as many, if not more, issues than the number we might have any impact on as members of a board of directors.[17]

For ideological reasons certain trade unions that are opposed to the existing social and economic order in their countries do not want participation in management. Conversely, private employer circles in many countries do not look forward to extension, particularly in management bodies, of the participation of representatives of trade unions which are opposed to the existing economic and social system.

Other criticisms are based not on doctrinal considerations but on practical observations, emphasising the problem of the training and the knowledge required to be able to assume management responsibilities.

However that may be, it must be recognised that the introduction of most of the more advanced systems of participation reflects a political choice which has only been possible in exceptional historical circumstances. In as far as such participation may lead to a change in social structures and the redistribution of power, the subject often arouses passions and gives rise to acute controversy. That is also why governments usually proceed with caution, paying attention to the arguments for and against participation and carefully assessing the pressures emanating from different interest groups before introducing reforms which may have marked repercussions on the balance of power in the nation.

Nevertheless, concepts and attitudes are changing. Discussions on workers' participation in decision-making in undertakings are being directed away from irredeemably contentious issues and towards a more flexible approach to industrial relations and to ways of modifying the existing power structure to bring it better into line with the rising expectations and aspirations and the growing abilities of workers, of their employers and of their respective representatives. As indicated in a publication for businessmen, many managers now recognise that an increasing desire among the workers to participate can be very beneficial for their undertakings.[18]

Notes

[1] Pierre de Calan: *Renaissance des libertés économiques et sociales* (Paris, Plon, 1963).

[2] Siegfried Balke: *Expansion of co-determination in the Federal Republic of Germany?* (Cologne, Bundesvereinigung der Deutschen Arbeitgeberverbände),pp. 13 and 15.

[3] André Jeanson: *La société démocratique*, Cinquantième semaine sociale de France, Caen, 1963 (Lyon, Chronique sociale de France, 1963), p. 315.

[4] George Strauss: "Participative management, a critique", in *ILR Research* (Ithaca, New York State School of Industrial and Labor Relations),Nov. 1966, p. 6.

[5] *Jeune Patron* (Paris), Apr. 1964, p. 28.

[6] *30 jours d'Europe* (Paris, Service de presse et d'information de la Commission des Communautés européennes), No. 237, Apr. 1978, p. 9.

[7] Balke, op. cit., pp. 3, 10–11.

[8] ibid., p. 13.

[9] ibid., p. 14.

[10] International Organisation of Employers: *Co-determination and private enterprise*, op. cit., pp. 28 and 29.

[11] *Involving people: CBI proposals for employee participation* (London, Confederation of British Industry, 1976), pp. 8–9.

[12] Walker, op. cit., p. 25.

[13] See for instance, the analysis of the views of the three major trade union confederations in Italy in Antonio Triola: "La participazione nel dibattito sindacale", in *Economia e Lavoro* (Padua), Oct.– Dec. 1977, pp. 647–669.

[14] Drouin, *op. cit.*, p. 37.

[15] A. Laval: "Remue-ménage autour de la participation", in *FO-Hebdo* (Paris, Confédération générale du travail – Force ouvrière), 14 Dec. 1973, No. 1369.

[16] See for instance ILO: *Workers' participation in decisions within undertakings, Oslo Symposium*, op. cit., pp. 44–45 and 77.

[17] T. R. Donahue, Executive Assistant to the President of the AFL-CIO, in a speech delivered at an international conference on trends in industrial and labour relations held in Montreal from 24 to 28 May 1976; reproduced in Frances Bairstow (ed.): *International Conference on Trends in Industrial and Labour Relations* (Montreal, Industrial Relations Centre, McGill University, 1977), p. 576. Nevertheless, in the autumn of 1979 the President of the United Automobile Workers became a member of the board of directors of the troubled Chrysler Corporation.

[18] See *Industrial democracy in Europe*, A Business International European report (Geneva, Business International, 1974), p. 5.

GENERAL OBSERVATIONS

4

The preceding summary shows that the concept of workers' participation is as complicated as it is important. Several general observations are already called for.

The first concerns the ambiguity of the term "participation".

The objections encountered in some countries and in some circles may be accounted for by the fact that the words "participate" and "participation" immediately evoke in many people's minds systems of workers' membership of the management bodies of undertakings. However, various forms of participation have been introduced in widely differing political, economic and social systems, and there are other ways of providing for the participation of workers in decision-making in the undertaking than through membership of its organs of management.

Of course the position varies greatly according to the politico-economic setting, in particular whether the undertaking operates under a system of collective or private ownership, with the resulting differences in power base and location.

In addition, the introduction and operation of workers' participation can be either facilitated or hindered according to whether or not the people working in the undertaking are in agreement with its basic structure.

Differences of philosophical doctrine do not necessarily prevent a measure of agreement from being reached on practical steps; on the other hand, even among people belonging to the same school of thought, deep-rooted habits may lead to radical opposition and almost insurmountable difficulties in reaching any agreement on the subject. Fundamentally, participation is very much a matter of individual outlook. It has been said that—

Members of an organisation seem to have somewhat ambivalent attitudes. In accordance with a natural wish to mould their own environment they are quite keen to participate, but at the same time they are afraid that by doing so they may lose their own independence and find themselves tied or restricted by their partners. It is far easier to keep one's independence and integrity by holding aloof from decisions than by agreeing to share in making them. As a result, members of an organisation seldom agree to participate in making decisions unless they are getting some substantial benefit in return.[1]

In any case, workers' participation in decision-making is not something that can be set once and for all in a particular pattern; it is rather a general trend which seems likely to become gradually more pronounced. It is essentially a dynamic process. Any definition of workers' participation can only be provisional because the practical circumstances in which it is to operate are subject to changes, social and cultural as well as economic and technical. Between the two extremes—a situation in which workers have no say in decisions and just have to obey orders given with the minimum of explanation, and the other in which they have to govern themselves and in fact make their own decisions—there are a host of other possibilities.

Generalisation would therefore seem to be very hazardous. It is noticeable that the advocates of reforms leading to greater workers' participation in decisions are increasingly aware of the diversity of situations and hence of the need for a corresponding diversity of methods.

It has been emphasised that an undertaking which seems to outsiders to have only one centre of decision may in fact comprise a whole web of centres of responsibility whose decisions, at least in theory, coalesce into a common plan. Only practical analysis of these centres of decision can show where responsibilities lie and suggest how to introduce greater industrial and economic democracy.

As is well known, not only is it very difficult to give a precise all-embracing definition of workers' participation in decision-making but also it is a very delicate matter to put participation into effect, since it impinges on the driving force of the economic machine. There is certainly much more general recognition now than previously that, in an increasingly competitive economic environment, management must have the necessary powers to run the undertaking effectively. That is why some reform proposals put the emphasis on "co-supervision" rather than "co-management".

SOME KEY FACTORS

At the end of this introductory survey we shall attempt in the present chapter to bring out some of the key factors in the operation of participation, though it is not easy to deal briefly with the findings emerging from research, studies, and exchanges of views and experience. These are fortunately becoming more frequent; we shall try to cover them more fully in later chapters.

Role of legislation and agreements

One question frequently discussed is whether participation systems should be brought into being by legislation or by agreements.[2] Two objects have to be taken into consideration: that of gaining the greatest possible support of the parties involved and that of maximum adaptability to the particular characteristics of the region, the industry or even the undertaking concerned so as to arrive at the best possible functioning of the system chosen. Much depends on national tradition: some countries resort to legislation to regulate industrial relations while others prefer to deal with these matters by negotiation at national, regional, local or even undertaking level. Nor is it uncommon in the first case for the law to lay down a number of fundamental rights and corresponding rules, leaving the details to be worked out by collective bargaining. Cases also occur in which the law recommends a system of participation without imposing it, or leaves it to subsequent regulations to apply such a system in specific undertakings or categories of undertakings, in some cases after an inquiry. There are also instances of agreements preceding the adoption of laws or regulations.

However, the choice between laws or agreements seems to be determined mostly by the form of participation selected. Bodies such as works councils seem to have been set up or developed according to whichever of these two traditions was current in the country concerned, whereas the generalised introduction of workers' representation, even minority representation, on the boards of directors or the supervisory boards of public undertakings (and even more so of private undertakings) can scarcely be achieved through negotiation alone.

In addition, since the attitudes of the parties concerned are so important an element in the functioning of participation systems, any introduction or reform of such a system must be preceded by explanations and consultations on the system's nature, aims and operation. A minimum of consensus between employers, intermediate staff and workers must be secured on the kind of system to be applied, and on aims and expectations.

Training

Everything points to the desirability of training programmes. These generally comprise an initial phase of information on and explanation of the participation scheme involved, addressed to those who will have to live with it and make it work.[3] Considerable experience has already been acquired in this field. In order to exert influence, whether through representation on management bodies or in the processes of consultation, negotiation or joint decision-making, workers' representatives must be capable of understanding the questions under discussion and appreciating the effect of the decisions to be taken. Business management has become a highly specialised skill requiring specialised training for those called upon to formulate decisions. This accounts for the growing importance, both for workers' representatives and for executives at different levels, of training programmes relating to participation, devised specifically for the scheme adopted or to be introduced.

Most of these training programmes are organised separately for management (as well as supervisors in some cases and sometimes shareholders' representatives on management bodies) and for workers' representatives (and sometimes rank-and-file workers); however, in certain cases there are joint sessions. Having regard to the considerable expense involved, the question of how to finance training programmes generally arises. In many cases the government is asked to help finance them, subject to safeguards for the independence of the trade unions or employers' organisations which often draw up and carry out the programmes. In the Netherlands employers contribute to the financing of trade union training institutions without exercising any control over the use made of these funds or over the programmes,[4] while in Norway a joint fund has been set up by the employers' and workers' confederations to finance either joint or separate training programmes for labour and management.[5] Paid educational leave can be very helpful for this type of training.[6] General educational systems and vocational training programmes could also do more to prepare people for participation.[7]

The extent of the training needed for participation will be appreciated if one considers the knowledge needed in fields as diverse as economic and financial questions, company and labour law, personnel policy and remuneration, work study and productivity measurement, working conditions, health and safety, business and production management. The better they have been trained to deal with such matters, the better the workers' representatives will discharge their duties on boards of directors, supervisory boards or self-management bodies. And of course many of the same subjects are touched on in works councils and by workers' spokesmen in collective bargaining. The frequent rotation of workers' representatives increases the need for training, as does the low level of education of many of the workers in developing countries.

Information

It is not enough for workers' representatives to be able to understand what is being discussed in participatory bodies: they also need to receive the necessary information.[8] The attitude of management and its readiness to participate is important in this connection. Often there is reticence resulting from the feeling that certain information must be kept confidential, and that it should be disclosed only if accompanied by an obligation on the part of the workers' representatives receiving it to keep it secret. Attempts have often been made to clarify the situation in this respect through legislation, which sometimes provides for appeals to a tribunal or other independent body to determine whether or not there has been misinterpretation of the relevant provisions. However, even legislation intended to be particularly precise as regards the information to be furnished and the rules to be observed in regard to confidential matters, such as a royal decree of 27 November 1973 in Belgium, has given rise to difficulties in practice.[9]

Moreover, although workers' representatives may have followed appropriate training courses, they may not be sufficiently well equipped to deal with certain items of information or certain problems. For this reason specialist assistance, sometimes from outside the undertaking such as that of chartered accountants, is provided for, for instance in Algeria, Belgium and France; it was also included in an agreement in Sweden in 1975. It is common practice, too, for members of works councils to be able to call on experts in certain subjects, either within the undertaking or from outside, in the plenary sittings of these bodies or in their specialised subcommittees.

It also happens that, sometimes simply for lack of time, managers submit complicated documents or abstruse statistics which could have been explained or presented in a simpler or clearer way. The necessary information may also be supplied too late for proper analysis, or there may be difficulties of mutual comprehension due to differences between management and workers' representatives in language and phraseology.[10]

Furthermore, management should provide information on improvements which have been achieved as a result of participation and greater effort on the part of the workers, for instance in regard to productivity or economics of various kinds, since participation should bring a sharing of the resulting profits.

There should also be a flow of information between workers' representatives and those who have elected them. In many countries there are arrangements such as liaison groups, regular meetings of trade union leaders with the rank and file, or regular general meetings of the workers which are intended to facilitate the communication of information. However, these meetings are sometimes restricted by the rules concerning the confidential nature of certain information or discussions, or sometimes by a restrictive interpretation by the workers' representatives themselves of what they may communicate. It has sometimes been stressed that, in the case of minority participation in supervisory boards

41

or boards of directors, it would be appropriate for workers' representatives, in reporting on decisions with which they were in disagreement, to give all the facts about these decisions and the stand which they themselves took up.[11]

Other factors

Another key factor which is repeatedly mentioned is the need to discuss important problems, not just minor matters, and to have these discussions with persons holding the power of decision or at the decision-making centre; the latter is sometimes a problem in the case of holding companies, grouped companies and multinational companies.

Generally speaking, the extent and the potential development of participation depend on—

(a) the degree of autonomy of an undertaking (this also holds true particularly for public undertakings);

(b) its structure and size (apparently participation is often less needed in small and medium-sized businesses because of their usually more flexible organisation and more frequent direct contacts between managers and their workers, though it is also more difficult in some respects);[12]

(c) the dispersion of its personnel (as for instance in agriculture, transport and the construction industry); and

(d) the degree of complexity of its technology.

The laying-down of, and respect for, various far from minor or accessory practical rules is also of great importance in achieving genuine participation. They should cover such subjects as the obligation to reply within a given period to proposals or requests made by workers' representatives, and to give reasons in the case of rejection, as well as for the representatives to give their reasons for a veto or refusal of approval in the case of a question requiring joint decision; the possibility of appeal to a conciliation or arbitration body or even to a court or tribunal in the case of a deadlock; the chairing and frequency of meetings; early preparation and despatch of the agenda and necessary papers; and the preparation of minutes.

Under many systems the term of office of workers' representatives is designed to be sufficiently long to enable them to profit from experience, while the number of successive terms for which they may serve is limited in order to ensure some decree of rotation and hence the participation of the largest possible number of workers.

It is important that the workers' representatives should have some protection and facilities (physical facilities and free time) to guarantee their independence, avoid reprisals such as arbitrary dismissal or transfer and enable them to perform their representative duties effectively.[13] Such arrangements, however, should not be allowed to lead to abuses that might discredit the workers' representatives in the eyes of their opposite numbers or of their constituents, not should they derive personal advantage from their representative functions.

Finally, it is difficult to overstress the importance of the time factor in the development and improvement of any participation system. Workers' participation in decision-making in the undertaking, as we have seen, is a complicated and essentially dynamic process. A far-reaching system such as that of self-management in Yugoslavia has undergone a series of reforms until quite recently,[14] although more than a quarter of a century has elapsed since it was introduced in the whole of the country's public sector. Parity representation of the workers on the supervisory boards of mining and iron and steel undertakings in the Federal Republic of Germany had been preceded some 30 years earlier by minority representation, and minority representation later introduced in other industries only became almost parity representation 24 years later,[15] and then only in companies with 2,000 or more workers. Time is essential also to cope with problems which, in one connection or another, arise in any participation system, particularly at the beginning. Hence the value of preliminary pilot experiments and later of research to establish the current situation in practice and the problems encountered. In the light of experience, management and labour may find it necessary to fix new targets, to change methods or the basis of representation, to introduce new areas of participation, to suspend certain activities or to introduce new ones.

In conclusion stress must be laid on a fundamental point, namely that in the long term, no system of workers' participation in decision-making within the undertaking will be viable if it neglects the needs of the undertaking or if it is hostile to trade unionism, leads to mistrust and opposition of the unions, or infringes in any way the principles of freedom of association.

Notes

[1] "Memento de psychologie sociale", in *Liaisons sociales* (Paris), Nov. 1964, p. 43.

[2] See ILO: *Workers' participation in decisions within undertakings, Oslo Symposium*, op. cit., particularly pp. 65–66.

[3] For further details see two mimeographed ILO documents connected with the symposium on the training of workers' representatives for participation in decisions within undertakings, held in Geneva in October 1977: *Background paper* (doc. EDUC/S.46/D.1) and *Report* (doc. EDUC/S.46/D.6).

[4] In the Netherlands the training of members of works councils is financed by a tax of 1 per cent on the total payroll of any undertaking statutorily required to have a works council, that is, any employing more than 100 workers.

[5] The Norwegian fund is financed to the extent of two-thirds by a contribution from employers amounting to 0.25 per cent of gross wages, the remaining third coming from a levy on workers' wages.

[6] In 1974 the International Labour Conference adopted a Convention (No. 140) concerning paid educational leave.

[7] ILO: *Workers' participation in decisions within undertakings, Oslo Symposium*, op. cit., pp. 57 and 78.

[8] Detailed claims in this respect are set out in European Trade Union Confederation: *Information rights of workers and their representatives in plants and undertakings*, Supplement to report on activities 1976–1978, pp. 80–82.

[9] See *Social and Labour Bulletin* (Geneva, ILO), No. 2/77, pp. 115–116.

[10] As has been noted in France and Tunisia. See M. Legendre, *Quelques aspects des relations professionnelles* (Paris, Service d'études pour le développement et l'animation, 1969), quoted in Walker, op. cit., p. 15.

[11] See for instance ILO/UNDP: *Report on the international seminar on workers' participation in decisions within undertakings, Belgrade, 2–11 Dec. 1969*, op. cit., p. 13.

[12] See for instance: "La participation et les PME", in *Prévisions et entreprise* (Paris), Nov. 1970, pp. 26–29; P. Voglaire: "Syndicats et participation dans l'entreprise: Questions aux syndicats", in *L'entreprise et l'homme* (Brussels), Aug.–Sep. 1972, pp. 345–350; Confederation of British Industry: *Practical employee participation in smaller firms* (London, 1976); and Marco Biagi: "Democrazia industriale e piccole imprese", in Wedderburn *et al*: *Democrazia politica e democrazia industriale* (Bari, De Donato, 1978), pp. 143–151.

[13] In 1971 the International Labour Conference adopted a Convention (No. 135) and a Recommendation (No. 143) concerning protection and facilities to be afforded to workers' representatives in the undertaking.

[14] See Chapter 5.

[15] See Chapter 6.

THE MACHINERY OF PARTICIPATION

THE MACHINERY OF PARTICIPATION

As shown in Part I, workers' participation in decision-making in the undertaking is based on a wide variety of ideas. There is a similar variety in its aims and in the objections to which it gives rise. These factors account for the great differences, by country and by undertaking, in the machinery established. Such differences extend not only to institutional structure and scope but also to the decision-making powers that are exercised. There are variations also in legal status according to the undertaking's degree of autonomy within the economy, the characteristics of the management and the respective roles of employers' and workers' organisations in the country or industry concerned. In addition to factors such as these, which are directly linked to the workers' place in the undertaking, arrangements are strongly influenced in practice by the constitutional and political system, by the level of economic, social and cultural development, by the history of relations between the various sectors of society, by attitudes and by other socio-cultural factors.

The purpose of the second part of this study is to describe the main types of institutional machinery now existing in different countries and different parts of the world, bringing out their principal characteristics (kind of participation, machinery, operation, nature of the powers granted to the workers and their representatives in matters of formulating and making decisions within the undertaking and in some cases of checking that they are carried out). Mention has also to be made of some of the problems which have arisen in this connection. These have often led to phasing the development of the machinery by a succession of reforms aimed at overcoming them. It appears essential to refer to the main characteristics of undertakings and the different labour-management relations systems under which participation takes place. No attempt, however, has been made, save in exceptional cases, to describe the general economic background or the major socio-cultural factors which in

47

practice exercise a decisive influence on the operation of the various participation schemes.

Workers' participation in decision-making in the undertaking may be strictly formalised, as in the case of workers' self-management councils or joint supervisory boards, both of which are often bodies vested with wide powers and having a definite place in national management practice. At the other end of the scale, purely informal relations with individual workers or groups may have strong repercussions on management decisions even where there is no formal sharing of decision-making powers. Between these two extremes there is a range of intermediate solutions allowing for varying degrees of formal participation such as works councils, other statutory bodies initially set up chiefly for purposes of consultation and collaboration, or voluntary joint committees and other arrangements negotiated by management and trade unions at the level of the undertaking. And of course for many years and in most countries, collective bargaining and other forms of relations between trade unions and the management of undertakings have allowed workers' representatives to participate in a number of decisions. These various arrangements for participation may, and often do, co-exist within the same national system or undertaking. Often they complement each other, but in other cases they may be in opposition to each other or mutually exclusive.

SELF-MANAGEMENT AND RELATED SYSTEMS

5

SELF-MANAGEMENT SYSTEMS

Conceptually, systems based on self-management undoubtedly represent the most far-reaching attempts at direct involvement of the workers in decision-making and management responsibilities. Self-management can be defined most simply as the management of undertakings by their workforce.

The main features common to these systems are usually the following. They are based on general legislation applicable to undertakings in the public sector in which management—but not ownership—rights have been transferred to the workers. The right to participate is granted to the whole of the workforce, whether manual or non-manual workers; those who, for any reason, leave the undertaking do not retain any management rights. The workforce usually exercises its rights through an elected body often known as a "workers' council", though in recent years some self-management systems have shown a trend to give greater importance to a workers' assembly or an assembly of workers' representatives. The competence of self-management bodies extends to all decisions taken in the undertaking, although special rules as to procedure and supervision may be laid down by legislation to avoid arbitrary action and to ensure the observance of certain standards. Self-management bodies have the right to dispose partly or wholly of the profits or net income of the undertaking, reinvesting certain sums, allocating others for social or cultural activities, or distributing sums directly in the shape of bonuses.

The various national systems differ considerably in most other characteristics and in their detailed application of the general principles mentioned above. The differences are also very pronounced if they are compared with other related systems which will be looked at later in this chapter, such as producers' co-operatives or undertakings owned and managed by trade unions.

The links between self-managed undertakings and local, regional and national governments, and with the planning authorities, have in the past few years been noticeably strengthened in most countries operating self-management systems. Even in Yugoslavia, where the principles of a market economy are applied to some extent, the regional and national governments have retained considerable powers, as have the banks. In all these countries the role of the ruling party and of the trade unions within the self-management system seems to have grown. There has also been a trend towards decentralising self-management authority down to the level of the establishment or production unit, or even of the workshop, and to speeding up turnover in elected posts by limiting the possibilities of immediate re-election.

Yugoslavia

The Yugoslav system is certainly the best-known example of self-management. It has been the subject of many studies and publications[1] and has already been in existence for over a quarter of a century. After a period of highly centralised economic direction and planning, with a series of nationalisations and a special effort to achieve reconstruction and industrialisation, self-management was introduced throughout the country by a basic law of 1950[2] respecting the administration of public undertakings and associations of undertakings by the workers employed therein. The law was applicable to mining, industry, commerce, communications and transport, larger farming or forestry undertakings, and other state or commune undertakings.

In fact there had already been cases of the introduction of self-management in undertakings in zones liberated from the occupying forces in the Second World War (for instance at the antimony mine and factory at Krupanj in Serbia where, in September 1941, the National Liberation Committee arranged the election of a workers' council to take over the entire management), and a whole series of self-management experiments in 1949 when, after a certain number of moves by workers and the economic blockade of the country, the federal Government and the trade unions issued a directive recommending the setting-up of workers' councils with extensive powers, but which generally still remained consultative only. These experiments initially concerned something over 200 large undertakings in very different regions, and at the time of the adoption of the 1950 Act workers' councils already existed, at least on an experimental basis, in 520 undertakings.

From 1953 onwards self-management was extended, subject to certain modifications, to various "non-economic activities" (public administration, education, health and social security services, scientific institutions, etc.) in which the workers in principle have the same self-management rights as those engaged in other activities. One of the principal modifications was the representation of users of these public services alongside the workers. Today this takes a form which will be described later in connection with "self-managing communities of interest".

The Yugoslav self-management system is based on "social ownership" as distinct from state ownership. Since 1950 it has undergone a series of reforms aimed at removing difficulties revealed by much research and confirmed by senior government leaders. The major milestones in these reforms in the past few years were a congress of workers involved in self-management, organised by the trade unions at Sarajevo in May 1971, which passed some 30 important resolutions; the adoption in the following month by the Federal Assembly of 21 amendments to the Constitution, broadly based on these resolutions; the promulgation in 1974 of a new federal Constitution[3] on which the existing system is based; the adoption since then of various laws, including one, in 1976, on "social planning" aimed at reconciling the advantages of common directives with the maximum of initiative from below; another in the same year, on "associated labour", comprising no less than 671 articles regulating the whole self-management system in detail; and one in 1977 concerning the determination and distribution of income.

Traditionally, the main self-management bodies at the workplace are the workers' assembly and the workers' council. In "non-economic" establishments the latter body is called simply "the council".

In line with the aim, characteristic of the reforms since 1963, of developing more direct participation of workers in self-management, "workers' assemblies", or general meetings, now have greater importance.[4] They take the most important general policy decisions, including decisions on the distribution of the net income of the production unit after meeting its fiscal and other obligations (allowance for depreciation, etc.). The assembly may appoint committees (for instance on recruitment,[5] grievances, housing, etc.), but in most cases these committees have only a consultative role. However, under the new Constitution, the assembly must always set up a self-management supervisory committee, or "workers' control organ" to see that workers' rights are respected. The assembly usually appoints a chairman and other officers to prepare the agenda for meetings.

The workers' council is elected by secret ballot of the staff from among its own members, usually for a term of two years (this is the maximum laid down in Article 102 of the Federal Constitution of 1974), with one-half being renewed each year. In order to ensure the turnover desired, no member may be elected for more than two successive terms. In addition, in line with a general principle, delegates may now be voted out by the electors at any time. The number of members on the council (usually between 15 and 70) must be proportionate to the size of the workforce concerned. Its composition, powers and functions are laid down by internal by-laws and regulations: in principle it proposes these itself and they are adopted by the workers' assembly or by referendum. As regards day-by-day management, the workers' council has quite broad powers of supervision, and even of decision, and is responsible for seeing that the workers are properly informed. It keeps track of the execution of programmes and periodically checks the accounts.

The workers' council generally appoints an executive committee and often various specialised subcommittees to which it delegates consultative powers or powers of decision in clearly defined areas of competence (for instance planning and programming, financial and commercial matters, investment, recruitment, discipline, grievances, education and training, safety and health, housing). Very important questions such as mergers or industrial diversification may be submitted to the workers by referendum, though in practice they are more often put before the workers' assembly. The assembly is not allowed to delegate its main powers of decision (for instance concerning activity programmes and distribution of income) to the workers' council.

It is the workers' council which elects the general manager and other top managers (generally as a group) for renewable terms of four years. The election follows an open competition organised by a committee consisting of representatives of the workers of the unit concerned, of the trade union and of the local authorities; this committee submits its proposals to the workers' council. The general manager and the other senior managers may not become or remain members of the workers' council. The council has the right to terminate their appointments; termination may be proposed in particular by the local assembly, the Communist League and the trade union. In principle, the management's chief task is to prepare the material on which the workers' decisions will be based and to help co-ordinate and execute those decisions. In practice it nevertheless wields considerable power in day-to-day management, particularly when decisions must be taken at short notice. The general manager may suspend the application of a decision of the workers' council or of any other workers' management body whenever it conflicts with the law; he must then refer the matter immediately to the competent authority.

One of the main reforms, introduced from 1956 onwards in order to bring the self-management bodies closer to the individual worker and to avoid the exertion of excessive influence by supervisory, executive and technical staff and highly skilled workers, consisted in decentralising management within the undertaking as much as possible by setting up workers' councils with the right to elect their own managers at the level of the workshop or department.

Thus the essential distinction is no longer one between undertakings (or institutions, in the case of "non-economic" sectors) and establishments; the ground structure is now that of "basic organisations of associated labour" corresponding to each technically distinct production or service unit whose output and costs can be determined and which constitutes a single production and management unit. This may for instance be a workshop or a factory department employing anything from 10 to 3,000 workers; in most cases the strength is between 100 and 500. Some parts of an undertaking such as the sales department, the drawing office, the stores or maintenance departments may, instead of being "basic organisations", form work groups which are likewise self-governing.

There is therefore the possibility of having, in one economic unit (or institution), a self-management structure existing at three levels: that of the unit (or institution) taken as a whole, that of its different factories or establishments and that of its workshops, departments or sections. The respective terms used at each of these levels are "composite organisation of associated labour" (which may for instance cover an organisation as vast as an agro-industrial combine), "organisation of associated labour" and "basic organisation of associated labour".

Self-employed workers such as artisans, truck owner-drivers, garage proprietors, those conducting family hotel or restaurant businesses as well as farmers now have in principle the same socio-economic status as the workers of organisations of associated labour and may associate freely, either by forming co-operatives or by resorting to other forms of association (such as basic organisations or "contractual organisations of associated labour", the latter being specially designed for self-employed workers and farmers).

Each unit of associated labour has its own by-laws and regulations and its own self-management bodies—assembly and workers' council—unless it has very few workers, in which case there is no workers' council but only an assembly. The workers' assembly of a workshop can thus decide all questions concerning internal affairs in the workshop, including the adoption of production and investment plans, internal rules and distribution of the income available.

Relations between these organisations at different levels, including the distribution of the gross income created in common, are regulated by "self-management agreements" which are generally drawn up in the workers' councils and approved by the assemblies or by referenda; at least half of the workers in each basic organisation which is party to the agreement must have signed it or accepted it in writing. In the event of a dispute between the signatory parties (for instance on quality of products, prices or delivery dates) the matter may be submitted to an internal arbitration body and, if necessary, to external self-management tribunals, to the normal courts of law or even to a constitutional court.

Previously, distribution of income among self-managed units was governed by the buying and selling relationships which existed between them. Now it is the self-management agreements that determine the distribution of the income obtained by a unit from its market sales of goods or services among the units that have contributed to its production.[6] Periodically, the workers are paid "advances" which are later readjusted in the light of the book-keeping results after deduction of the various liabilities such as interest repayments, taxes due and statutory reserves. If a basic organisation of associated labour does not succeed in providing its workers with the legal minimum wage, assistance is obtained from other basic organisations (a solidarity fund for this purpose is common); if the situation persists, the organisation must prepare and implement a reorganisation plan. If the reorganisation plan is ineffective, the workers are transferred to another basic organisation within the same organisation (or composite organisation) of associated labour, or may even be transferred elsewhere, possibly after retraining.

Self-management agreements also regulate relations within or between self-managing communities of interest; these associations are responsible for co-ordinating the interests of the providers of certain public services or utilities and their users, for instance in education, health, social security, housing, transport and power and water supply. The assembly of a community of interests has two chambers, one constituted by the delegates of the workers of the public service concerned, the other by the delegates of workers, retired people and others who are users of the service concerned. An agreement concluded at the end of the year for the following year between the delegates of the two chambers settles such matters as the resources to be employed, the financial arrangements and the prices to be charged. Agreements of this kind have to be submitted for the approval of the workers of all the basic organisations which are party to them. When important questions of general interest are at stake the agreement of the assembly of the local authority or republic must also be obtained.

To avoid the imposition of planning by central government and to allow the greatest possible scope for the initiative of individuals and of self-managed units, a certain number of "social rules" are laid down by "social compacts" instead of by laws or regulations. Planning subsists, but the Social Planning Law of 1976 endeavours to promote initiative from below in planning matters. The social compacts cover all self-managed units in a given territory in respect of important questions which

54

are common to them. They are concluded at different levels by those units, the economic chambers, socio-political organisations such as the trade unions and the executive councils (or governments) of the provinces, the republics or the federation. The first social compact concluded at federal level regulated minimum living and working conditions on building sites, whilst one of the most important concerned employment policy.[7] A social compact concluded in April 1972 in the republic of Croatia concerned income distribution, limiting the spread of individual incomes to a ratio of 1 to 5 and fixing the minimum and maximum individual monthly incomes of workers. These provisions then had to be included in the self-management agreements of 130 industries and economic and non-economic associations. It is also by such social compacts that special funds are established to come to the help of organisations facing exceptional economic difficulties or to deal with unemployment and underemployment problems in certain regions or industries.

In the absence of self-management agreements or social compacts, a certain number of matters continue to be regulated by legislation.

It is often stressed in Yugoslavia that genuine self-management in undertakings can develop only if relations at the other levels of social organisation and in society as a whole are similarly self-managing in nature.[8] Self-management arrangements have now penetrated all socio-political activities. As from 1953 the Constitution set up producers' councils or chambers attached to all assemblies from the commune up to the federation. Under the 1963 Constitution these bodies were known as "self-management community councils". Under the 1974 Constitution a system of "delegations" has been established, strengthening direct democracy and the links with the workers concerned in each case. Delegations are elected by secret ballot for a term of four years in the organisations of associated labour, in local communities and in the socio-political organisations (Communist League, Socialist Alliance, Confederation of Trade Unions, ex-servicemen's federations and Youth League). These delegations in turn elect from among their own members delegates to the assemblies of local communities, autonomous provinces, republics and the Federation. The assembly of a republic for instance comprises a chamber of associated labour, a chamber of communes and a chamber of socio-political organisations. All the delegates must maintain close contact with the bodies that have elected them (and which can dismiss them at any moment) so as better to express the point of view of their constituents. At the beginning of 1976, it was estimated that 100,000 delegations, comprising a total of over 1 million persons, had been elected. By 1978 the number of these delegations had doubled and some 2.5 million persons had been elected to serve on them.[9]

In a self-management system of this kind, the role of socio-political organisations such as the party and the trade unions has sometimes been questioned. In practice this role is quite important. It should be borne in mind that Yugoslavia does not have a plurality of political parties. The role of the trade unions, which was questioned particularly around 1968, was laid down in clearer terms in the new federal Constitution and in the Associated Labour Law of 1976. Trade unions have the duty of facilitating the functioning of the self-management bodies, especially through training programmes for workers and workers' representatives and by forestalling disputes of any kind which might arise between workers and their organisations of associated labour, or among those organisations themselves, and by contributing to their settlement. They have the right to arrange for the conclusion or revision of self-management agreements and to promote the conclusion of social compacts. The Associated Labour Law of 1976 gives them extensive disciplinary powers, not only to conduct hearings before disciplinary committees at the workplace or to submit an appeal against a penalty—even if the workers concerned have not themselves taken the initiative to do so—but also to initiate disciplinary proceedings, in the interest of the personnel, against a worker whose unsatisfactory work or absenteeism is damaging the unit of which he is a part.

There has thus been a succession of reforms aimed at avoiding the growth of bureaucracy and strengthening the individual worker's direct participation by maximum decentralisation of the self-management system and by limiting the influence of supervisory, executive and technical staff and of the best educated and most highly skilled workers, which could otherwise easily prevail. Other problems subsist, some of which seem to be inseparable from this high degree of participation, such as the often considerable amount of time spent in meetings,[10] and the risk (less since the recent reforms) that managers will avoid submitting certain decisions to the self-management bodies on the pretext that they have to be taken urgently, or that managers will carry out price adjustments too readily, with resulting inflationary effects.

The Yugoslav head of state referred to a number of other problems in an address delivered in 1974:

. . . Trade enjoys a privileged position in comparison with production. This is especially applicable to the large-scale foreign trade and wholesale enterprises which are in a monopoly position vis-à-vis the producing enterprises. In selling the latter's products, or procuring what the producing enterprises need, on the domestic or foreign market, they appropriate a disproportionate part of surplus labour[11]. . . .

Vast social resources are concentrated in banks and property insurance companies while the workers who created those resources have the least to say about them. Moreover, they are highly dependent on the banks and insurance companies which operate as autonomous centers of economic power and are actually the principal factors of decision-making on the conditions under which organisations of associated labour operate and on their development.

Direct links have not yet been established between material production on one hand, and public and communal activities in the fields of education, science, culture and health, on the other. . . . Most frequently it is the state that acts as intermediary between them, regulating the work of these public and communal activities, determining the obligations of the economy as regards their financing, making the decisions on their development, and so on. Even where special communities of interest have been formed, those who provide the resources for financing these activities do not yet make the decisions on them, nor do those who perform these activities. And in those communities, it is usually a small circle of persons, acting independently, who hold a monopoly on decision-making. [12]

It was with a view to solution of problems of this nature that the Associated Labour Law provided for the distribution of the "collective income" through self-management agreements among all units contributing to it, that the present system of self-managing communities of interest was put into force and that the representatives of basic organisations were given increased powers in the self-management bodies of the banks where they deposit the funds of the organisations.

It will be seen that the task of implementing so highly developed a system of participation through successive reforms is a tremendous one. In the beginning, owing to many workers' lack of knowledge and experience, the workers' council had only limited powers of decision, and the most important decisions were taken jointly with the general manager. Yugoslavia provides a good example of the dynamic character of participation in decision-making, already referred to, and of the importance of the time factor.

Algeria

Self-management came into being in Algeria in 1963 after the proclamation of independence and at a time when, with the departure of the previous owners and managers, the workers took over the operation and management of various undertakings. Two decrees, dated 22 and 28 March 1963, provided the legal basis for machinery comprising a workers' assembly, an elected workers' council, an elected management board and a manager appointed by the Government; the decrees also laid down the procedure for sharing out the income of self-managed undertakings. [13]

No further regulations were issued in the following years to clarify and consolidate the legal status of these undertakings; the introduction of self-management amounted in fact to a tacit form of nationalisation or socialisation. Thus, while in law the self-managed undertakings kept, in varying degrees, the autonomy which they had enjoyed when they had been privately owned, they were in practice integrated into official or semi-official organisations, particularly as concerns the purchasing of supplies and the marketing of products, especially in agriculture.

At first the Algerian experiment did not extend to all sectors of the national economy. In agriculture self-management was introduced in virtually the whole of the modern farming sector; but in manufacturing industry, where it has not been continued in its initial form, it was limited to about 300 factories employing some 15,000 workers.

Originally, self-management frequently made it possible to continue operations when immediate closure seemed inevitable; however, the system encountered a whole series of major obstacles to its operation and development. They are both internal and external in origin.[14] The autonomy of the undertaking as regards the distribution of its income and other matters was often challenged; the slow turnover of management staff and of members of the self-management bodies, the workers' lack of training and information and the lack of a clear definition of the relationships between the management bodies slowed down the movement and bred conflicts. Nor were the economic conditions of the time and other factors favourable to the growth of self-management, and very soon it gave way to centralised direction by the State, particularly in industry, while in agriculture the management was taken over by the government departments responsible for the supervision of the undertakings in question.

Today self-management properly so-called applies officially only on large farms, under an ordinance of 17 June 1975 instituting a policy of decentralisation and autonomous management and amending an ordinance of 1968 on self-management in agriculture and several decrees issued in 1969. Under the present system, the management of large nationalised farms is entrusted by the State to "workers' collectives". A collective is a "group of producers" (all the workers on the farm), with elected bodies to express its collective views on the management of the undertaking subject to the directives of the national economic and social development plan, and to protect the common interest of its members. These bodies are: a workers' assembly, a workers' council (above a certain size of farm), a management committee and a chairman. The assembly is the supreme body. It has powers of management and supervision and elects, from those of its members who are permanently employed on the farm, the workers' council or management committee (if there is no workers' council) and the chairman. It adopts the annual production plan and the development and equipment plans within the limits of the national plan, and decides on the organisation of work and job allocation of workers. It also adopts the scale of basic pay and bonuses for each job, approves the annual accounts and expresses its opinions on the use of the undertaking's funds. The workers' council applies the general policies laid down by the assembly, elects the management committee and supervises its work. The management committee is responsible for taking all the necessary decisions for the running of the farm along the lines laid down by the assembly, for instance decisions on the purchase of supplies, on the marketing of produce, on short-term borrowing and on the recruitment of seasonal workers. The chairman, now appointed for three years instead of one year as previously, is relieved full time of his other duties so that he can represent the workers' collective as required; the law provides that the Government shall put a qualified technician at his disposal to help him with his technical tasks, but the technician may not overrule the decisions of the collective's self-management bodies. More recently the post of manager has reappeared; he is the representative of the State in the undertaking. He is responsible to the management committee and is regularly informed by the chairman of the decisions of the self-management bodies.

The income of self-managed farms, for which strict accounting procedures are prescribed, is distributed at the end of the financial year between the farm's own funds (statutory reserve, operating funds and investment fund), the income of the workers' collective (workers' dividends and welfare fund) and the local authorities, in accordance with rules laid down by decree. During the course of the year, each member of the collective draws an advance on his share of the income; this is determined by the assembly on the basis of the estimated income of the farm and the minimum agricultural wage. The people's assemblies for the region (*wilaya*) and for the district are responsible for co-ordinating, encouraging and supervising the activities of the self-managing agricultural undertakings in their respective areas, being assisted in this task by the all-purpose local agricultural co-operative service. For some time now there has been considerable development of co-operatives that supply farms and market their produce.

After entry into force of the ordinance of 1975, elections were held in the agricultural self-management bodies to reinvigorate them. The party (the National Liberation Front) had an important part to play in the explanatory, promotional and training programme that accompanied this reform.

In addition, the Algerian Government has since 1965 applied itself to seeing that workers are not just wage earners but "producers-cum-managers", and it adopted in 1971 a code and charter for the socialist management of undertakings.[15] These provisions are applicable to non-agricultural public undertakings. They provide for the election for a term of three years of unit assemblies to act as trade union councils[16] and undertaking assemblies elected by the unit assemblies.

The assemblies have between seven and 25 members according to the size of the workforce, and meet at least twice a year (undertaking assemblies) or at least four times (unit assemblies). They are expected to contribute to formation of the undertaking's general policy by issuing opinions and recommendations on the budget estimates and proposals of the undertaking and on programme proposals, including investment proposals (the latter have to be submitted to the supervising department). The assemblies are required to supervise the management and to give their opinion on the annual balance sheet and on the accounts. They must be associated with the management in deciding personnel policy, in particular in regard to recruitment, termination of employment, pay, training, health and safety and working conditions. They manage welfare activities. Both unit and undertaking assemblies are to have standing committees to deal respectively with economic and financial matters, social and cultural matters, personnel and training matters and—with an equal number of management representatives—discipline and health and safety.[17]

Regulations have been issued to lay down the powers of undertaking and unit assemblies. They include—

(a) supervision of the execution of the plan and issue of an annual report showing the successes and shortcomings of the management as well as the lessons to be drawn from them (the assembly must denounce any form of abuse, waste or misappropriation of funds at any level at which it occurs, and must propose to the manager of the undertaking or unit, as the case may be, the measures to be taken and the prosecutions to be set in motion);

(b) distribution of the income of the undertaking;

(c) formulation, with the undertaking's management board, of personnel policy (including pay scales) and staff training policy; and

(d) election from among its members of representatives on the management board and various committees.

The assemblies must report on their activities at least once a year to their electors. They may consult experts in specific fields, such as analysis of the financial situation of the undertaking or unit.

The management must form a coherent group in order to ensure co-ordination. The management board, which in principle meets once a month, brings together under the chairmanship of the general manager the principal managers and two staff representatives elected by the workers' assembly. The management is required to attend the meetings of staff assemblies in an advisory capacity.

Today, the structure of the larger undertakings is such that units have the same bodies as undertakings: an assembly, a management board (which likewise comprises two representatives elected by the personnel) and a manager. As mentioned above, it is these unit assemblies which elect the members of the undertaking assembly.

A decree has defined the composition, powers and operational procedures of the management boards of undertakings and units. Boards now have from nine to 11 members at undertaking level and from seven to nine members at unit level.

Initially, this new system was introduced experimentally in several undertakings before a vast national explanatory campaign. By 1975, 27 undertaking assemblies had been set up, having been elected by 540 unit assemblies representing almost 150,000 workers in the power, commerce, transport, posts and telecommunications, tourism, finance, and public works sectors. The second national conference on the socialist management of undertakings, which met in the same year in Algiers, requested the extension of the system to all the production of goods and services, including undertakings belonging to local authorities. This conference also passed a resolution on general policy to reduce bureaucracy.[18] In 1979 socialist management applied in 57 undertakings, totalling some 300,000 workers, with more than 750 unit assemblies.[19]

In 1975 an ordinance[20] laid down the relationships between the undertaking, the department to which it reports and other departments of state. The supervising department has powers of direction and supervision over the undertaking; for each undertaking, it prescribes sectoral targets corresponding to the national plan, approves the plans of the undertaking (which are then submitted to the Government for adoption), and puts the necessary resources at the undertaking's disposal. In addition, it approves, sometimes with the other departments concerned, the budget, the draft personnel regulations and the proposed organisation chart of the undertaking. It makes recommendations to the Government for posts of general manager and itself appoints the assistant general managers and the managers of undertakings and their units. In addition, it supervises the management of undertakings.

There is also provision for the establishment of co-ordinating councils to promote joint programming of investment, production, supplies and marketing by undertakings in the same industry or trade, and to set up joint machinery for foreign trade, distribution, management organisation, research, health and safety, and vocational training.[21] Co-ordinating councils consist of the workers' assembly chairmen and the general managers of all the undertakings concerned, a representative of the party, a trade union representative and a representative of the government departments responsible for finance and planning.

Among problems recently reported are the considerable size now attained by some undertakings, which has led to the need to introduce intermediate or specialised centres of decision not provided for in the legislation, and to the tendency of some managers to exceed their powers.[22] It has also been found that problems are looked at solely from the point of view of the workers' interests, though the terms of reference of workers' assemblies are wider. Mention is also made of anti-worker tendencies among some executives keen on asserting their powers, and the persistence of technocratic ideas tending to cut down the role of the workers because of their alleged inability to understand the problems.[23] The Algerian trade union movement (UGTA), which played a very active part in the explanatory campaigns preceding the new system, will also have to make a considerable contribution towards its application in undertakings, particularly through workers' education. According to one prominent Algerian, socialist management of undertakings does not as yet amount to either self-management or joint management, but to initiation of the workers to management problems.[24]

Poland

In Poland workers' councils sprang up spontaneously in 1956 in many undertakings on the workers' initiative, as a result in particular of tension aroused among the workers by the centralised system of planned management of the economy at a time when the trade unions had ceased to provide an effective channel of communication.[25] The movement was rapidly recognised by the highest political authorities in October 1956, and the workers' councils were granted legal status by an Act of 19 November 1956.[26]

Undertakings were granted much wider management autonomy, while continuing to operate within a centralised planning system, especially in respect of prices and other major aspects of economic policy. Proposals aimed at granting full independence to undertakings within some form of indirect planning were firmly rejected; however, a special procedure was introduced for arbitration in the event of disputes between the undertaking and the central government departments responsible for economic affairs. A limited form of profit-sharing was introduced directly in the shape of bonuses and indirectly through welfare measures. Existing official and trade union bodies for consultation and co-operation in undertakings were maintained, and the functions of the trade unions at higher levels considerably strengthened. Within the limits of plan targets, collective agreements were again concluded in most industries, particularly on wages and fringe benefits.

The machinery for self-management in undertakings was revised by law of 20 December 1958[27] aimed at the formal association of the trade union and party organisations in the undertaking with management decisions; it conferred overriding authority on the "self-management conference". The self-management bodies in Polish undertakings are the self-management conference, the workers' council of the undertaking and the workers' councils in workshops.

The self-management conference, which meets at least every three months, consists of the workers' council, the undertaking's trade union council or committee and the executive committee of the cell of the Polish United Workers' Party; it may co-opt representatives of youth organisations and technico-scientific associations. Since 1978, in order to increase participation in self-management, representatives elected annually by secret ballot in the various departments of the undertaking also take part in the conference (at the end of 1978 it was estimated that 60 per cent of the members of these conferences were rank-and-file workers).[28]

The workers' council, meeting in principle once a month, consists of members elected by the workers (or, in the case of a large undertaking, of members of the shop councils), a representative of the trade union council and a representative of the party executive committee, up to a limit of 50 members in all, of whom in principle two-thirds should be manual workers, or half in the case of an undertaking with a large technical staff. The workers' council may be dissolved, or some of its members deprived of their membership, if the majority of the workforce decide accordingly; similarly, the trade union has the right to dissolve a workers' council in exceptional cases expressly provided for by law, particularly when the activities of a workers' council obviously run counter to the interests of the undertaking, its personnel or the national economy. The workers' council has a presidium or executive committee consisting of its chairman and secretary together with members elected by the council from among its members or from among the chairmen of shop councils, as well as of the chairman of the trade union council and of the secretary of the party executive committee (that is of from five to 11 members in all).

In large undertakings shop workers' councils each consist of between three and seven elected members plus a representative of the trade union and a representative of the party.

The decisions of these bodies take the form of resolutions. The general manager of the undertaking, without being a member, takes part ex officio in their meetings and is required to submit all relevant documents. Various committees, set up mostly by the workers' council, are responsible for studying specific problems.

The self-management conference has exclusive competence, which it may, however, delegate to the workers' council of the undertaking, in respect of the adoption of works rules, distribution of the "undertaking fund" (which varies from 5 to 10 per cent of the wage fund, according to the undertaking, after targets have been fulfilled), the allocation of bonuses and material incentives, the construction of housing and the provision of institutions such as rest or holiday homes and libraries. It supervises the activities of the management, reviews the balance sheet and the functioning of the undertaking, and examines and adopts the latter's annual and long-term plans in the light of directives and indices in national economic plans. It lays down broad principles with regard to organisation and productivity, health and safety and employment and vocational training policy, and decides on major investments. Since 1978 the departments of large undertakings may each have their own self-management conference.

In addition to the duties delegated to it by the conference, the workers' council approves the monthly and quarterly programmes, sees that the resolutions of the conference are implemented by the management and organises discussions on production jointly with the management and the trade union council. It exercises general supervision over the economic and financial activity of the undertaking, and pays attention to the lowering of production costs and the improvement of productivity and quality, health and safety, and work discipline. Taking account of the collective agreement, it adopts, in agreement with the trade union council of the undertaking, directives on pay, pay scales and output norms. Its presidium makes recommendations on the appointment, or in certain cases the dismissal, of the general manager by the supervisory department of state, supervises the management of the wage fund and the payment of bonuses, gathers the opinions of workers at their meetings or assemblies and analyses personnel and promotion policies.

At their own level shop councils have a role corresponding to that of the workers' council; they examine monthly programme proposals and in collaboration with the shop manager and the shop trade union council they organise implementation within the workshop of the resolutions of the conference, the workers' council and the production conferences.

Sometimes the personnel is consulted by referendum on production questions or financial or welfare questions which are then discussed by the self-management conference.

All workers are under the orders of their management, since the self-management bodies do not have the power to give them instructions directly, and a detailed procedure is provided for settling any disputes between the management and the self-management conference or workers' council. The general manager is responsible to the supervisory department for the efficient operation of the undertaking. He has the power of decision in all fields where it is not allocated by law to a self-management body (in which case he may present all the proposals or observations he considers pertinent). He may also suspend the execution of a decision of a self-management body if he considers it contrary to law or to the Plan; it is then for the self-management conference or, if the original decision emanated from the conference, for the supervisory department to come to a decision.

Various surveys carried out by research institutes had shown that the workers were relatively passive towards the self-management bodies when it was their impression that they had little influence on changes in the policy of the undertaking. However, it has been observed that the rising educational level of the working population in general has strengthened interest in self-management and the ability to contribute to it effectively. Article 13 of the Constitution as amended in February 1976 has enshrined the right of workers in all undertakings to participate in decision-making.

The rule mentioned earlier under which, in principle, two-thirds of the members of a self-management conference had to be manual workers, was aimed at avoiding a situation common at the start of self-management in which there was a preponderance of executive, supervisory, technical and other non-manual staff on the self-management bodies. However, recent inquiries show that only a small minority of manual workers take an active part in self-management, except in connection with supervision of the distribution of bonuses and other rewards, and that the proportion is even lower in small undertakings and in undertakings generally employing less well educated and skilled workers such as former agricultural workers, who only adjust progressively to industrial work and who often keep their small farms, or women who, on top of their day's work, have to cope with household duties.[29] Other problems encountered include occasional poor communication between the workers and the bodies responsible for representing them, overlapping competence between the workers' council and the trade union, and the attitude of certain managers who are not always sufficiently ready to accept the role that should be played by the self-management bodies.[30] It also happens, as in many other countries, that the documents presented to the workers' representatives contain too many insufficiently analysed statistics and are written in esoteric language.[31]

In the past few years the autonomy of Polish undertakings seems to have grown, and planning, while remaining centralised, seems to have become even more flexible, being undertaken in close consultation with the personnel of undertakings and their self-management bodies.[32] In 1978 the self-management system, applied initially in manufacturing industry, construction and state farms, was extended by a decision of the Council of Ministers to state undertakings in other fields such as commerce and transport. It has aroused greater interest since the end of 1970, as has been evident from discussions at the seventh congress of the trade unions and the many articles which appeared in the press at the time. In 1972 a charter of rights of general managers of undertakings was adopted by the Council of Ministers. In 1978 the National Conference of Self-Management Delegates, after listing the weak points of the self-management system and denouncing in particular the formalism which hindered the real participation of workers in decision-making, recommended a strengthening of workers' self-management and issued a number of guidelines with this in view. Also, as in other countries of Eastern Europe, there has been a trend towards the merging of production units into groups of undertakings; in Poland this has raised problems of adaptation of the system and its structures. However, under a law of 12 December 1969, merged undertakings retain their self-management bodies, with periodic meetings of their representatives being organised at the level of the group of undertakings; some groups have their own self-management bodies.

Although for some years the self-management bodies' powers of decision were limited by the central planning system and by restrictions as regards the distribution of incomes, these bodies, especially the workers' councils, nevertheless succeeded in adjusting to the situation, and they had a varying degree of influence, always significant, on the policies and practices of undertakings. In spite of, or perhaps thanks to the complexity of its machinery, the system seems to have permitted a number of checks which have given workers by no means negligible possibilities of participation in many fields; and in the context of the country's socio-economic régime, these possibilities were such as to facilitate adaptation to circumstances. In addition, particularly over the past ten years or so, growing attention has been paid to the "humanisation of work" and to human relations in general in undertakings, and this has had the effect of strengthening the participation machinery. On the basis of the work of specialists or research institutes, endeavours are being made to improve the machinery or to introduce suitable provisions in the social plans of undertakings.[33]

Israel

A type of self-management is provided by the egalitarian communal "kibbutz" organisation in Israel. Initially limited to agriculture, the kibbutz has tended to move into industrial production such as metal-working or wood-working, the manufacture of furniture or plastic products and food processing. In 1976 kibbutz industrial units numbered about 250, employing an average of 50 people each; in 1977 they contributed one-twentieth of the country's total industrial production, and their productivity was estimated to be 30 per cent above the national average.[34]

In principle each kibbutz has a general assembly which usually meets once a week to discuss its farming activities and once a month for its industrial activities. It elects several committees (for instance to deal with technical problems, marketing, job allocation and training assignments) and a management board. This board generally consists of a general manager, a production manager, an economist, a treasurer and a number of workers' representatives appointed by the unit assemblies that are found in the larger kibbutzim. Only technical problems are within the exclusive competence of the management board. Investment and production plans are approved by the general assembly. The way work is organised is decided by the unit assembly.

Under this system the concept of a wage has disappeared and there is no resort to material incentives such as output bonuses. Each member lives as a member of a community on the common funds of the kibbutz, and receives only a small annual allowance for personal expenditure. The principle that all members take their turn is applied not only for the post of manager but for the rest of the leadership that is elected by unit assemblies and often participates in production work, and for members of the various committees.

While participation at management level is very highly developed, there remain problems at the level of execution and of the individual job (general working conditions, work tempo, monotony, manpower shortages, lack of information and communication, tension between production workers and technicians or maintenance workers). Special projects have been launched to deal with these problems.[35]

Tanzania

In Tanzania a vast self-management experiment has now been going on for some ten years in the community villages known as "ujaama". By 1973 these already covered 20 per cent of the population and by 1976 there were about 8,000 ujaama villages covering some 85 per cent of the population.

This arrangement has its origin in the tradition of collective farming by the extended family or clan, which after several experiments became the official rural development policy of the country after President Nyerere's Arusha declaration of 1968, advocating a form of African socialism for Tanzania.

Initially, the system was characterised by communal organisation of the ujaama village as a whole. Since 1973 this has been superseded by a form of collective farming by "blocks" of family holdings within a general co-operative framework for the purchase of supplies, equipment and consumption goods and the sale of produce. One of the main objects was to give these village communities better opportunities for the use of modern farming techniques and equipment, better access to agricultural advisory services, loans and material facilities (piped water, irrigation, electricity, schools and dispensaries), together with the benefits of larger-scale production.

To be set up officially an ujaama village must contain at least 250 families. It then has a village assembly, consisting of every resident of 18 years or over, which approves the community's budget, admits or expels members, and elects every year from among members of 21 years or older a village council to act as management committee. The council has a chairman, generally somewhat senior in age, a secretary, mostly young and better educated, and a treasurer. Often various subcommittees are set up to deal with problems such as those of education or finance. In practice, a council of elders is in many cases still found, dealing in particular with disciplinary questions. Local officials and representatives of the national trade union confederation (JUWATA) and its youth league play a part in the organisation of these village communities.

The achievements vary. Problems have been encountered, such as the preponderating influence of better educated and dynamic villagers who are already better off, or the growing remoteness of the plots to be cultivated as the population becomes concentrated in the villages. In most cases, marketing of produce continues to be carried out by quasi-government bodies outside the ujaama framework. However, many of these villages have succeeded, with their own resources, in building access roads and irrigation systems, in setting up dairies and poultry farms and in starting reafforestation programmes. Some have carpenters' shops or smithies.

Madagascar

In Madagascar, in the agricultural sector, a very old communal farming institution—the "fokonolona"—is a form of self-management at village level where in practice the council of elders still plays a considerable part. Certain public works, such as the construction of access roads and irrigation networks, can be carried out on a communal basis under the fokolona system.[36]

In the mining, industrial, commercial and service sectors, in parallel with a series of nationalisations, an ordinance dated 27 December 1976[37] promulgated a "charter for socialist undertakings" which, now amended by an ordinance dated 1 May 1978,[38] establishes the new structure of socialist undertakings.[39]

The introduction and preamble to this charter emphasise that its aim is to eliminate bureaucracy and conflict by introducing the organised participation of workers at all levels of policy-making, administration, organisation and supervision in socialist undertakings. It provides that the worker has the right to share in the fruits of his labour and that "as a producer, manager and responsible member" he participates in policy decisions, management and supervision of the operation of the undertaking and in the organisation of its work. This new system has features both of co-management and self-management, but conceptually the latter seems to predominate. As in the Algerian system of socialist management of undertakings, the workers' assembly, the specialised committees and the workers' committees all play important roles. In addition the preamble provides that important decisions have to be taken on a joint basis. It mentions "non-interference by the administration in the management of the undertaking" and the sharing of its income according to work performed and merit.

According to this charter, a socialist undertaking is an economic unit under independent management, in which the State owns at least 51 per cent of the capital either directly or through undertakings which it controls. All undertakings set up after promulgation of the charter and all state economic operations must take the form of socialist undertakings if they meet the requirement as to their financing.

Socialist undertakings with similar or complementary objectives must be constituted into a distinct sector of the economy under the authority of a policy council representing the State. That council collects information and proposals for national and regional development plans and lays down the programmes and targets for implementation of those plans in the sector and the undertakings belonging to it.

The policy council, which is appointed by decree, includes representatives of the State (its chairman is one of these), members of the National People's Assembly, representatives of the management committees of socialist undertakings in the sector, delegates elected by the workers and, if appropriate, representatives of the socialist co-operative movement in the sector. The council appoints one or more auditors or auditing bodies that do not have the right to become involved in the management of the undertakings.

Each socialist undertaking is administered by a management committee and a manager.

The management committee consists of representatives of the State, appointed by Prime Minister's order on the recommendation of the policy council, delegates elected by the workers of the undertaking and, in appropriate cases, one or more nominees of investors known as "participants" (minority shareholders) approved by the Government and, in certain cases, representatives of the local authorities. This committee reports to the policy council, to which it submits programme proposals and proposals to change or extend the undertaking's activities. It concerns itself with the fulfilment of targets. The members have to deposit surety-bonds with the undertaking in a blocked account as a guarantee for action taken in the course of management.

The manager puts the programmes and the management committee's decisions into execution, in accordance with the principles of respect for majority decisions taken after discussion, and of unity of command once those decisions have been taken. He is appointed by Prime Minister's order on the recommendation of the management committee, of which he is a member ex officio though he cannot be its chairman.

The charter provides that the workers shall form a workers' general assembly, to consider the estimates and budget of the undertaking and lay down its general policy within the framework of the national plan.

A workers' committee of each establishment is elected by this assembly from among active members of the trade unions indicated in the charter. In their turn they elect the workers' committee for the undertaking. The latter committee is responsible to the workers' general assembly, to which it reports on its activities. The workers' committee, which elects from among its members the representatives of the staff of the undertaking to sit on the policy board and the management committee, participates in the formulation of the general policy of the undertaking and in the supervision of its management; it also co-ordinates the management of the welfare activities of establishment committees or manages them directly itself.

In addition, standing committees can be set up within the undertaking or each of its establishments to take charge of economic and financial affairs, social and cultural affairs, personnel matters, training, discipline and health and safety. The workers' committee appoints its representatives on these committees from among its own members or, if necessary, from among members of the general assembly; however, on the disciplinary and health and safety committees there is parity with representatives of the management. Other committees can be set up temporarily if so decided by the workers' committee or the workers' general assembly.

The net income of the undertaking (that is, after deduction of overhead expenses, debt repayments, deposits, statutory payments into reserve and other funds and other charges, such as the dividend paid to members of the management committee) is distributed among the shareholding participants, the workers (mainly through the financing of the undertaking's welfare activities), the State (in the form of taxes) and the nation. This last share goes to the National Investment Fund; it may be reinvested in the undertaking, invested in a priority sector or placed in an interest-bearing national loan fund.

Peru

In Peru, alongside the public sector, the private sector, which consists of small businesses, and the "reformed" private sector (where a system of co-determination has been introduced as described below), a legislative decree dated 30 April 1974[40] launched a self-managing sector to which the term of "socially owned undertakings" is applied.

The establishment of undertakings in that sector is normally financed by an initial contribution from the State, repayable later.

Any newly engaged worker must pass a skill test (which obviates the need for a trial period) and swear to exercise his rights and fulfil his obligations in conformity with the ethical principles of social ownership. Temporary and casual workers have the same rights and obligations, except the right to occupy an elective post.

In addition to access to information on the situation of the undertaking these rights include continuing technical and vocational training, as well as training in participation in decision-making at all levels. In addition to remuneration for work performed, each worker is entitled to an equal share of the annual surplus.

As part of their obligations, the workers of a socially owned undertaking are required to ensure that the undertaking works efficiently and to play an active part in its self-management bodies. There are special penalties aimed at reducing absenteeism.

The main management bodies of a socially owned undertaking are the general assembly of the personnel, the board of directors, the management and a number of special committees.

The general assembly of the personnel (held at least once a year, with secret and compulsory voting) approves the undertaking's programme, management and balance sheet, decides on distribution of the available surplus, elects or dismisses the members of the board of directors and ratifies the appointment of the general manager (whom it may dismiss, subject to appeal to the relevant regional authority).

The board of directors is an executive body entitled to approve actions taken by the management, and supervise and periodically evaluate the undertaking's plans and programmes.

The management includes the general manager and subordinate managers, who are appointed for an indefinite period.

Apart from an honour committee, which is responsible for examining workers' grievances, and a training committee, there are other specialised committees which have responsibility for advising management and for giving workers the possibility of direct knowledge of, and participation in, the operation of the undertaking. They are set up in each unit (department, workshop, section, etc.) and also serve as centres for cost control. These committees deal with suggestions, examine the accounts of their unit, participate in the preparation of plans and programmes, and recommend promotions or disciplinary measures. Members are elected for one year by all the workers in the unit.

The regional authorities on which the socially owned undertakings depend for supervision and encouragement of their activities are themselves administered by a general assembly consisting of three delegates from each affiliated undertaking, elected by that undertaking's general assembly, and a board of directors of three to six members. At the national level there is a "socially owned sector assembly" consisting of the chairmen and delegates of the regional authorities, and a national social ownership commission consisting of 12 representatives of the State and three workers' representatives from that assembly.

Initially, the socially owned sector was intended to play an important part in the Peruvian economy, perhaps leading to the remodelling and readjustment of the government machine. In practice, its scope has been limited, on account of financing problems, lack of management experience, and administrative delays. At the end of April 1976 three socially owned undertakings had been established, and employed just over 2,000 workers in all; 53 were in the process of being set up, representing a total workforce of some 45,000 persons; 74 plans for the establishment of undertakings had been approved; and 313 were under examination. In addition, the co-operatives (including credit co-operatives) had been requested to convert themselves into socially owned undertakings in the interest of better co-ordination of their activities both in the towns and in the country. There had also been a trend for "social interest agricultural associations" to convert themselves into socially owned undertakings; in April 1976 there were 57 of these associations, bringing together some 60,000 families over a cultivable area of 2.5 million hectares.

However, in the autumn of 1976 the Government declared that "social ownership" would henceforth be reserved for the poorer rural areas. Most of the projects that had been approved were not implemented or were rapidly abandoned. In 1979 there were a total of about 5,300 units or undertakings (including 52 socially owned undertakings) in the four sectors that were more or less self-managed, viz. the co-operatives, the Indian and rural communities, the social interest agricultural associations and the socially owned undertakings in the narrow sense. One of the few large socially owned undertakings surviving is the Lima public transport corporation.

Libyan Arab Jamahiriya

In the Libyan Arab Jamahiriya, after the publication by the head of state of his "green book"[41] setting out his ideas on direct democracy and people's power, people's committees have come into being in private and public undertakings, retaining or rejecting the former managers as they wish. At the People's General Congress held in December 1978 the head of state enunciated the slogan "partners not wage-workers".[42] For the time being, however, people's committees may not be formed in the petroleum industry, banks or insurance companies.

Some experiments

In some other countries self-management has been tried in a few undertakings only, or has been very short-lived. However, the size of the undertakings involved or the point in time at which the experiments were made have sometimes given them prominence.

In Malta the largest undertaking in the country—the Malta Drydock Corporation—a state-owned ship building and repairing yard, has been administered since 1 April 1975 by a board consisting of workers elected by the whole personnel.

From September 1971 up to that date it had been managed by a board consisting half of members appointed by the Government and half of members appointed by the trade union, with an independent chairman approved by both categories of member.

After a referendum of the workers organised by the Government to find out whether they preferred continuation of the old arrangement or whether they were prepared to take over full responsibility for management, and in accordance with amending legislation adopted by the Maltese Parliament on 14 March 1975,[43] the affairs of the corporation came under the direction of a board consisting of eight members elected by the undertaking's workers plus a chairman appointed by these members. Members of the board stay in office for two years.

The board meets whenever required, usually twice a week and in any event not less frequently than once every six weeks. The chairman has a casting vote only. The board is under a series of obligations to keep the Prime Minister informed of the corporations' activity.

The board lays down the corporation's policy, which is then implemented by a management committee consisting of five senior managers and five workers' representatives. The workers share in the profits of the undertaking, the distribution being decided by the board.

In addition, in accordance with model regulations for government departments and nationalised or quasi-government undertakings issued in 1978, works committees with delegates elected by secret ballot have been formed.

As with other forms of participation in Malta (see below), various difficulties have had to be overcome, such as the educational level of workers, the abstruse wording of documents submitted for discussion,

73

poor communication, the attitude of some managers towards workers' representatives and the need to extend participation down to workshop or bench level.[44] Moreover, at the beginning of 1977 the workers, on the advice of their trade union, decided not to sit on any management boards pending consultations with the Government.[45] Since 1978 these experiments seem to have been vigorously pursued within the framework of a new policy of development and participation. Already from 1975 on, participation in the management of undertakings had been reinforced by the work of internal committees (energy-saving committees, etc.) and by now there are annually elected establishment committees (18 in 1979) operating in all sections of the undertaking, and collaborating with the board on productivity, working conditions and welfare.

In Portugal, at the time of the revolution of 25 April 1974 and for several months afterwards, the management of a number of undertakings was taken over by their workers, often after the departure of the owners or managers; according to an unofficial estimate made by the Ministry of Labour at the end of 1975, almost 200 small and medium-sized undertakings were involved.[46] An Act dated 14 October 1978 set up a national institute of self-managing undertakings (INEA) to advise, assist and supervise these undertakings. A further Act dated 16 October 1978 dealt with their internal organisation in cases in which their legal situation had not been regularised. This latter Act provided in particular for an annual inventory of the assets of the undertaking and the election, by secret ballot, of a management committee of three to seven members for renewable terms of two years. Periodic reports on the economic and financial situation of the undertaking have to be sent to the proprietor and to the INEA, which has the power to dismiss a management committee or some of its members. The penultimate chapter of the Act deals with the final determination of the status of the undertakings (by direct settlement with the proprietor, acquisition or expropriation of the undertaking by the State or its acquisition by the personnel). The board of INEA consists of seven representatives of government departments and seven representatives of self-managing undertakings.[47]

In Argentina self-management was tried out in 1973 in a large public electricity generation and distribution undertaking serving Buenos Aires and its suburbs and employing some 25,000 persons at the time.[48] A self-management committee was set up at the head office, and there were councils at the level of the departments and sections. Consumers also were represented on these bodies, through the municipalities. An Act of 5 July 1976 put an end to this experiment, which thus lasted less than three years.

In the spring of 1976 the Government of Jamaica decided, after nationalising three sugar refineries and the sugar-cane plantations belonging to them, to entrust them to self-management by their workers through co-operatives.

PRODUCER'S CO-OPERATIVES AND OTHER RELATED SYSTEMS

One form of self-management rarely described as such but through which workers nevertheless exert direct influence on the management of their undertakings is that of the producers' co-operative, which has been in existence for some 150 years. In many countries, whether industrialised or developing, such co-operatives play an important role, especially in agriculture, the food-processing industries, building and public works, various engineering and electrical industries, glass manufacture, printing, transport and services; in the last-named sector they have been growing fairly rapidly over the past ten years. The Mondragón network of producers' co-operatives which started up in Spain some 20 years ago is often cited as a particularly successful large-scale example of a producers' co-operation. Today it consists of about 60 undertakings employing some 13,000 persons in all.[49] Being formed by workers who want to follow their trade together, all of them were originally new undertakings. Since the 1970s, however, it has not been uncommon in certain industrialised countries for such societies to take over bankrupt private undertakings, thereby helping to preserve jobs threatened by economic recession; in some cases they also attract young people and so facilitate their entry into productive employment.

In principle, the worker members of these producers' co-operatives (which they own) assume all the responsibilities for their management.[50] As in any co-operative, supreme authority lies with the general meeting of members, which elects the board of directors or the management board, as the case may be, as well as the supervisory board, and the auditors. It also discusses and adopts, or rejects, the programmes and budgets, approves the accounts and the balance sheet, decides on the distribution of the surplus, particularly remuneration for work done, and on the amounts to be paid to reserve, decides in the last resort on the admission or exclusion of members, settles disputes, and keeps track of the proceedings of the often numerous committees which it sets up with various terms of reference.

In these co-operatives an effort is made to keep all the worker-members informed through the committees, whether they are office-bearers or not. Also, general briefing meetings are usually organised several times a year on technical or general subjects such as supplies, sales, organisation of services, solidarity arrangements, capital repayment, etc., as well as regular meetings of members of the elective bodies, heads of departments or "brigades" and delegates of various groups.

In order to help their members take decisions more effectively, co-operatives in France belonging to the General Confederation of Workers' Production Co-operatives decided to supply not only an annual balance sheet but also statements of the societies' assets and liabilities at least once every six months. Since 1965 an increasing number of them have prepared reports on progress in co-operation dealing with membership, development and distribution of the society's capital, the promotion of members within the undertaking, their training (and the special budget devoted to this), information, consultation and the course of decision-making, working conditions and their effects (absenteeism, accidents, lost working days, labour turnover, hours of work), the welfare budget and application of the profit-sharing agreements provided for by law.

It will be noted that, in these producers' co-operatives, there is a closer link between participation in decision-making and participation in the resulting proceeds than in other types of undertaking through arrangements for the final distribution of the proceeds between "income for work" (which, in principle though not in law, takes the place of wages), additions to joint-stock capital and endowments for provident institutions (which have been maintained or even increased in spite of the growth of social security systems).

In several (mostly industrialised) countries, other kinds of co-operatives, including in particular consumers' co-operatives, have made arrangements allowing their workers to participate in management.

In Sweden, for example, the statutes of consumers' co-operatives affiliated to the Kooperativa Förbundet (the co-operative alliance and wholesale society) provide that three persons elected by the works council or any other body recognised by the management committee of the society as representing its workers have the right to attend and vote at all general meetings. In Switzerland the statutes of co-operatives affiliated to the Swiss Union of Consumer Co-operative Societies provide that the employees who are members of it may elect their own representatives in the same proportions (one delegate per 200 members) as others to the annual delegates' meetings, and that they have the same rights as other delegates.

Another form of workers' participation in decision-making, less direct than in the above cases, exists when workers' organisations are themselves the owners of undertakings. There is a well known example in Israel, where the General Federation of Labour (Histadrut), through a special subsidiary (Hevrat Ovdim), operates a considerable sector of the economy. It contributes about one-quarter of the gross national product (excluding government services), and includes some large undertakings, industrial or commercial, the industrial ones employing about 15 per cent of the country's labour force.[51] In principle, every member of the Histadrut is a co-proprietor participating in the elaboration of the policy of the undertakings. But the fact that the trade union movement's ownership of undertakings represents an element of workers' participation in the over-all economy of the country does not guarantee that the workers employed in these undertakings have a right to participate in their management. Their situation may not differ fundamentally from that of trade unionists employed in other undertakings.

The managers of Histadrut undertakings are appointed by Hevrat Ovdim. They enjoy considerable autonomy in the running of their undertakings. Since 1956 various attempts have been made to involve the workers directly in management, particularly through the setting up of special committees which, however, met with only limited acceptance, particularly on the part of managers. There have been a series of forms of participation: bipartite productivity councils (introduced also in the private sector)—these became active again after the 1967 economic recession; bipartite works councils with elected workers' delegates (not more than one-third of whom were to be trade union officials), with competence to discuss all problems other than those of wages and fringe benefits—these practically went out of existence between 1960 and 1963; and parity representation on the management of wage and salary earners elected by trade union general meetings—this has spread progressively since the adoption by the Histadrut at the end of 1968 of a charter on participation, parallel with a system of profit-sharing.

By 1976 there were 50 or so Histadrut undertakings with this form of parity representation. The workers' representatives on the management are elected for three years and may not serve more than two consecutive terms. They carry on with their usual jobs, do not receive any special remuneration and may not concern themselves with subjects which are the prerogative of the trade unions. There continue to be reports of resistance from the managements of some undertakings, and of some workers' representatives' lack of appropriate training.

In other countries too, though on a more limited scale, trade union owned undertakings are to be found, as well as teaching and training establishments, and credit, housing and other organisations, many of them set up a long time ago. In recent years there has been particular interest in union-owned or union-supported undertakings in Austria, the Federal Republic of Germany,[52] Malta and Sweden; in Argentina and Panama; in Australia, India, Japan, Malaysia and Singapore; and in Ghana and Tunisia. In some countries these undertakings form only a very small sector of the national economy, but in others, particularly in Asia, they are beginning to play a more important role. By establishing such undertakings and through the services they offer (in food processing,

77

for example) some rural workers' organisations are endeavouring to increase their membership. On the other hand some trade unions hesitate, on principle, to engage in economic activities.

In the past few years there have been cases in a few countries, such as Belgium, France, Italy, Japan, Malta and the United Kingdom, of workers going in for a form of self-management during industrial action accompanied by factory occupation when an undertaking has been about to close down on account of serious economic difficulties. The case of the LIP company in France was widely discussed.[53] In circumstances of this kind, some undertakings have been transformed into producers' co-operatives, sometimes with state help (as in the case of the Triumph motor-cycle factory at Meriden in the United Kingdom).

In this connection mention may be made of a special form of supervision in the Netherlands which can be regarded as participation in a broad sense. Since 1971 the law has given trade unions the right to demand from the courts an inquiry in the event of alleged mis-management of an undertaking in which they have members; up to that date only shareholders had such a right.[54] Proceedings must be instituted through a complaint to the management or to the supervisory board; when the complaint emanates from a trade union, it must have been supported by the works council; if no satisfaction is obtained within a certain time, an action can be opened in the chamber of the Appeal Court of Amsterdam that deals with disputes relating to company law. If the chamber deems an inquiry justified, independent experts are appointed with right of access to all information concerning the undertaking. If mis-management is proved, the chamber may suspend or cancel decisions taken by the undertaking's management bodies, suspend or dismiss one or more of their members and temporarily appoint new members from outside. When mis-management is not proved, the undertaking has a right to compensation.

In France consideration has been given to the introduction of arrangements for alerting those concerned within the undertaking and subsequently the commercial court and asking for an outside expert opinion on management, not only on behalf of the shareholders but also on behalf of workers' representatives (the works committee or, if there is none, on behalf of the personnel representatives) or of a minimum proportion of the workers of the undertaking.[55]

In Austria in establishments employing over a given number of workers, a works council having objections to make in regard to the management may raise the matter with the manager and if no agreement is reached the parties may request the establishment of a joint arbitration board. If that fails, or if the matter is one of general interest, the works council may bring the matter to the notice of a state economic commission. When the objection relates to the proposed closure of an establishment, closure may be suspended for a period of at most four weeks from the date on which the manager's decision was communicated to the works council.[56]

In Belgium, under a national collective agreement of 27 November 1975, any employer employing on average at least 50 workers must, in circumstances such as a three months' delay in paying social security contributions or value-added tax, immediately inform the works council or, in its absence, the trade union delegation in the undertaking, as well as the section of the Ministry of Economic Affairs that is responsible for detecting undertakings in difficulty.

Notes

[1] The ILO publication *Workers' management in Yugoslavia* (Geneva, 1962) already contained an extensive bibliography.

[2] ILO: *Legislative Series*, 1950—Yug. 2.

[3] ibid., 1974—Yug. 1. New constitutions introducing similar reforms were adopted shortly afterwards in each of the six republics and two autonomous provinces.

[4] A recent study of the role of these assemblies was analysed in the *Social and Labour Bulletin* (Geneva, ILO), No. 3/77, pp. 218–219.

[5] Since the end of the 1950s decisions on recruitments and dismissals have been taken by the self-management bodies and not by the management (Section 126 of the Labour Relations Law, which came into force on 1 January 1958).

[6] For an example of the calculation of workers' contribution to the collective income, see report on the "14th of October" undertaking at Kruševac in *Yugoslav Trade Unions* (Belgrade), July–Aug. 1977. Account is of course taken of the level of skill required and the hardship and risk exposure of jobs, and there is generally a system of special rewards for workers with the highest output. For a brief analysis of the law adopted in 1977 on distribution of income, see ibid., Jan.–Feb. 1978.

[7] In this connection see ibid., Jan.–Feb. 1976. *Yugoslav Survey* (Belgrade), Aug. 1975, pp. 78–84, reports on the social compact on prices policy concluded at federal level in 1975.

[8] See B. Kavčič: *Workers' participation in decisions within undertakings in Yugoslavia*, Communication to the Oslo Symposium (Geneva, ILO, mimeographed document SWPDU/D.65), p. 4. (The other mimeographed documents bearing the reference SWPDU quoted later in the present work are likewise written communications submitted by participants in the symposium on workers' participation in decisions within undertakings organised in Oslo by the ILO in 1974).

[9] Figures given in *Yugoslav Trade Unions*, May–June 1978.

[10] See for example the figure of 26.8 working days of eight hours each on average per worker per year mentioned in a study by Ivan Segota relating to a shipbuilding yard in Rijeka, quoted in *International Herald Tribune* (Paris), 22 Sep. 1975, p. 5. It is also current practice for the workers assigned to a specific task to meet in little groups to discuss production problems. However, in practice many meetings are held outside working hours.

[11] This is the part of the income allocated to strengthening the material basis of work, raising productivity, improving the workers' standard of living and increasing the wealth of the community as a whole.

[12] Extract from President Tito's report on the struggle for the further development of socialist self-management in Yugoslavia and the role of the League of Communists of Yugoslavia to the Tenth Congress of the League, in *Socialist Thought and Practice* (Belgrade), June–July 1974, p. 42. See also extracts from a resolution of the Eleventh Congress of the League, on the role and tasks of the League of Communists in the struggle for the development of socialist self-management and the material and social progress of the country, published ibid., Sep. 1978; extracts from the report of the President of

the Confederation of Trade Unions of Yugoslavia to its Eighth Congress, published in *Yugoslav Trade Unions*, Nov.–Dec. 1978, pp. 2 ff.; and a report by President Tito to a special meeting of the Central Committee of the League of Communists on 60 years of revolutionary struggle on the part of the League, in *Socialist Thought and Practice*, June 1979, where he drew attention to excessive consumption, exaggerated investment ambitions, rising prices, unbalanced trade and employment problems.

¹³ Decree No. 63–95, dated 22 March 1963, on the organisation and management of vacated undertakings, and Decree No. 63–98, dated 28 March 1963, laying down the rules for the distribution of the income of self-managed farms and undertakings (ILO *Legislative Series*, 1963—Alg. 1). Both in its general principles and in its detailed provisions this legislation closely followed the model set in Yugoslavia at the beginning of the 1950s.

¹⁴ On the initial phase of self-management in Algeria see for example H. Temar: "Le choix des organes de l'autogestion dans l'Algérie de l'ouest", in *Revue algérienne des sciences juridiques, politiques et économiques* (Algiers), Dec. 1964, pp. 7–36; J. Teillard: *Autogestion en Algérie* (Paris, Centre de hautes études administratives sur l'Afrique et l'Asie modernes, 1965); and Serge Koulytchizky: *L'autogestion, l'homme, l'Etat: L'expérience algérienne* (Paris, Mouton, 1974).

¹⁵ Ordinance dated 16 November 1971 respecting the socialist organisation of undertakings (ILO: *Legislative Series*, 1971—Alg. 2), and the principles enunciated in the national charter adopted in 1976. These provisions were supplemented by a profit-sharing system first introduced on an experimental basis by a presidential circular dated 12 July 1976 (see *Social and Labour Bulletin*, No. 4/76, p. 313).

¹⁶ The "unit" was defined in a decree dated 25 October 1953. In the goods-producing sector, the criterion for defining a unit is the homogeneity of the technical production process and of the organisation of the work and the autonomy of the management, while in the service sector, units are established on a territorial basis. Between meetings of an assembly its responsibilities may be discharged by the trade union executive.

¹⁷ A series of decrees adopted on 28 December 1974 laid down the rules for the constitution, operation and duties of each category of committee (ILO: *Legislative Series*, 1974—Alg. 1).

¹⁸ *El Moudjahid* (Algiers), 23 Dec. 1975, p. 2.

¹⁹ Statement of the Algerian Minister of Labour and Vocational Training at the 65th Session of the International Labour Conference. See *Provisional Record*, International Labour Conference, 65th Session, Geneva, 1979, p. 12/6.

²⁰ Ordinance No. 75–76 dated 21 November 1975 (*Journal officiel de la République algérienne*, No. 100, 16 Dec. 1975, pp. 1062–1063).

²¹ Decree dated 29 April 1975 concerning co-ordinating councils in socialist undertakings (ibid. No. 36, 6 May 1975, p. 406).

²² See M. Atcheba: "Gestion socialiste: Tout est en place", in *Révolution africaine* (Algiers), June 1975, pp. 21–22.

²³ *Bulletin économique* (Algérie Presse Service), 1975, No. 10: "Point de la situation sur la gestion socialiste des entreprises", p. 37. A more recent article spoke of difficulties "due essentially to the negative attitudes of some workers" (in the broad sense, including supervisory, executive and technical staff) who had "not yet succeeded in freeing themselves from the shackles of the old management system", and to mistakes in the choice of men elected at workers' assemblies, both causes generally due to lack of positive encouragement and of continuous support on the part of the trade union bodies concerned. The result is said to be that many unit assemblies play only a minor role or are diverted from their true purpose into futile tasks. See "Gestion socialiste des entreprises: Bientôt la Direction nationale de la construction", in *Révolution africaine*, 25–31 Oct. 1978, p. 19.

²⁴ Ismail Hamdani, quoted in "La gestion socialiste: Un fondement de la démocratie", ibid., p. 11. However, an article entitled "La gestion socialiste des entreprises à la Pharmacie centrale algérienne: Deux années d'expérience" states that some units are making great advances towards self-management (ibid., p. 17).

²⁵ See in particular O. Lange: "Outline of a reconversion plan for the Polish economy", in *International Economic Papers* (London and New York), 1957, No. 7 (translation of an article in Polish which had appeared in *Zycie Gospodárcze* (Warsaw), 16 July 1956), and J. Rosner: "Management by the workers in Poland", in *International Labour Review*, Sep. 1957, pp. 257–277.

²⁶ ILO: *Legislative Series*, 1956—Pol. 3. This Act was repealed in 1958 (see following note).

²⁷ ibid., 1958—Pol. 4.

²⁸ Figure given by T. Jaworski: *Development of workers' self-management in Poland* (Warsaw, 1979), p. 7.

²⁹ See for instance Z. Rybicki et al.: *Workers' participation in management in Poland*, op. cit.,

pp. 14–16, which also stresses that active participation in self-management is more difficult to arrange if over-ambitious production targets are set, with resulting strain and less scope for workers' initiative; one must be particularly on one's guard in this respect at the level of groups of undertakings.

[30] ibid., p. 20.

[31] See International Institute for Labour Studies: *Further data on the operation of workers' participation in management in Poland*, doc. WPM 5 (App.) (Geneva, 1971), p. 12.

[32] See for example M. Kabaj and S. Wróbleski: *Workers' participation in management: A review of Polish experience* (Warsaw, Institute of Labour and Social Studies, 1977), p. 7.

[33] See Edmund Wnuk-Lipinski: "Job satisfaction and the quality of working life: The Polish experience", in *International Labour Review*, Jan.–Feb. 1977, pp. 53–64.

[34] *Labour in Israel* (Tel Aviv), Feb.–Mar. 1978, p. 9.

[35] See for instance Naphtali Golomb: *Brief report on the QWL* [quality of working life] *projects in kibbutz industries*; idem: *Similarities and dissimilarities of four socio-technical projects to improve the quality of working life of four kibbutz plants*, which emphasises for instance (p. 4) that in practice the powers of the general assembly vary greatly from one undertaking to another (both Ruppin, Ruppin Institute, Kibbutz Management Center, no date).

[36] For further details see Sennen Andriamirado: "Heurs et malheurs des fokonolona", in *Autogestion et socialisme* (Paris), Sep. 1977, pp. 51–64.

[37] See *Journal officiel de la République démocratique de Madagascar*, 31 Dec. 1976, pp. 3058–3065.

[38] This ordinance was ratified after amendment by an Act dated 5 December 1978 published with the revised text of the ordinance ibid., 9 Dec. 1978, pp. 2538–2552.

[39] On the difficulties of state-owned undertakings see *Madagascar Matin* (Antananarivo), 18 Jan. 1980, p. 1, and 19 Jan. 1980, p. 1.

[40] ILO: *Legislative Series*, 1974—Per. 1.

[41] Muammar Al Qadhafi: *The Green Book* (Tripoli, Public Establishment for Publishing, Advertising and Distribution, no date, 3 vols).

[42] Quoted in Roland Delcour: "Libye: En réunissant le Congrès général du peuple le régime a célébré la mise en œuvre de la 'démocratie directe'", in *Le Monde*, 23 Dec. 1978, p. 4, which reported that the Government and the public sector employed about 300,000 workers, while there were only 40,000 to 50,000 workers in the private sector.

[43] An Act to amend the Malta Dockyard Act, 1968, Supplement to *Government Gazette*, No. 13069, 14 Mar. 1975.

[44] See G. Kester: *Workers' participation in Malta: Issues and opinions* (Msida, Malta University Press, 1974), p. 112; idem: *Transition to workers' self-management: Its dynamics in the decolonizing economy of Malta*, Research Report Series, No. 7 (The Hague, Institute of Social Studies, 1980).

[45] See *Free Labour World* (Brussels, International Confederation of Free Trade Unions), Mar.–Apr. 1977, p. 33.

[46] See Yvon Bourdet: "Révolution et institutions", in *Autogestion et socialisme* (Paris), Jan.–Mar. 1976, p. 21.

[47] See *Diário da República* (Lisbon), No. 237, 14 Oct. 1978, pp. 2151–2153, and No. 238, 16 Oct. 1978, pp. 2168–2174.

[48] See Osvaldo H. Villas Figallo: *La participación de los trabajadores en una empresa de servicios publicos: Informe sobre el proceso de autogestión en SEGBA* (Geneva, ILO, 1974, doc. SWPDU/D.68).

[49] See for example Ana Gutiérrez Johnson and William Foot Whyte: "The Mondragón system of worker production cooperatives", in *Industrial and Labor Relations Review* (Ithaca, Cornell University, New York State School of Industrial and Labor Relations), Oct. 1977, pp. 18–30.

[50] Sometimes, however, not all workers in a co-operative undertaking can become members. This is the case with apprentices and auxiliary workers when, as in the building industry or the docks (where such co-operatives are highly developed), the level of employment depends on the amount of work to be done. Laws may also exclude foreign workers from belonging to such co-operatives. Conversely, there are sometimes members who are no longer workers, for instance retired members who wish to keep their shares in the co-operative. In all such cases, the regulatory provisions set limits both to prevent non-workers from having too great an influence on management and to avoid a restriction of membership to a privileged élite of workers.

[51] Estimates published in International Consultants Ltd.: *Trade and investment in Israel*, A businessman's guide (Tel Aviv, Bank Leumi Le-Israel, 1978), pp. 11 and 67.

[52] Parity representation of the personnel on the supervisory board, and the institution of a labour director elected by this board with the agreement of the representatives of the personnel, were introduced in 1971 by way of collective agreements in the Alt-Volksfürsorge life insurance company and the Neu-Heimat building group, and in 1972 in the Bank für Gemeinwirtschaft, all owned by the trade unions.

[53] The workers of LIP, who temporarily managed some of the activities of the undertaking (mainly watch assembly) preferred the term "self-defence" to that of "self-management", because they considered that self-management was possible only in an appropriate economic and social setting. See for instance E. Maire, C. Piaget, C. Acquier, A. Burgy: *LIP 73* (Paris, Editions du Seuil, 1973); C. Piaget: *LIP: Charles Piaget et les LIP racontent* (Paris, Stock, 1973); F. H. de Virieu: *LIP, 100.000 montres sans patron* (Paris, Calmann Lévy, 1973). In the end, part of the undertaking was converted into a producers' co-operative.

[54] For details see C. Hak and J. de Jong: *Workers' participation in decisions within undertakings in the Netherlands* (Geneva, ILO, 1974, doc. SWPDU/D. 4), p. 6. The right to an inquiry is now governed by an Act dated 8 April 1976 published in *Staatsblad* (The Hague), No. 228, 1976.

[55] See *Rapport du Comité d'étude pour la réforme de l'entreprise*, présidé par Pierre Sudreau (Paris, La documentation française, 1975), pp. 135–140. The proposals of the Minister of Labour following this report (see *Le Monde*, 16 Apr. 1976, p. 29) did not retain the right for the workers or their representatives to lodge a complaint with the commercial court, but granted it to the public prosecutor. The works committee has no right to take action under the proposals recently considered by the legislature.

[56] Sections 111–112 of the Federal Act dated 14 December 1973 on collective labour relations (ILO: *Legislative Series*, 1973—Aus. 2).

MEMBERSHIP OF MANAGEMENT BODIES

6

In a number of countries workers' representatives sit as full members on the supervisory or management bodies administering the company, undertaking or establishment in which they are employed. This arrangement, often known as "management participation system", "co-determination" or even "co-management", has certain distinctive features.

When it operates in the private sector a fundamental distinction must be made between cases in which workers' representatives on these bodies are equal in number to those of shareholders and cases in which they are in a minority. The "Green Book" on participation published in 1975 by the Commission of the Economic Communities states that in the case of minority representation "there is no fundamental shift in the ultimate balance of power as regards decision-making. On the other hand a situation of parity, or indeed any situation in which the shareholders' representatives cease to hold an absolute majority, produces such a shift."[1] There is generally strong opposition in employers' circles to any arrangement under which shareholders' representatives are not in the majority. As we have seen, various arguments are advanced in this connection, such as that it infringes private ownership, making the workers' representatives joint holders of the right to dispose of the capital of the undertaking; that it jeopardises the market economy, which frequently relies on rapid decisions in response to fluctuations in demand; that it gives too much power to the trade unions since they would in most cases play a preponderant role in any parity representation arrangement,[2] and that they might be represented by persons not employed in the undertaking concerned; and that parity representation would interfere with collective bargaining, particularly because of the influence of workers' representatives on the appointment, and more especially the reappointment of members of the management.[3]

Another important distinction must be made between representation on a supervisory board, a board of directors and, in certain cases, a management board. Admittedly, a supervisory board usually appoints and can dismiss the management board or management team, and lays down the general policies of the undertaking. As has been emphasised in the above-mentioned "Green Book", however—

> ... The existence of a separate supervisory body ... facilitates the drawing of a relatively sharp distinction between the function of management on the one hand, and the supervision or control of management on the other. The managers can then be left free to manage, subject only to the powers of the supervisory body to replace them in the event of a basic difference of opinion or to disapprove certain proposals of an important kind. Conversely, the members of a supervisory body can be given the power to ensure that the managers are adequately performing their functions without being caught up in the actual administration of the company's affairs.[4]

The commission on reform of the undertaking appointed in France in 1974 under the chairmanship of Pierre Sudreau systematically used the term "cosurveillance" (co-supervision) rather than that of "cogestion" (co-management) when it dealt with the minority participation of workers' representatives on supervisory board.

In practice, another distinction can be drawn between systems under which managers are not allowed to be members of the boards of directors or supervisory boards (the commonest situation) and those in which they are.

Workers' representatives on boards of directors or supervisory boards, though usually having the same rights and obligations as shareholders' representatives,[5] are in a minority on those boards in most countries operating this form of participation and never form more than half of the membership. Usually, a fixed number of seats is reserved for workers' representatives, and the statutes or rules of the company or undertaking, whether public or private, do not undergo any substantial change, especially in regard to its aims, which are not modified in any way.

Normally there is no express provision for the workers to participate directly in the profits or other income of the undertaking; in any event there is no link between such participation and representation on the boards except in Peru under the "industrial communities" system, and in proposals being studied in some countries such as Denmark. Nevertheless it is obvious that, particularly when workers have parity representation on boards, their representatives will influence the undertaking's general policy, including decisions on the distribution of profits, in a direction favourable to the workers. In the course of discussion and compromise, their ideas will blend with those of the other members to finish up with a coherent policy which will be that of the board as a whole. Boards normally hold their sittings in private and opinions expressed by members and the reasons for decisions are therefore not disclosed; the aim is not usually that of direct participation by all the workers in decision-making, except in the very general sense that they are aware that their representatives take part in the discussions and decisions of the boards. Moreover, the undertaking is generally not equipped for such direct participation.

Arrangements for workers' participation on the boards of directors or supervisory boards of undertakings vary according to whether they apply in both public and private undertakings or in public undertakings only.

It seems that in the industrialised countries more attention has in general been paid to workers' representation on boards of directors or supervisory boards in the private sector than in the public sector, where there is almost always greater security of employment and easier access by workers' representatives to information. In the developing countries, on the other hand, interest in this form of participation is greater in government or nationalised undertakings for reasons given briefly above and which will be analysed later.

People in favour of adoption of participation arrangements of this kind in the private sector argue that, in addition to improving access to the information needed for collective bargaining, they offer the opportunity for prior consultation, at an early stage, on matters of major interest to the future of the personnel (such as the closure or relocation of an establishment, mergers and other so-called "rationalisation" measures, or changes in manufacturing processes) which may not have previously been systematically discussed in other participatory bodies such as works councils or in the course of collective bargaining, which may take place after such decisions have been taken or primarily at regional or national levels or at the level of the industry.[6]

PRIVATE SECTOR

Industrialised countries

After describing the system of workers' representation on supervisory boards in the Federal Republic of Germany, which is undoubtedly one of the best-known forms of workers' participation in decision-making and one of those that have attracted most attention, both within the country and abroad, the following pages go on to describe the provisions adopted some time ago in Austria, Spain and France, and then those adopted more recently in three Scandinavian countries, Luxembourg and the Netherlands.

Federal Republic of Germany

The system in force in the Federal Republic of Germany,[7] which comprises minority or parity representation of the workers (according to

85

the industry and size of undertaking) on supervisory boards, is undoubtedly one of the best-known forms of workers' participation in decision-making and one of those which have attracted most attention, both inside the country and abroad.

While works councils operate at the level of the production unit (and will be looked at later), the right of participation in management is exercised at the level of the undertaking or of the industrial group, whichever is the responsible legal entity.[8] This right applies both in private companies and in public undertakings. In this connection it should be noted that in the Federal Republic of Germany publicly owned undertakings have no special status (with the exception of a few which are statutory corporations) and that there is no statutory provision for a management structure different from that of private concerns.

Under the law of the Federal Republic a characteristic of joint stock or other companies is their two-tier management structure. A supervisory board, elected by the shareholders' general meeting, has the duty of general policy guidance for, and supervision of the activities of, the company concerned; in accordance with the articles of association, it approves decisions of major importance such as the closure of establishments, the opening of new factories, major production changes or investments above a certain volume. It does not meet more often than four or five times a year, and elects the management board, which is the top management body responsible for the conduct of current business.[9] In practice, one manager is usually responsible primarily for technical matters, another for commercial questions and the third for personnel and welfare questions.

The system introduced by the Act of 21 May 1951[10] applies in the mining and iron and steel industries, but only to companies (including holding companies) employing at least 1,000 workers. As regards the mining industry, it is specified that this covers coal-mining and its associated activities, lignite mines and iron-ore mines (it was estimated in 1977 that the sectors covered by this Act employed some 600,000 workers).

Under this system the workers nominate, for subsequent confirmation by the shareholders' general meeting, a number of members of the supervisory board equal to the number appointed by the shareholders or owners (five, seven, eight or ten for each of the two groups, the commonest number being five). An additional independent member, who in practice plays the part of mediator, is appointed jointly by the two sides or, failing agreement, by a court. Two of the worker members—one wage earner and one salaried employee—come from within the personnel of the company (the chairman of the works council is generally one of these two) and are elected by the works council or the councils of the establishments belonging to the company; the remaining worker members do not necessarily have to be and usually are not in fact in the employment of the company: they are appointed by the trade union concerned, in practice after consultation with the works council. In addition to the independent member already referred to, who is usually known as the "eleventh man" (in the case of a supervisory board of 11 members), at least one of the workers' representatives and one of the shareholders' representatives (again in the case of an 11-man board), must have no direct interest in the undertaking, or links with a workers' or employers' organisation concerned, and must not be workers or employers from within the undertaking. These "supplementary members" are intended to represent the public interest; although unlike the "eleventh man", one is close to the workers and the trade unions, the other to the shareholders.

While the supervisory board as a whole appoints the management board of the company, one of the three members of that board may be appointed or removed only with the consent of the majority of the worker members of the supervisory board. This person, who is therefore in fact a workers' appointee, is known as the "labour manager", and is in charge of all labour and personnel matters in the company, while also participating on an equal footing in all general decisions coming within the competence of the management board as a whole.[11]

Under the general provisions of an Act of 11 October 1952[12] applicable in other sectors of the economy, the workers appointed one-third of the membership of the supervisory board of undertakings having such boards or permitted to have them (certain partnerships, for instance), with the exception of businesses with a single owner (irrespective of size) or family undertakings employing fewer than 500 workers. The workers' representatives were elected by direct secret ballot by all the company's workforce (wage earners and salaried employees), candidates being lawfully designated by the workers and works councils but not by the trade unions as such although in practice there were trade union lists of candidates. If more than one seat was reserved for workers, at least two of the representatives—one wage earner and one salaried employee—had to belong to the personnel of the undertaking, and one of them was usually the chairman of the works council. These provisions continue to apply to undertakings employing between 500 and 2,000 workers in industries other than mining and iron and steel; according to a recent estimate, they cover about 1 million workers.

These workers' representatives on supervisory boards are full members, having all the rights and emoluments pertaining to their office and taking part in all deliberations and decisions.

For more than a quarter of a century, and with increasing insistence in the 1970s, the German Confederation of Trade Unions has fought for the extension of a parity system of workers' representation on supervisory boards, such as that existing in mining and iron and steel, to companies above a certain size, or at least with a certain level of turnover, in other industries. This claim was vigorously opposed by the German Confederation of Employers' Associations. Finally, a Bill was drafted reflecting a compromise between the Social-Democratic and the Liberal parties in the government coalition and, with some amendments, this was adopted by a very substantial majority in the federal parliament in 1976.

Under this new Act, dated 4 May 1976,[13] the supervisory boards of joint stock or limited companies and of limited partnerships (with a few exceptions such as primarily educational or scientific undertakings and undertakings having information or the expression of opinions as their main function), if normally employing more than 2,000 workers and not subject to the legislation applicable in the mining and iron and steel industries, must be composed as follows:

(a) if the undertaking does not have more than 10,000 workers, six members representing the shareholders and six representing the workers (four employees of the undertaking and two trade union representatives);

(b) if it has more than 10,000 but fewer than 20,000 workers, eight representatives of the shareholders and eight of the workers (six employees of the undertaking and two trade union representatives); or

(c) if the workforce exceeds 20,000, ten representatives of the shareholders and ten representatives of the workers (seven employees of the undertaking and three trade union representatives).

Below the level of 8,000 workers, the worker members of supervisory boards are elected by direct vote, unless the personnel opt for indirect election by an electoral college. This second arrangement is the rule if the workforce exceeds 8,000, but the workers may opt for direct elections.

Wage earners and salaried employees elect their members of electoral colleges separately (unless they opt for a common vote) by secret ballot and proportional representation.[14] The electoral college then elects those members of the board who must be company employees (wage earners or salaried employees), again by secret ballot and proportional representation. Among the salaried employee members of the supervisory board there must be a proportionate number of executives (at least one in any case). The trade union representatives are also elected by the electoral college by secret ballot, using proportional representation, from lists of candidates submitted by the trade unions. The recall of any worker member of a supervisory board before the end of his term is possible under conditions specified in the Act.

The supervisory board elects a chairman and vice-chairman from among its members by a two-thirds majority. If this majority is not reached, a second vote is taken, with the shareholders representatives electing the chairman and the workers' representatives the vice-chairman. It should be noted in this connection that if the votes are equally divided in the supervisory board, and if on a second count there is still no decisive vote, the chairman has a casting vote, though this is never the case with the vice-chairman.

The supervisory board elects the management board by a two-thirds majority. If no such majority can be achieved the election is by a simple majority after a complex mediation procedure, and the chairman of the supervisory board has a casting vote. One member of the board, the labour manager, must be made responsible for personnel and social matters, but the rule applicable in the mining and iron and steel industries that this member must be appointed with the agreement of the majority of the workers' representatives on the supervisory board does not apply under this new Act.

It was thought that this new Act, which came into force on 1 July 1976, would, by the end of the two years' transition period, apply in some 600 firms employing in all about 4 million workers. However, the first elections under the Act, which took place in August 1978, concerned only 457 firms.[15]

It is clearly too early for there to be any in-depth evaluations of how this new arrangement is working in practice. The employers' organisations considered that the new legislation went too far, particularly in giving, in their opinion, excessive powers to the trade unions. Some employers' organisations and some firms affiliated to the German Confederation of Employers' Associations instituted proceedings before the Constitutional Court in July 1977, asking it to declare that the 1976 Act was unconstitutional in that it was incompatible with two basic rights guaranteed in the Constitution, namely that of private citizens to dispose of their property as they wished and that of freedom of association and collective bargaining between equal parties independent of each other.[16]

The trade unions reacted strongly to this move, even going so far as to withdraw temporarily from the national economic and social concertation body; for their part, they considered that the new law did not go far enough. They point out that because their own incomes and their security of employment are at stake, the workers have a vital interest in the performance of their undertaking, its competitivity and financial soundness. They doubt whether there is genuine parity on the new supervisory boards in view of the casting vote of the chairman, who is generally appointed by the shareholders, and the representation of management executives who, they fear, tend to vote with the shareholders' representatives in order to avoid deadlocks. They also criticise the possibility of appointing the labour manager without the approval of the workers' representatives.

The employers' appeal was rejected by the Constitutional Court in a judgement dated 1 March 1979.[17] According to an analysis by the German Confederation of Trade Unions in which it emphasised that the court's decision was strictly related to the 1976 Act, it follows from this judgement that the Constitution is not an obstacle to a policy of further reforms. The Confederation of German Employers' Associations, at a meeting of its central committee on 7 March 1979, stressed on the contrary that, on the basis of the reasons given by the Court, "the judgement . . . on this Act contains important limitations on any trade union claims aimed at an extension of co-determination".

The operation and the practical effects of the system of participation at board level up to the adoption of the 1976 Act, and particularly of the parity system in the mines and in iron and steel, have given rise to much research, and a great deal has been published on the subject.[18] It seems that the participation bodies have been operating satisfactorily in terms of the statutory provisions described above in almost all the undertakings concerned. In practice, situations in which it has not been possible to arrive at a compromise have been very rare. In the supervisory boards in the mining and iron and steel industries decisions have generally been taken unanimously. In fact one of the criticisms that has sometimes been made is of over-frequent resort to compromise, with a comparative specialisation or distribution in practice of the power of decision, with the workers' representatives being concerned primarily with the repercussions of economic decisions on labour and with personnel matters, and the shareholders' representatives with other problems. In practice the management board tries to anticipate the stand that would be taken by the various parties on the supervisory board and itself attempts to find a compromise, often by consulting the works council. Agreement on one point is sometimes achieved at the cost of concessions on others. Mention has also been made of the importance assumed by informal decision procedures, such as unofficial contacts or group meetings for preliminary negotiations.[19]

Many studies have looked at the problem of "dual loyalty". It appears that in practice labour managers appointed with the approval of the workers' representatives have in most cases experienced no serious difficulty in participating in the full range of decisions of the management boards. Moreover, in the iron and steel industry, where labour managers find themselves facing trade union representatives on the other side of the bargaining table, they have more than once vigorously opposed wage claims by the trade unions, and the latter have accepted this attitude.

However, it has also been noted in a number of instances that workers' representatives on supervisory boards, having at their disposal information supplied by the shareholders' representatives, tend to see problems not only from their own point of view but also from that of the shareholders, and thus become inclined to compromise.

It has also been observed that a considerable proportion of the chairmen of works councils, who are in general members of supervisory boards, have held those posts for more than ten years, which leads to a risk of their becoming professional "representers" and losing contact with the rank and file; however, this problem exists in any participation system. Conversely, it has been emphasised that being a member both of the works council and of the supervisory board gives one a very thorough understanding of the daily realities of the undertaking, which the shareholders' representatives cannot have, and that this leads to a better discussion on the supervisory board. Another weakness sometimes mentioned relates to the slowness of decision-making, but this does not seem to have been particularly serious or widespread if one considers the importance of the role of the management board in the day-to-day running of affairs and if one looks at the country's economic achievements.

The trade unions have often remarked that the system of participation in iron and steel, and perhaps more so in the mines, has prevented problems of redundancies, rationalisation and technical change from leading to serious consequences or social tension (from the end of 1957 to the middle of 1973, the numbers employed in the mines fell from 600,000 to 200,000). Employers' circles reply that the problems in the coalmining industry were solved, not through workers' representation on the boards of undertakings but because of the very high manpower demand in other industries during that period.

The report published in 1970 of the commission chaired by Professor Biedenkopf gave a generally favourable verdict on parity representation as it had operated up to that time in the mines and in iron and steel, and recommended its extension to other industries, while keeping a certain priority for the representation of shareholders' interests.

Admittedly, various studies have shown that, as in other countries, workers on the shop floor often have only a vague knowledge of the representation of their interests at board level. It must also be remembered that participation at that level—however important—is only part of a whole[20] in which another body—the works council—participates very actively in many respects, and that collective bargaining in the Federal Republic takes place in principle at the level of the industry, not at that of the undertaking. In addition there is a broad consensus of opinion in favour of the existing economic and social structure.

Austria

In Austria the works councils of public and private companies used to elect two representatives as full members of supervisory boards. As in other countries with similar arrangements, this system was criticised by the unions on the ground that the shareholders' representatives, being in the majority, could settle the main problems outside the boardroom, in which case the official meetings become a mere formality. For that and other reasons, the Austrian trade unions have asked for the introduction of parity representation on the model of the mining and iron and steel industries in the Federal Republic of Germany. They have come up against the opposition of private employers. An Act dated 14 December 1973 concerning collective labour relations[21] raised to one-third the representation of workers on the supervisory boards of companies with capital exceeding a certain level.

Spain

In Spain an Act dated 21 July 1962[22] provided for limited workers' representation (in the proportion of one-sixth, in principle, of shareholders' representation) on the boards of directors or similar bodies of joint stock and other companies employing at least 500 workers. The board chooses the workers' representatives from a list submitted by the works council and, once appointed, those chosen automatically become members of the council if they were not members already. Under this legislation there must be at least one workers' representative on subcommittees and permanent working parties concerned with questions other than those of the ordinary conduct of business whenever the resulting decisions may have direct repercussions on the workers' interests. Any decisions of boards of directors or similar bodies which do not include the worker representatives provided for are null and void.

In practice, though applied in just over 300 undertakings, this minority worker representation on boards had little effect, particularly on account of restrictive provisions such as those prohibiting the communication to workers of information on business matters. A survey carried out in 1967–68 in about a hundred undertakings on the basis of a questionnaire revealed that 75 per cent of the workers and 50 per cent of the employers questioned were not satisfied with this participation system (55 per cent of the workers considered that no change in the power structure of the undertaking had resulted and 47 per cent thought that management had ways of nullifying its effectiveness, while 32 per cent of the employers thought that it did not solve any of the problems of an undertaking and 26 per cent that the workers' representatives were ill-prepared to perform their functions). In addition, 57 per cent of the workers thought that boards of directors held secret sittings; this was, however, denied by all but two of the firms covered by the survey.[23] The system has now fallen into disuse, and some claim that it is one of the institutions that should be reformed in the light of the new Constitution.

France

In France an ordinance of 22 February 1945 provides that the works committee shall be represented in an advisory capacity on the board of directors or the supervisory board of a joint-stock company. Subject to certain conditions, an Act dated 29 December 1972 raised the number of such representatives of works committees to four, of whom one represents first-line supervisors and another represents engineers and executives. Some companies with both management and supervisory boards set up voluntarily under an Act of 24 July 1966 give worker representatives on their supervisory boards the same rights as shareholders' representatives. Following the Sudreau report already referred to on reform of the undertaking, the Government decided to encourage "co-supervision" in larger undertakings.

During the first half of 1978 a Bill was drafted providing that joint-stock companies employing more than 500 workers should give representation with voting rights to their executive, supervisory and technical staff, though on a minority basis in relation to the shareholders; depending on the results of this arrangement, it was envisaged that it would be extended to other categories of workers. However, there was much opposition in employers' circles[24] and in most of the trade unions. On 15 November 1978 the Economic and Social Council accordingly issued an unfavourable majority opinion on this Bill, though it accepted that voluntary experiments along these lines should be facilitated by law. After debate in parliament in the spring of 1980 there was some talk of adopting legislation that would compel any joint-stock company with over 500 workers to admit to its supervisory board two representatives of the personnel, re-eligible for a three-year term, one to be elected by the salaried staff (including foremen and kindred staff) and the other by other categories of personnel. Parliament went into recess before the law could be adopted.

Already under an Act dated 2 January 1978[25] in all undertakings under an obligation to form works committees, the head of the undertaking was to seek, with the elected representatives of the supervisory staff and their trade union delegates, ways of improving the supply of information to, and consultation with, the said supervisory staff in fields concerning the general policy of the undertaking. In undertakings employing more than 500 workers, the head of the undertaking, in collaboration with those concerned and particularly their elected representatives and trade union representatives, was to prepare a report on ways and means of developing concertation between the undertaking's management and the executive, supervisory and technical staff. This report was to be distributed to all members of such staff in the undertaking and to the labour inspection service, and was to mention the nature and purpose of all consultations that had taken place and the opinions expressed on those occasions; it was also to deal with the advisability of introducing methods or forms of regular consultation.[26]

There has also been some talk of promoting the establishment of new kinds of co-operative society, including "worker-shareholders' companies", but no legislation has been adopted on the subject. Consideration is being given to the adoption of an Act entitling workers to express their views on conditions of work and job content.

Denmark

In Denmark two Acts dated 13 June 1973, respectively on joint-stock and other limited companies, have given workers of these two types of companies employing at least 50 persons the right to elect two members to the board of directors; they are now entitled to elect one-third of the total number of members of the board. The statutes of the company may provide for a higher number of workers' representatives, but members of the board elected by the shareholders' meeting must always remain in the majority.[27] A request to exercise this workers' right of representation may be made by the majority of the workers' representatives on the works committee (known as the collaboration committee), by one or more trade union organisations representing more than one-tenth of the personnel of the undertaking, or directly by at least one-tenth of the workers. It must be approved by a vote of the personnel as a whole. The same procedure applies in the case of a wish to terminate workers' representation. Although there is no rule concerning proportional representation, it is the normal practice to have one representative of the wage earners and one of the salaried employees. One of these representatives is generally the chief trade union officer in the undertaking. Management staff may sit on the board, though they may neither be in a majority nor take the chair.

In response to proposals from the trade unions, a Bill was presented to the Danish Parliament at the beginning of 1973 by the government in power at the time with the object of creating a national investment fund to be constituted by employers, both public and private. This contribution, initially 0.5 per cent of the payroll, would rise by 0.5 per cent each year until it reached 5 per cent. In most cases, two-thirds would be invested in the undertaking, the remaining third being invested in accordance with the directives of the central fund. The workers were to have a number of representatives on each management board corresponding to their share in co-ownership of the capital up to a limit of 50 per cent. Discussions are continuing on proposals of this kind in the context of "economic democracy", but Danish employers would like to limit arrangements to the traditional workers' shareholding and profit-sharing systems which are widely practised.[28]

Norway

In Norway an Act dated 12 May 1972,[29] which came into force in 1973, added a new body to the shareholders' general meeting in mining and manufacturing undertakings with more than 200 workers, namely the corporate assembly, a third of whose members must be elected by the personnel. Decisions on major investments and on matters of rationalisation or reorganisation having considerable effect on the personnel must be referred to that assembly, which has the right to examine the accounts of the undertaking either in plenary sitting or in committee. The assembly appoints the board of directors on the basis of proportional representation if a third of its members ask for this, which may result in the appointment of one-third (at least two) of the members of that board by the workers' representatives. Mining or manufacturing companies employing from 51 to 199 workers must, if the majority of the personnel ask for this, proceed with the election of workers' representatives on their boards; there must be at least two of these, but not more than a third of the total. In companies below this size, representation is optional, though it may be required by the company statutes or be the subject of an agreement.

In November 1973 a similar system was introduced by the Government in the construction industry (however, for the time being without a corporate assembly) after a labour-management agreement had been concluded on the subject. Another agreement led to the introduction of a somewhat similar arrangement in the newspaper industry; this has been in force since 1974 and has been approved by the Government. A royal decree dated 18 October 1974 extended the system as from 1975 to commerce, transport, and hotels and catering. Other sectors, such as agriculture, fisheries and power, have been covered since the beginning of 1976.

Today, workers' participation in the management bodies of Norwegian undertakings is governed by an Act dated 4 June 1976 and a decree dated 10 December 1976 applying this Act, both of which are applicable to joint-stock companies in all sectors, including state-owned undertakings, with the exception of banks,[30] insurance companies,[31] press undertakings and agencies, and shipping companies trading abroad. Undertakings in the construction sector are covered by the new Act but are subject to different regulations. Also, special rules have been promulgated for state-owned undertakings; these give more limited powers to the corporate assembly, inasmuch as the Government has the final say in matters affecting the public interest. The new Act defines the supervisory powers of corporate assemblies and indicates the type of comments which they may send to the shareholders' general meeting in addition to recommendations which they may make on any subject. Total or partial exemption from the application of the Act may be requested by a company or its personnel. Such requests go to a committee of seven members, of whom three are independent while two are appointed on the nomination of the main workers' organisations and two on the nomination of employers' organisations.

In 1975 the Norwegian Employers' Confederation and the Federation of Norwegian Industry carried out a survey of the application of the provisions concerning workers' participation in the management bodies of undertakings.[32] The survey dealt mainly with the results of the first elections under the Act of 1972, and showed that, in joint-stock companies with 50 to 200 workers where workers' representation on boards is optional, the workers of 54 per cent of the companies had exercised their right to be represented. In joint-stock companies with more than 200 workers, 64 per cent of the workers, on the average, had voted in the elections. The participation rate in this vote was roughly the same in all sectors, with the exception of iron and steel, where it was a little lower, and the printing and allied trades, where it was particularly high (84 per cent). The survey also showed that 33 per cent of the representatives elected were non-manual workers, although they only constituted 28.5 per cent of all the workers. However, in 16 per cent of the companies covered, no representative of the non-manual workers had been elected (when the Act was adopted, it had commonly been thought that non-manual workers would be under-represented on the boards).

According to another survey carried out at about the same time,[33] more than half of the heads of Norwegian companies thought that the workers' members of boards made a useful contribution to meetings, while 48 per cent thought it neither positive nor negative and only 1 per cent thought it negative. Among the respondents, 78 per cent thought that the workers' representatives had shown as much concern for the profitability of the undertaking as the other members of the board, while 22 per cent thought them "less interested". While 79 per cent of the respondents considered that the workers' representatives had not up to that time influenced the running of the company, 55 per cent stated that the proceedings at board meetings had been influenced by their presence. Among the effects mentioned were "more penetrating discussions", "longer meetings" and "new aspects raised". However, it was mentioned by 12 per cent of the respondents that important decisions were often taken at unofficial meetings at which the workers were not present.

The Director of the Norwegian Institute of Personnel Administration, after stressing the special training usually received by workers' representatives on boards, stated in a recent manual for board members that "in many cases, these representatives are among the most competent members of boards of directors; it just seems that up till now many boards did not function as they should have done. Participation is a challenge to any board, perhaps in particular to the representatives of shareholders".[34]

Sweden

In Sweden, under an Act of 1972,[35] every joint-stock company (except insurance companies and banks) employing at least 100 workers has been required, if the trade union delegates in the undertaking so demand,[36] to give seats on their boards to the representatives of their workers (and two substitutes) designated by the local trade unions which are parties to a collective agreement with the undertaking. If more than four-fifths of the workers bound by the agreement belong to the same local union, that union appoints the representatives; otherwise they are chosen by the two local unions representing the largest number of workers. In practice, the unions see to it that one of the two titular representatives (both of whom have to be members of the personnel of the undertaking) is a wage earner and the other a salaried employee. However, these representatives may not take part in deliberations concerning a labour dispute or in negotiations likely to lead to collective agreements. The two substitutes attend meetings of the board but without the right to vote. The introduction of this form of participation was largely the outcome of the campaign launched by the two main workers' confederations (LO and TCO) at the beginning of the 1970s to develop "industrial democracy".

An extensive survey of the first results of this participation was carried out in 1975 by an official agency in collaboration with the Ministries of Industry and of Labour and the employers' and workers' organisations.[37] This survey took account of the fact that the process of decision-making generally covers various stages from preparatory work up to supervision of execution, with the board and its members participating in one or several of these stages, with a varying degree of influence. For instance, in certain matters participation is passive (receiving information), and in regard to investments below a certain sum an undertaking may be so organised that the board may merely give formal sanction to decisions actually taken by the management.

It came out that on the average the workers had not exercised their right to board representation in only 9 per cent of the undertakings covered by the legislation, the proportion being 3 per cent in undertakings with more than 500 workers but 15 per cent in undertakings with fewer than 200 workers. It was also found that in 18 per cent of the undertakings which had introduced this type of representation, the boards had working parties which, in seven cases out of ten, did not contain a workers' representative. It should be noted, however, that most of those working parties were already in existence before the new legislation was adopted, and that only about 20 per cent had been formed at the time of its adoption.

The survey also showed that workers' representatives on boards received the same documentary information as shareholders, but that in a number of cases it was not received long enough before meetings and was incomplete.

In spite of the absence of specific information on the point, it appeared that in many cases the power of decision was exercised more by the management than by the board, particularly in subsidiaries of foreign companies and in family businesses. In certain admittedly exceptional cases, such important matters as changes in production policy and in the structure of undertakings had been decided without prior consultation with the board.

A fair proportion of replies expressed the opinion that with the participation of workers' representatives, board meetings had become more lively and that more consideration was given to personnel problems. Critics of the system mostly alleged either that decisions were taken unofficially outside the boardroom or that meetings became longer and more formalistic. Some employers attributed this change to increased caution in discussions or to lack of information on the part of the workers' representatives, some of whom stated that participation in decision-making on the boards of larger groups of undertakings was in many cases somewhat theoretical but that it did provide interesting information.

A problem often mentioned was that of insufficient communication between workers' representatives on boards and other workers, in spite of the existence in many undertakings of a liaison group or similar body. It seems that the problem was partly due to the confidentiality, official or implied, of some of the information received.

Nevertheless the official agency which carried out this survey (the National Industrial Board) came to the conclusion that, on the whole and in the majority of undertakings, the reform had produced encouraging results. According to that agency, the Act on workers' representation on boards was to be regarded as a useful addition to other measures aimed at improving democracy in working life.[38]

The principal recommendations made by the agency were limited to proposing that workers' representation should be put on a permanent basis (the initial legislation had been adopted for an experimental period of three years) and that it should also apply to undertakings with a smaller number of workers. These proposals were adopted in an Act of 3 June 1976[39] confirming this form of workers' participation on boards and extending it downwards to companies employing from 25 to 100 workers—which more than quadrupled the number of companies covered—and making similar participation possible below 25 workers if the shareholders are in agreement. It should also be noted that if the board appoints an executive committee, one of the workers' representatives has the right to sit on it. The agency refrained from making detailed proposals on internal rules of procedure, but drew special attention to problems of the frequency of meetings, early receipt of the documents needed, and rules relating to confidential information.

Another subject that has been much in the public eye in Sweden over the past few years is that of the constitution of employee investment funds. A study of this subject was made at the request of the Swedish Trade Union Confederation.[40] According to that body, the main objects sought were keep up a high investment rate and thereby safeguard employment, while guarding against concentration of capital and hence of economic and decision-making power in the hands of a limited number of people and of large companies, particularly through self-financing; strengthening the influence of the workers through participation in the ownership of capital; and remedying an unwanted side-effect of the policy of wage solidarity (whereby the most prosperous companies pay lower wages than they could afford and thus make additional profits).

This study, known as the "Meidner Report", proposed that part of the profits of larger companies in the private sector should be put into an employee investment fund by a transfer of shares (no money payments being made). The Meidner Report was discussed at the June 1976 Congress of the Swedish Trade Union Confederation, which decided to continue study of the subject without pronouncing on the details of such a system. The Confederation showed itself in favour of decentralised funds and a decisive role for local trade unions, particularly in the selection of workers' representatives to sit on the boards of companies in which the funds were to be invested.

In 1976 a group of Swedish industrialists and economists known as the "Waldenström Group" put forward a counter-proposal suggesting the constitution by voluntary agreements of funds derived from a specified proportion of wages and salaries. The funds would be managed by the workers and their assets would be invested in shares negotiable after a period of five to ten years.[41]

In February 1978 a working party of the Swedish Confederation of Trade Unions and the Social-Democratic Party published a report proposing that 20 per cent of the profits of companies employing more than 500 persons should be placed in investment funds managed by the unions, giving rise to the issue of shares.[42]

The employers' confederation is strongly opposed to such proposals, which it considers would do irreparable harm to the system of private enterprise and the market economy. In particular it fears that such a concentration of powers in the trade unions could lead to a corporatist state.[43] For its part, the Social-Democratic Party did not centre its electoral campaign in 1979 on these proposals in view of the complexity of the problem and the controversy which it had aroused among the public. It considered that a three-year period of reflection and study was still necessary, and its congress in September 1978 decided to present a detailed report on the subject only in 1982. In any event a report was awaited in 1980 from a commission composed a representatives of the different political parties and of the trade unions and employers' organisations, which had been set up to study the implications for the workers of increases in company capital.

Luxembourg

In Luxembourg an Act dated 6 May 1974[44] introduced workers' representation on the boards of directors of companies employing at least 1,000 workers, holding a state concession for their principal activities or financed by the State to the extent of 25 per cent or more. In the first type of company, representation is at the level of one-third; in the second, there is one director for every 100 workers (with a minimum of three and a maximum of one-third of the members of the board). The workers' members of the board are elected, under a system of proportional representation, by ballot of the personnel representatives. In principle, only members of the personnel of the undertaking are eligible for election, but in the iron and steel industry the most representative trade unions may directly appoint three representatives who do not necessarily have to be employees of the undertaking. The workers' members of the board may be removed by the personnel representatives or the trade unions from which they hold their appointment, and the Act exonerates them from the statutory obligation to deposit shares as surety for their behaviour in their management capacity. In addition, this Act added to the auditor of these companies an independent auditor whose appointment is subject to the unanimous approval of the members of the board representing the shareholders and the workers. A Bill under discussion provided that joint-stock companies might opt between the traditional structure with a single board of directors or a structure comprising a supervisory board and a management board, but the provisions of the above-mentioned Act would remain applicable either to the board of directors or to the supervisory board.

Netherlands

In the Netherlands, for joint-stock and limited liability companies with more than 100 workers and with a capital of a certain amount, an Act dated 6 May 1971, as amended by an Act of 8 April 1976 that has already been referred to, altered the rules governing the composition of the supervisory board, which now appoints, and could dismiss, the management board. The supervisory board has to approve important decisions such as those relating to major investments and changes affecting an appreciable proportion of the workforce.

Under the Act, members of the supervisory board are co-opted. Both the works council and the shareholders' general meeting or a committee appointed by it may veto these appointments, although an appeal against such a veto lies to the national tripartite Economic and Social Council. Candidates may be sponsored by the shareholders' general meeting, the works council and the management, but they must not be members of the personnel of the undertaking or of a trade union participating in the determination of the conditions of employment. Both the works council and the shareholders' general meeting may oppose the appointment of a candidate if they regard him as unsuited for the duties of member of a supervisory board or if, in their opinion, the appointment would upset the balance in the composition of the board. The object of these provisions was to ensure that members of the supervisory board would enjoy the confidence of both shareholders and workers. There are provisions for exceptions, in particular in undertakings in which more than half of the shares are held by companies having the majority of their personnel working abroad.[45]

According to a survey of a representative sample of 231 companies carried out in 1973 by the Netherlands labour inspectorate, in 19 per cent of these companies the works council had proposed candidates for the supervisory boards, and their proposals had been accepted in 81 per cent of the cases; the right of veto had not been exercised in any of these companies.[46]

The management board's decisions on any important management question affecting the position of the company and its workers, such as new investments or financial participation by other undertakings to the extent of over 25 per cent of the capital, the issue of shares or bonds, workforce reductions and closures of establishments, require the prior approval of the supervisory board.

The Federation of Netherlands Trade Unions (FNV, which resulted from the merger of the Roman Catholic and the Socialist trade unions) is compaigning in the long term for a self-management system under which a works council converted into a genuine workers' council will supersede the supervisory board, and in the short term for the works council to be able to appoint at least as many members of the supervisory board as the shareholders, with the two groups possibly (especially in large undertakings) in their turn appointing a third group up to a maximum of one-third of the board. This Federation is also in favour of growing co-ownership of undertakings by the workers through a national collective fund managed by the trade unions. Instead of the present supervisory boards, the Federation of Protestant Trade Unions (CNV) is in favour of boards with considerable powers, half of whose members should be appointed directly by the personnel.

Plans and proposals

Finland

In Finland a Bill drafted in 1976 after several years of study and discussion provided in its original version for representation of the workers on boards of directors.

Ireland

In Ireland in March 1980 the Ministry of Labour published a report[47] as a basis for discussion between employers and workers with a view to promoting voluntary experiments in workers' representation in the management organs of private firms, as well as the setting up of supervisory boards. This initiative was a sequel to the studies and proposals of the European Communities and to the measures taken in the public sector of the Irish economy and described in a later section. Consideration is being given to the adoption of legislation once a consensus has emerged in these matters, in order to provide a flexible statutory framework for undertakings wishing to introduce workers' representation along these lines.

United Kingdom

In the United Kingdom the Trades Union Congress discussed in 1974 a report asking for parity representation of workers, through the medium of trade union representatives, on bodies of a supervisory board type in private or public undertakings, with the right to veto important decisions of the management or of the shareholders' general meeting (on subjects such as closures, mergers or investments on a certain scale).[48]

British employers' organisations, while looking with favour on an extension of workers' participation in decision-making in undertakings especially through consultative procedures, affirmed their opposition to the imposition of participation on management bodies.[49]

A committee of inquiry on industrial democracy was appointed in December 1975 to study what would be the most appropriate ways of arranging worker representation on the boards of directors of private firms. This committee, known as "the Bullock committee" from the name of its chairman, published its report in January 1977.[50] The document contained a majority report signed by the chairman and six other members, a minority report signed by three members who were company directors, and a dissenting opinion on certain particular points by the solicitor of the committee.

The main report proposed giving trade union members and shareholders equal representation on boards of directors, with these two groups appointing a third, smaller, group co-opted with the agreement of a majority of each of the first two groups. This formula, described in the report as "2X + Y" would have been applicable in any company, group of companies or subsidiary employing 2,000 persons or more in the United Kingdom, with certain special provisions for groups of companies and multinational companies. All full-time workers (whether union members or not) would have been asked to approve the system by secret ballot before any company was obliged to accept workers' representatives on its board. (A ballot could only have been asked for by one or more trade unions recognised as representing at least 20 per cent of the workers.) Similarly, a further ballot could have been organised under similar conditions after five years to check whether the majority of the workers still desired such representation.

The Bullock report aroused much controversy among all concerned, particularly on the point whether or not workers should be represented on boards of directors, and on the role of the trade unions in that respect. In trade union circles opinion was far from unanimous on the principle of representation on a board of directors or a supervisory board.

In May 1978 the Labour Government published a White Paper on industrial democracy,[51] submitting to Parliament the policy which it intended to follow and the broad lines of the draft legislation which it intended to put forward at a later date on the subject of workers' participation in decision-making in public and private undertakings.

According to the White Paper, the Government favoured negotiated

103

arrangements rather than detailed formulas imposed by legislation, but held that in the absence of such arrangements it should be possible to enforce certain statutory rights of workers to participation.

It proposed that legislation should impose on all companies employing more than 500 persons in the United Kingdom an obligation to discuss with the representatives of their workers all major proposals, in particular relating to investment plans, mergers and takeovers, the expansion or contraction of establishments, and major organisational changes.

In spite of controversy on the subject of workers' representation on boards of directors, the Government favoured granting workers the statutory right to be represented at that level in their companies in the absence of voluntary agreement on the point, except where the personnel voted against such representation. To encourage this representation, it contemplated opening up the possibility of opting for a two-tier structure—a policy board responsible for deciding the policy to be followed and for taking the major decisions, on which both workers' and shareholders' representatives would have seats, and a management board appointed and supervised by it which would be responsible for current management, with participation in decisions concerning current management being arranged at lower levels.

The White Paper recalled that the trade unions had insisted that, in the case of workers' representation on the top board, this should be on a parity basis, while the employers' associations had been opposed to such an arrangement, fearing in particular that it would lead to deadlocks, to a lack of independence of the parties and to upsetting the balance in favour of the trade unions in collective bargaining, with the risk that the confidence of investors would be destroyed. Accordingly, while not excluding parity representation as a long-term objective, the Government considered that it would be better to proceed by stages on the basis of experiment, starting with one-third representation of employees, companies being free to introduce higher proportions through voluntary agreements.

At its second national conference, held at Brighton in November 1978, the Confederation of British Industry reiterated its opposition to any legislation which would impose trade union nominees on boards of directors. Emphasising that the workers themselves were not unanimously in favour of representation at that level, it insisted on the desirability of flexible arrangements and voluntary experiments, and adopted a motion recommending that the Confederation should prepare a code of conduct for the promotion of participation on a voluntary basis. Already in 1977 it had published a document proposing such a code, the establishment of a participation agency, and the development of consultative "steering committees" in undertakings.[52] A survey carried out at the beginning of 1978 had shown that about 70 per cent of the larger undertakings had made arrangements for the information and consultation of their personnel. At its third national conference, in November 1979, the Confederation approved a resolution on industrial democracy and gave its support to guidelines on employee involvement which emphasise the need for improved communication and consultation in undertakings.[53]

In 1978 the liaison committee between the Trades Union Congress and the Labour Party put out a document demanding early legislation on the subject.[54]

The Secretary of State for Employment in the Conservative Government which came into power after the 1979 elections declared in reply to a parliamentary question that the Government welcomed closer involvement by workers, whether trade unionists or not, in the decisions which affected them at their place of work. It believed this was best achieved through voluntary agreement. In its view, it would be wrong to impose by law a particular system of participation on every company.[55]

Switzerland

In Switzerland in 1971 the trade unions set on foot a procedure for amending the Constitution to state that the Confederation (i.e. the federal Parliament) has "the right to legislate on participation of workers and their organisations in decisions in business and in the public service". In the minds of the trade unions, such participation could have gone as far as representation, even parity representation, of the workers on boards of directors. In 1973 the federal Government put up a counterproposal to the effect that the Confederation would have "the right to legislate on an appropriate participation of the workers which would safeguard the operational possibilities and efficient management of the undertaking". Lively discussion ensued: employers' circles insisted on limiting participation to the level of production, as distinct from management, and there was great controversy on the possible representation of workers by trade unionists from outside the undertaking. Finally, a popular vote in March 1976 rejected both of the texts proposed—that of the trade union initiative quoted above and a counterproposal of the federal Parliament phrased as follows:

The Confederation has the right to legislate on appropriate workers' participation in production management, such participation to safeguard the possibilities of decision-making and of efficient management.

Only workers employed in the undertaking may exercise the participation rights deriving from the foregoing clause.

After this vote, however, the authorities expressed the view that the question of participation remained open. The employers' organisations considered that it would be better to deal with participation matters on a practical rather than a political plane, that is to say through discussions and negotiation between employers and workers. The trade union organisations were of the opinion that the best course would henceforth be to seek to take advantage of other constitutional provisions and announced that they would prepare proposals for the strengthening of participation on the basis of legislation and collective agreements.

Subsequently, a committee of the lower chamber of Parliament (the National Council) drafted a possible new text as follows:

> The Confederation may legislate on appropriate workers' participation in undertakings.
> Participation shall be limited to workers employed in the undertaking. The Confederation shall determine by means of legislation the cases in which, exceptionally, persons from outside the undertaking shall be eligible.
> The efficient management of the undertaking and the unity and decision-making powers of the management should be safeguarded.[56]

A number of other proposals have been made in parliament by individual members. Among employers avowed opposition to workers' participation in management continues.

European Communities

The Commission of the European Communities has concerned itself with workers' representation on the management bodies of undertakings for a considerable time. It submitted a draft Statute for European Companies to the Council of Ministers, first in 1970, then in 1975 after a revision which took account of the opinion of the European Parliament expressed in July 1974 and after thorough consultations with the representatives of employers and workers in the Community, including discussions in the Economic and Social Committee.

According to the last version of this draft,[57] in undertakings operating in several States Members of the European Communities, having adopted the statute (adoption would not be compulsory), and wishing to adapt their legal status to the requirements of the common market as a whole, the supervisory board would consist of one-third of shareholders' representatives appointed by the general meeting, one-third of workers' representatives (elected in principle by two successive ballots, and of whom a minority might be non-members of the personnel but deemed capable of appreciating the situation of the undertaking in its macro-economic and sectoral context), and one-third of members co-opted by the other two groups by two-thirds majority or, if necessary, designated by a legal arbitration body. (The earlier draft provided for two-thirds of representatives of the shareholders and one-third of representatives of the workers on the supervisory board, although the company's own statutes might provide for a higher proportion of workers' representatives.) The co-opted members should be chosen from among persons representing general interests not directly linked with those of the shareholders or the workers or their respective organisations. However, there would be no workers' representatives on the supervisory board if the majority of the personnel decided against it.

According to normal practice, the supervisory board, being responsible for regular supervision of management without directly intervening in it, would designate the members of the management and would have the right to remove them for serious reasons. It should be kept informed of the management's activities and the state of affairs of the company. The supervisory board or a third of its members would have the right to examine all the company's books and to appoint one or more auditing or other experts, as might seem necessary. Management decisions relating to closure or relocation of establishments or of important parts of establishments, major restrictions, extensions or modifications of the activity of the undertaking, major modifications in its organisation and the introduction or termination of long-term cooperation with other undertakings would require prior authorisation by the supervisory board.

There are appropriate provisions in this draft for groups of undertakings. This draft statute contains many other provisions, mostly designed to facilitate transnational activities in the European Common Market. Even after its adoption, however, the statute would not have binding force. On the other hand the Commission of European Communities prepared in 1972 a draft fifth directive aimed at co-ordinating the legislation of Member States on joint-stock companies; this directive would have imposed on companies employing 500 workers or more a system of workers' participation in the election of members of the supervisory board, a body which would also have become compulsory. There should have been a choice: it would have been possible for not less than one-third of the board's members to be elected by the workers or their representatives, or from persons proposed by them; alternatively, it would have been possible to adopt a system simular to that obtaining in the Netherlands. The rights of the supervisory board to information would have been similar to those indicated above for "European companies", as also the cases in which the management board would have had to obtain the prior authorisation of the supervisory board.

This draft was prepared before the entry of Denmark, Ireland and the United Kingdom to the European Communities. The dual management structure of companies (supervisory board and management board or directorate) is not current in all nine countries of the Communities, and workers' participation—even minority participation—on supervisory or boards of directors could hardly be unanimously accepted by employers and their associations, or even by trade unions in those countries. As already emphasised in the first part of this report, one of the main problems resides in the co-responsibility which derives from the right to genuine co-determination: a number of trade unions are apprehensive about being associated in decisions which may have unfavourable repercussions on the workforce, without in practice having sufficient opportunity, especially in the case of minority representation, to influence various aspects of management; they prefer to defend the interests of workers by lodging claims and following them up by negotiations. In some cases also, they more or less completely reject the prevailing economic and social system.

For instance, in Belgium the General Federation of Labour is opposed to co-determination, and has declared its aim to be that of workers' supervision[58] through trade union action, carried out primarily by the undertaking's trade union delegation. In complete independence, it would propose whatever action it considers appropriate, in the course of systematic consultations with the management and after receiving very full information on any proposals (prior to the taking of decisions) and on the situation of the undertaking, and would if necessary press for the abandonment or modification of certain projects or decisions proposed.

In France the three major trade union confederations —the General Confederation of Labour (CGT), the General Confederation of Labour - Force ouvrière (CGT-FO) and the French Democratic Confederation of Labour (CFDT)—are not in favour of workers' representation on boards of directors, or even on supervisory boards. The CGT advocates a system which it calls democratic management of the undertaking,[59] while the CFDT favours self-management[60] and the social ownership of the means of production. Only the French Confederation of Christian Workers (CFTC)[61] and the French Confederation of Executive and Supervisory Staff (CGC)[62] have spoken clearly in favour of such representation.

In Italy too, the three major trade union confederations have, for a long time, opposed the presence of workers' representatives on the management bodies of private undertakings and have concentrated on the development of consultation and collective bargaining. In the past few years, however, their unified federation has taken a more flexible attitude towards the draft statute for European companies, and has accepted that such representation might be tried experimentally on the multinational level in Western Europe.

Also, some trade union organisations such as the Trades Union Congress in Great Britain and the Irish Congress of Trade Unions have insisted that workers' representatives on supervisory boards must be chosen exclusively from among trade unionists.

On the employers' side, the Union of Industries of the European Community has protested vigorously against the idea of minority representation of shareholders on supervisory boards.

Having regard to the fact that a two-tier structure of management bodies does not exist throughout the Common Market, the Commission of the European Communities decided in 1975 to revise its draft fifth directive. It published a "Green Book" entitled *Employee participation and company structure*[63] as a basis for wide-ranging discussion and the preparation of a new draft. That new report describes and analyses existing participation structures and practices, including collective bargaining, in companies of the member States, brings out the possibilities of participation that are made available in various ways in several of those States, and comes down in favour of the gradual adoption of the above-mentioned two-tier structure. The maintenance of a single management body such as a board of directors, and of a single information and consultation body such as a works council, is contemplated for a transitional period, though the hope is expressed that Community legislation will in certain cases confer on the workers' representatives the right to approve or object to decisions proposed. In addition, it was announced that the amended fifth directive should not contain uniform rules as to the methods of designating workers' representatives, but that all the workers should be able to participate in their election, and that workers' representation on the supervisory board should be introduced only if a majority of the workers were in favour of it.[64]

In an opinion voted on 2 February 1978, unanimously except for one abstention, the Economic and Social Committee of the European Communities commended the intention of the Commission to take better account, in the harmonisation of company law, of existing legislation and practices in the nine member States so as to give a more flexible tenor to the future directive. While recognising that divergent opinions remained, it considered that the directive might provide for two practical measures which would ensure continuous and convergent development. The first would be the optional introduction of the two-tier system (supervisory board and management board) in the member States which did not yet have it. The second would be the establishment, in large companies which did not yet have any body including workers' representatives, of a special body on which the workers would be represented would enjoy certain minimum rights to information and consultation.[65]

In May 1979 the Legal Commission of the European Parliament discussed a report and a draft resolution containing proposals in relation to the revised draft fifth directive, which would be applicable to

109

undertakings employing not fewer than 250 workers instead of 500, so as to include, in particular, highly automated or highly capital-intensive undertakings, or as from a certain level of turnover. These proposals were akin to the arrangements described above in connection with the revised draft statute for European companies, and provided in particular, for a supervisory board composed of one-third of shareholders' representatives, one-third of workers' representatives and one-third of persons co-opted by members in the other two categories, with a workers' delegate on the management board. For a transitional period of five years, it would also have been possible to retain the system with no more than a board of directors but with at least one-third of its members being designated by the workers or their representatives. The agreement of the workers' representatives would have been necessary before any measure was taken to change conditions of work or methods of organisation, to establish general rules regarding recruitment and dismissal, to proceed with mergers or large-scale redundancies, or to take relief measures in that connection.[66] A draft resolution stating that "the object to be achieved is workable parity representation of the workers" was put to a vote, but the quorum was not reached. The matter was referred back to the Legal Commission of the new elected parliament; its rapporteur submitted a report which was discussed in the Legal, Economic and Social Commissions in 1980. Amendments were put forward and the matter is still under consideration.

The Commission of the European Communities approved in October 1980 a proposal concerning a directive to be submitted to the Council, the Economic and Social Committee and the European Parliament, on procedures for informing and consulting the employees of undertakings with complex structures, including groups of undertakings and transnational undertakings.

Other

By resolution No. 564 of 9 May 1974 the Consultative Assembly of the Council of Europe called upon the governments of its member States to consider the possibility of enacting legislation to set up, in all companies employing more than 1,000 persons, a supervisory board composed to the extent of at least one-third of representatives of the workers, without prejudice to collective bargaining procedures. The European Social Charter adopted in October 1961 already provides in Article 6 that "with a view to ensuring the effective exercise of the right to collective bargaining, the Contracting Parties undertake (1) to promote joint consultation between workers and employers; (2) to promote, where necessary and appropriate, machinery for voluntary negotiations between employers or employers' organisations and workers' organisations with a view to the regulation of terms and conditions of employment by means of collective agreements."

Under an agreement signed on 1 March 1975 between the management of the multinational Scandinavian Airlines System (SAS) and 33 Danish, Norwegian and Swedish trade unions, the personnel are represented on the board and on the committee of shareholders' representatives, which to some extent plays the part of a supervisory board. To begin with, these personnel representatives had no voting rights.[67]

In Japan some big firms have seats for workers' representatives on their management bodies and others are considering such an arrangement. It is a common practice for ex-leaders of the undertaking's trade union, if they have shown themselves to be able and dynamic in trade union affairs, to be promoted later to a high rank in management. According to a survey carried out in the autumn of 1978 by the Federation of Japanese Employers' Associations (Nikkeiren), two-thirds of the 352 big firms that replied had ex-members of the trade union committee on their management board, in an average proportion of about 16 per cent. It should be mentioned that in practice the management board in Japan has no intermediate body between itself and the shareholders' general meeting, and is more autonomous in relation to the owners and shareholders than in other countries.[68]

Developing countries

In the developing countries workers' representation on management bodies in the private sector seems to be rather unusual, although in some of these countries the subject is attracting more and more attention. It seems that, in addition to the strong resistance of employers and the fears of governments about putting off foreign investors, there are a number of other factors that account for this situation. These factors include the special importance of the public sector, in which workers' representation has been introduced in many countries without always producing conclusive results. There is also the hesitation, or even the opposition, of the trade unions, which generally prefer collective bargaining. As the Under-Secretary of Labour of a developing country emphasised at the Oslo symposium in 1974, the weakness of trade unionism in some of these countries means that workers on the boards of private companies might become "captives of management".[69] In some countries trade unions, because of their multiplicity, would even have difficulty in designating the small number of workers' representatives required. Two other points must also be borne in mind: that the educational level of most of the workers is often still too low to enable them to participate effectively in management, and that a higher priority is often given, even by the workers themselves, to other economic and social objectives. Nevertheless there have already been, in certain developing countries, experiments in participation in management in the private sector which deserve a brief mention.

In Algeria part of the code for the socialist management of undertakings applicable to the private sector provides that two officers of the trade union section of the undertaking shall attend meetings of the board of directors or management board.

In the Republic of Korea, where the federation of trade unions is campaigning for workers' representation on boards of directors, there is sometimes found, instead of the joint council (similar to a works council) provided for in the legislation, a "junior board" whose role is basically advisory but which may also have powers of decision limited to fields predetermined by the top management of the undertaking. It has also happened that, in undertakings in difficulty, the trade unions temporarily designated a group of workers to sit on the board of directors.

In Egypt the decree of 1961 introducing a system of workers' participation in management (which will be described later in connection with the public sector) was also applicable in the private sector, except in family businesses and partnerships. Under that decree, two members of the board of directors (one manual worker and one salaried employee) represented the workers, being elected by the personnel by secret ballot under the supervision of the Ministry in charge of social affairs and labour. The other members were elected by the shareholders' general meeting; one at least and three at most were chosen from senior executives (managers or heads of departments) out of a maximum total of seven members of the board. This decree was amended in particular by a presidential decree of 1963 which, as with public undertakings, raised the maximum number of members of the board to nine, of whom the personnel must elect four by secret ballot for a term of two years from among the workers of the undertaking. Only private undertakings included in a list drawn up by ministerial decision are now subject to this scheme.

In India a commission set up to examine the operation of the law on monopolies and restrictive commercial practices submitted a report in the autumn of 1978, in which it pronounced in favour of workers' representation on the boards of directors of private firms employing at least 1,000 workers, leaving it to the Government to fix the proportion of workers' representatives on these boards. The question was also considered by a tripartite commission on workers' participation in management and equity, which had been set up by the Government in 1977,[70] but its report has not been made public.

In Iraq private undertakings are, in principle, subject to the same rules as regards personnel representation on their boards of directors as undertakings in the semi-public sector that is covered in the next section.

In Jamaica, in accordance with the recommendation of an advisory committee on workers' participation, guiding principles have been laid down for the development of participation at different levels and in different types of undertakings, including workers' representation on the boards of directors of private undertakings. Accent has been put on the launching of pilot experiments in voluntary agreement with the trade unions and with the help of a workers' participation unit (a central consultative body attached to the Ministry of Labour). The introduction of participation and its adaptation to the characteristics of the undertaking must be assisted by the setting up of an internal steering committee including top and middle-level management, delegates of the personnel and members of the various categories of personnel. At the very least, this provides for direct possibilities of dialogue between the workers' representatives and members of the board of directors.[71]

In Malta a hotel complex financed by foreign capital has two elected workers' representatives among the nine members of its board of directors.

In Pakistan, under an ordinance of 1969, amended several times (in particular by an Act dated 16 April 1976), the management committee of any factory employing at least 50 persons must include in its membership 50 per cent (previously 20 per cent) of workers' representatives, with a minimum of one such representative.

The workers' representatives must be selected by the trade union responsible for collective bargaining in the factory or elected by simple majority by secret ballot by all workers in establishments where there is no such trade union (a case which hardly ever occurs in practice). These workers' representatives take part in all meetings of the management committee except those bearing on commercial or financial matters. No decision may be taken on the following subjects without the written opinion of these representatives: elaboration of employment rules, change of material working conditions in the factory; regulation of the length of the working day and of breaks; fixing of holiday dates; questions relating to discipline and the conduct of workers in the undertaking; promotions; on-the-job training; recreational activities and workers' welfare. The management has a period of six weeks in which to answer the questions raised and to make its final position known. When, after joint discussions, the management rejects the proposals of the workers' representatives, the union may treat the issue as a labour dispute.

The latest amendments provided for the establishment, at undertaking level, of joint management boards composed, to the extent of 30 per cent, of workers' representatives, the remaining members being employers' representatives chosen from senior executives and managers of the undertaking. These councils are responsible for seeing to the improvement of production and productivity, for determining basic wages and piece rates, for redeployment of workers, and for studying and adopting new methods of remuneration.

Up to the adoption of the 1976 Act undertakings managed by the state or local authorities were excluded from this participation system. Moreover, little information is available on the degree of strictness with which the legislation has been enforced. According to an estimate made in 1977, only about one-tenth of private undertakings in practice had this worker representation on their management bodies. The fact that decisions of a commercial or financial nature are not submitted for discussion considerably diminishes the bearing of the system, since many decisions have financial implications. In addition, the duties attributed to workers' representatives on these bodies make the latter, in spite of their name, more like works councils although, as will be seen, there is specific provision in Pakistani legislation for such councils with functions set out elsewhere in this volume.

In Peru, under legislative decrees dated 27 July 1970 and 1 September 1970,[72] supplemented by another dated 6 January 1972, "industrial communities" of a co-operative type, managing part of the funds deriving from the profit-sharing system, were established in private industrial undertakings employing at least six full-time workers. These "communities" should have a number of representatives on the board of directors corresponding to their share of the capital, up to an initial limit of 50 per cent, with a minimum of one representative. This system was extended with variations to mines, fisheries and telecommunications, and a similar arrangement was introduced in public undertakings, where the representation of workers was permanently fixed at two members. At its peak, this experiment covered some 2,000 undertakings employing in all more than 200,000 workers.

The system of "industrial communities" subsequently came under strong, substantiated, criticism due partly to financial difficulties and partly to lapses in its administration. The organisation to which most of the large undertakings and many of the medium-sized undertakings belong (Sociedad Nacional de Industrias) proposed another system, which would involve the distribution of shares to each worker. On 1 February 1977 the Government promulgated legislative decree No. 21789[73] changing the system of "industrial communities" to some extent. Whereas before 15 per cent of the net profits of the undertaking were converted each year into theoretically non-transferable "labour shares" which became the property of the industrial community, and carried with them the right, in proportion to their share in the total capital of the

114

undertaking, to a given number of workers' representatives on the board of directors, henceforth only 13.5 per cent of the profits would be paid over to the industrial community, which could now distribute the proceeds in the form of securities other than "labour shares". Even the latter became individual shares which could be assigned to third parties on certain conditions. The labour shares held by workers of the undertaking remain the basis for determining the number of their representatives on the board of directors, those representatives being elected for a term of one year and re-eligible not more than once. At present, this system is functioning in only about a hundred undertakings.

In the Syrian Arab Republic, under a legislative decree of 5 October 1961, two members of the board of directors of any joint stock company must be elected by the personnel.

PUBLIC SECTOR (IN MARKET ECONOMY COUNTRIES)

There are workers' representatives on management bodies in a fairly large number of countries, industrialised and developing, either in the whole of the public sector (most frequently the case in the developing countries) or in certain nationalised undertakings or services such as railways, airlines, posts and telecommunications, or gas, water and electricity supply.

Introduction of this representation clearly does not raise the same questions of principle as in the private sector. However, it is exceptional for the number of workers' representatives to be equal to the number of representatives of the public authorities or of management. In recent years it has been introduced in a growing number of developing countries, particularly those in which the modern sector is composed mainly of public or semi-public undertakings.

Industrialised countries

Besides countries mentioned earlier, such as the Federal Republic of Germany and Austria, where the legislation on workers' representation on management bodies is generally applicable to public undertakings as much as to private ones, and a number of other countries in respect of which the situation is described in some detail below, workers' representation on the boards of directors of some undertakings (such as railways or the national airline) is also to be found in industrialised countries such as Australia, Belgium, Canada (Province of British Columbia), Italy and Switzerland.

115

France

In nationalised industries in France postwar legislation mostly provided for direct representation on boards of directors at the level of the undertaking. In general, workers had one-third (sometimes fewer) of the seats on these boards (or on the supervisory board in undertakings which had opted for this possibility under an Act of 24 July 1966); boards of directors also included representatives of the Government and generally of consumers or users. Later expert members were appointed also. Ordinarily, the worker members are appointed by the most representative trade union organisations (as in coal mines, gas, electricity and the railways); they are sometimes appointed by the works committee (Renault, Alsace Potash Mines) or elected by the personnel (Air France). The government representatives and the expert members are selected by the government department concerned, thus in general increasing the influence of the Government.[74] The representatives of users or consumers are selected mostly by representative bodies such as chambers of commerce and industry, but sometimes by the Government. As regards the worker representatives the highest administrative court, the *Conseil d'Etat*, has ruled that the public authorities have discretionary power to appoint representatives nominated by "one of the most representative organisations" and not necessarily "the most representative organisation".[75]

Although the powers of the boards of nationalised industries were originally similar to those of boards of directors in the private sector, they have tended to be narrowed down under pressure from the government departments concerned and on account of the growing number of decisions requiring the prior consent of those departments. In February 1979 the government decided that, in non-subsidised public undertakings in the competitive sector, the board members representing the Government should henceforth be chosen from outside the government department directly concerned, from among officials of other departments who, during their civil service careers, had acquired experience and skill which would be useful for the public undertaking concerned. The purpose was to make a clearer distinction between supervision by the government department directly concerned on the one hand and management of the public undertaking on the other, thus making the management fully responsible for its decisions and allowing the Government to form a better appreciation of the quality of management. In addition, in public undertakings operating public utilities or state monopolies, or receiving state subsidies, government representation would in future be more diversified, without excluding some representation of the department directly concerned on their boards.

In France nationalisation also affected other sectors such as insurance and banking; in the latter, employee representation is especially well developed.

The appointment of trade unionists to the boards of directors of nationalised or public undertakings is a well established practice in several other countries. However, those concerned usually sit in a personal capacity with no obligation to account for their activities to the workers or their organisations.

United Kingdom

In the United Kingdom trade unionists were expected to sever their links with the trade union movement if they were appointed as full-time members of a board of directors; however, an amendment to the law on nationalisation of the steel industry some years back increased workers' participation in that industry, and the requirement to sever links with the trade union movement was lifted. A thorough study of the first years of operation of this participation has been made.[76] The majority of the workers and of the local trade union officials expressed favourable views on participation.

A working party was appointed some years ago to study the development of participation in the public sector, which employs more than 7 million workers, as had been done by the Bullock commission for the private sector, without, however, gathering any external opinions.[77]

In another connection, a 1975 Act dealing with industry made the National Enterprise Board responsible for developing industrial democracy in undertakings under its supervision. A similar requirement was enjoined on the Scottish and Welsh development agencies.

A 1977 Act on the aircraft and shipbuilding industries provided that the industrial democracy already under study in those two industries should be developed. A similar policy applies in the other nationalised industries. In the railways several pilot experiments have been undertaken, basically on consultation and negotiation since the main trade unions do not wish to have worker-directors in the industry.[78]

High-level consultative committees have been set up in electricity distribution. Various experiments in associating personnel representatives with major decisions, including those of investment policy, have been made in several nationalised industries, and new structures have been worked out for the gas industry. In British Airways a council has been set up for the discussion of long-term planning. By agreement the Post Office, which employs some 500,000 persons (of whom 90 per cent are unionised), changed the composition of its central board of directors as from 1 January 1978 for an experimental period of two years so that it

117

comprised seven representatives of management, seven trade union representatives and five independent members. Regional consultative boards and local committees were also to contain equal numbers of management and trade union representatives. To the regret of the unions concerned, this participation scheme was allowed to lapse at the end of the experimental period. As an alternative, the management of the Post Office proposed the setting up of two national joint boards to discuss issues of general policy before decisions were taken; the unions did not regard this proposal as satisfactory.[79]

Ireland

In Ireland an Act on workers' participation in state undertakings was adopted on 29 March 1977. Under the Act, individual sets of regulations have been issued covering seven different public undertakings, engaged in peat production, air transport, sea transport, road and rail transport, electricity supply, sugar manufacture and the production of fertilisers, and employing about 45,000 workers in all. The Act provides for the election, by secret ballot with proportional representation, of workers' representatives on the boards of directors of these undertakings, where they hold one-third of the seats. Only the trade unions have the right to put up candidates (who must have at least three years' seniority), or to appoint the members if the number of candidates does not exceed the number of seats to be filled. However, the personnel may, by a majority preliminary vote taken by secret ballot before each triennial election, request that this representation system should not apply in their undertaking; such a preliminary vote may be requested by a trade union or by a group consisting of at least 15 per cent of the personnel.

Israel

In Israel the Ministry of Finance, which is responsible for applying the 1975 Act on state companies, issued regulations on 20 June 1977 providing for the election of two employee representatives on the boards of directors of public undertakings (with the exception of banks) employing 100 workers or more. Candidates must have spent at least three years in the undertaking concerned and must not be holders of managerial or executive posts, in particular.[80] They may be proposed by the works council or by a tenth of the personnel entitled to vote. The electors may not vote for more than four candidates. The government department to which the company reports appoints two workers' representatives from the six candidates who have received the highest number of votes. Those representatives carry on with their usual jobs, and their pay does not change. Their term of service is for three years, and they may not serve more than two consecutive terms.

Developing countries

It has already been mentioned that over the past few years a growing number of developing countries have introduced workers' representation on the management bodies of their public undertakings. The purpose has been to give the personnel a greater interest in improving the quantity and quality of output and the efficiency of the undertaking, to make management methods more flexible and, in a general way, to contribute to strengthening popular participation in development and the better fulfilment of national plans. It had also often been found that rigid administrative and budgetary rules hampered the management of these undertakings, which had to operate under the dual constraints of a government wage policy and a pricing policy aimed at keeping the prices of the goods and services which they supplied within the means of the consumer and at endeavouring to prevent increases in the cost of living. Moreover, in some cases members of management bodies had been chosen more for their political connections than for their managerial abilities. Sometimes, too, the displacement of expatriate senior personnel or the establishment of new industries in the public sector had outstripped the training of national managers. All these factors may have played a part in the desire to improve the decision-making process in public undertakings through participation.

In some developing countries workers' representation was introduced as part of a policy of more or less complete socialisation of the economy, or was decided primarily on the initiative of the government. In several countries, too, it will be seen that the ruling political party plays an active part in participation. In some socialistically oriented developing countries, workers' representation emerged at the time of independence, or shortly after, and was the main element in the whole system of industrial relations, while in other countries it is only one of a number of elements in the system. For instance, in India and Pakistan, where it co-exists with collective bargaining, the latter remains far more important than workers' participation in management bodies.

In most developing countries the workers' representatives on the management bodies of public undertakings are in a minority, sometimes a very small minority. Only in a few countries such as Benin, Egypt and Tanzania does the number of such workers' representatives approach parity. Sometimes too, representation is not at the level of, or is not limited to, the board of directors, but exists on executive or management committees; and in some countries, account has to be rendered periodically to general meetings of the personnel.

Most frequently, the government as such, and usually also the department or departments of government directly concerned, are strongly represented; even where it is not expressly laid down that the boards may only make recommendations to the higher authority to which the undertaking reports, it is not uncommon for the main decisions to be taken by that authority, or for decisions to be subject to that authority's approval. In that case, if decisions or recommendations which have been agreed in the undertaking are not put into effect, there may well be a sense of frustration among both management and labour.

In some countries minority representation of the personnel has given rise to criticisms, such as that there is a risk of loss of contact between the workers' representative and the workers themselves since the representatives are sometimes retired trade union leaders who have never worked in the undertaking, and that representatives lack experience or are reluctant to be associated with decisions which may be unfavourable to the personnel. For that reason various other arrangements have been tried, in the public as in the private sector, to broaden the possibilities of co-decision through other bodies such as works councils (which will be dealt with in the next chapter) or to develop consultation to such an extent that in fact it almost amounts to participation in management. In addition, as has been seen, works councils often play a complementary role in workers' participation where it exists.

Benin

In Benin after a series of nationalisations, workers' representation was introduced in 1973 on the boards of directors of companies entirely or partly owned by the State. In 1976 this representation was raised from one to five workers out of a total of 12 to 15 members, comprising a chairman appointed by the minister in charge of the department directly concerned, representatives of the other departments concerned and a representative of the National Revolutionary Council. The workers' representatives are elected by the undertaking's trade union council. The general manager attends meetings of the board in an advisory capacity.

The management committee of each undertaking, which meets at least once a month, includes, in addition to the general manager and the other managers, a representative of the Government and, since 1976, five workers' representatives (instead of one as previously) who are elected by the trade union council of the undertaking. Similar workers' representation is provided for in private companies, but is difficult to ensure in practice.

General meetings of the workers are held at regular intervals to examine the reports of management committees, as well as of boards of directors at the end of the financial year, to collect suggestions and criticisms, and to hold wide-ranging discussions on all matters concerning the undertaking and its workers. Such meetings also take place at the level of the departments or other units in the undertaking.

Welfare activities are managed directly by workers' representatives through a special committee. An active role is also played by a "committee for the defence of the achievements of the Revolution" elected by the workers, which has, among other responsibilities, that of making suggestions on the running and sound management of the undertaking.

Congo

In the People's Republic of the Congo an ordinance and a decree, both dated 18 May 1973, introduced in all undertakings in which the State has an interest and in all departments of the Government and of other national administrative entities a system known as that of the "three co's"—co-determination, co-decision and co-responsibility.

Under the heading of co-determination, the management must associate the party and the trade union with the study of problems relating to the running of the undertaking, service or production unit which are of interest to workers and their families; co-decision implies associating the party and the trade union with the actual taking of decisions concerning those problems; and co-responsibility implies that the consequences of a decision jointly agreed by the party, the trade union and the management must be shared by this triarchy.

To make the triarchy effective, there is provision for the establishment, at the level of each undertaking or department concerned, of a management committee, a committee on recruitment and promotion, a standing committee on production and a committee for the supervision of production. The management committee consists of members of the management, representatives of the trade union of the undertaking or department and members of the party cell. The manager is responsible to the management committee, which is in turn responsible to the workers' general meeting.

Egypt

In Egypt, as has been seen, workers have been members of the boards of directors of public and private undertakings since 1961. Originally, however, they held only two seats out of seven. It was in that year that a major programme of nationalisation was launched, so that the public sector came to account for about 80 per cent of the Egyptian economy. Parity of representation was introduced in October 1963 by a series of presidential decrees, confirmed later at the time of the revision of the legislation on public sector organisations and companies at the end of 1966, at which time it applied to more than 400 public undertakings.

Under this legislation all companies belonging to the public sector are run by a board of directors consisting of at most eight members plus a chairman; half represent the workers, the other half and the chairman being appointed by presidential decree. The worker members are elected for two years (up to 1963, their term was for one year only) directed by the personnel, by secret ballot under the supervision of the ministry responsible for social and labour affairs. The chairman of the trade union committee has the right to attend meetings of the board, but without the right to vote.

For a long time the boards' main function was to make proposals to the higher bodies to which the undertakings reported. In 1975, in a desire to cut down bureaucracy, the Government did away with these bodies, set up special committees to co-ordinate the activities of groups of undertakings belonging to the same field of activity, and considerably increased the autonomy of the management.

During the early years of this participation system, the contribution of elected members of boards of directors was not unanimously admired. Often management complained that they did not have the qualifications required to participate effectively in deciding the policy and programmes of the undertaking and that they lacked the necessary experience to discuss technical and administrative problems; it was not uncommon for managers to show very scant confidence in them and to keep information secret, particularly concerning personnel questions. It blamed them for being primarily interested in personnel questions (so as to win the support of their workmates) and for disrupting the work on the pretext of seeking information. It was even claimed that electoral campaigns took up a lot of time and reduced productivity. On their side, the workers' representatives sometimes blamed the chairman and other members of the boards for lack of collaboration, unsatisfactory practical arrangements (late distribution of the agenda, faulty minutes in which opposing points of view were too briefly summarised), insufficient interest in personnel matters and, in general, for their autocratic attitude and marked reservations about participation, and for the frequency of the occasions on which they met outside the boardroom to come to agreement.[81] Also, there were sometimes overlaps between the activities of the workers' representatives on the boards and the trade union committee, with members even outbidding each other with a view to obtaining more votes at the next elections.[82]

Substantial training (including joint sittings of workers' representatives and managers) was provided in order to remedy these weaknesses and, from 1963 on, the term of workers' representatives was raised to two years in order to take advantage of the experience they had acquired. An Act in 1966 defined more clearly the duties of boards of directors; other legislation increased the frequency of their meetings (to a minimum of once a month), made it impossible for senior executives to be elected as worker representatives, and laid down that at least half of those representatives should be skilled workers.

India

In India representation of the personnel by one worker was introduced on the boards of directors of some public undertakings in 1971, and in the nationalised banks in 1973, although such appointments raised difficulties in a number of cases beacuse of the plurality of trade unions. Here, too, attempts have been made to make the management of these undertakings less burcaucratic, because some managers had retained habits from the civil service from which they had come. As in many other countries, the managers did not always seem very receptive to participation.[83] A desire for equal representation on the boards of public undertakings has been expressed by various sections of the trade union movement. The "joint management councils" which, despite their name, are more comparable to advisory bodies of the works council type, will be discussed later, as will also the joint councils advocated in the government directives of 30 October 1975.

Iraq

In Iraq, since the adoption of Act No. 60 of 1970, wage earners have had two representatives (out of a minimum of seven members) on the boards of directors of public undertakings, which constitute the largest sector of the economy. These representatives have an equal number of substitutes, both full members and substitutes being designated by the trade union organisation. In undertakings in which the State holds at least 50 per cent of the shares, in addition to the two wage earners' representatives a representative of the salaried employees is elected by the whole of the personnel (wage earners and salaried employees) to sit on the board, which has from seven to nine members in all. These boards lay down the policy of the undertaking and supervise its execution, but most of their decisions are subject to the approval of the government department directly concerned. In public undertakings in the food, energy, textile, chemical and paper, leather and footwear, and construction industries (which are answerable to the Ministry of Industries) there is not a board of directors but a consultative committee at the level of each undertaking, chaired by the general manager of the undertaking and consisting of its senior executives and two workers' representatives designated by the trade union organisation. This consultative committee submits "resolutions" for the approval of the board of directors of the group of undertakings in each industry. This board is composed of a chairman, the respective managers of each affiliated undertaking and two trade union representatives from the industry concerned. Its decisions are submitted to the Minister of Industry for ratification, which is assumed in the absence of a reaction within two weeks. If the Minister is not in agreement, the board must change its decision; if it maintains its original position, the question is settled by a committee of the various ministers concerned.

Mali

In Mali, under an ordinance dated 11 April 1969, public undertakings—which in fact means practically all the 40 or so large establishments in the country—each have a board of directors consisting of seven to 12 members, of whom two are selected by the personnel, the others being representatives of the government departments concerned and persons appointed for their recognised special knowledge. Each board is chaired by the minister to which the undertaking is answerable, or by the minister's delegate. When the minister is not in the chair the decisions of the board are not effective until they have received his approval, which must come within a maximum of two weeks. Exceptionally, the minister may delegate the general manager of the undertaking to chair the board of directors. The board meets at least twice a year, and discusses the main issues connected with the running and management of the undertaking. It examines and approves the annual production plan and the investment plan drawn up by the general manager, as well as the balance sheet. It also discusses how much of the profits should be paid into the welfare fund.

In addition, in each undertaking or production unit in the public sector, a management committee has been set up in order to associate its workers with the management of the undertaking. This committee is composed of the department chiefs and not more than four representatives of the workers. It must be consulted in particular on questions of work organisation, improvement of working conditions and productivity and disciplinary matters. It must also be kept regularly informed of the progress of the undertaking and its financial situation. It administers the welfare fund. In practice, the composition of these committees and their scope activities vary a great deal, some undertakings giving a very broad interpretation to their terms of reference while in others the committees are little more than additional channels of communication with the workers.

Mozambique

In Mozambique Legislative Decree No. 17/77, which came into force in April 1977, laid down model by-laws for state undertakings. It is provided that these undertakings should have a manager, a management board and workers' general meetings, all three being responsible for good management, for raising production, for improving quality, for eliminating waste, for maintaining discipline and for fulfilling plan targets.

The manager is appointed by the government department directly concerned and he may have assistants, of whom at least two are elected for two years by the workers' general meeting. The manager's duties are to draw up the annual budget, the operating plans, the annual report and the accounts, which are submitted for approval of the government department concerned after consultation with the workers' general meeting; to submit pay scales for the approval of the department, taking account of the guidelines provided by the Ministry of Labour; and to recruit and deal with the promotion of personnel on the recommendation of the management board.

The management board consists of the general manager, the heads of various branches of the undertaking, representatives of the workers' organisation for the undertaking and representatives of the party (FRELIMO) cell in the undertaking, and is chaired by the manager. The board must meet at least once a month. Its competence extends to study of the basic problems facing the undertaking and of measures to raise productivity and improve quality, to promote greater interest in the job, to improve occupational safety and health, and to improve training and the living and working conditions of the workers.

The model by-laws provide for several workers' meetings: the workers' general meeting for the entire undertaking, attended by all the personnel (or by their delegates in the case of large undertakings or dispersed establishments), and branch meetings of the workers in each department. The general meeting takes place at least twice a year to conduct a critical examination of the undertaking's operations and to make practical suggestions for its development; to examine the operation and investment plans, the budget and accounts, and to decide on the distribution of the welfare fund; and to take disciplinary action on cases submitted by the manager or the management board. The branch meetings have to take place at least four times a year to examine the results of the department concerned and to study ways of carrying out the programme of work.

Pakistan

In Pakistan undertakings managed by the state or the local authorities have, since 1976, had to apply the participation system described earlier in connection with private undertakings. It seems, however, that in practice most public undertakings have neither the management committees nor the joint management boards provided for. This seems to be due to various reasons such as the novelty of the concept of joint management, the reluctance of trade unionists, who prefer to maintain their influence through collective bargaining, the lack of interest in the new arrangements on the part of the general run of workers, who continue to put their trust in traditional forms of trade union action, and the concern of middle managers not to see their powers reduced.[84] In addition, as has been seen, the powers of workers' representatives on the bodies, despite their names, correspond more to those met with in consultative bodies of the works council type (although the legislation of the country also provides expressly for works councils).

Syrian Arab Republic

In the Syrian Arab Republic, where nationalisation has been very far-reaching, and where there was talk first of workers' management then of "democratic management", there are today, under a legislative decree of October 1961 as amended by a legislative decree of 1974 applicable to the public sector only,[85] two worker representatives elected by the workers and one representative appointed by the executive committee of the General Confederation of Trade Unions on the board of directors of each public undertaking. In the case of an undertaking with several establishments or of a public economic body, the number of trade union representatives is raised to two, and they are in that case appointed by the appropriate departmental trade union federation.

Also, an Act of 4 January 1978 provided for the setting up of a production council in each establishment or undertaking in the public sector. This council comprises the general manager, the members of the board of directors (or management committee), the chairman and various representatives of the trade union organisation, party officials working in the establishment and a maximum of five wage earners, considered to be the most able in the undertaking, appointed by the board of directors or the management committee. The functions of the production council are, in particular, to draw up the annual plan for the undertaking or establishment; to formulate policy for the raising of productive capacity; to appoint production committees in sectors or units of the undertaking or establishment in which there is need for them, and to revise the previous year's plan to take account of any deficiencies that may have been revealed.[86]

The production council is convened by its chairman every three months; it may also meet on other occasions when called upon to do so by its chairman or by a majority of its members, on condition that such a meeting does not necessitate travel outside the district.

Undertakings or establishments whose special organisational structure or activities make the application of this Act difficult may be exempted on the recommendation of the minister concerned, subject to the agreement of the General Confederation of Trade Unions.

Tanzania

In the "parastatal" sector in Tanzania there is an authority, corporation or holding company that frames general policy for each industry, whereas actual production is carried out by subsidiaries. A presidential circular of 10 February 1970[87] provided that at least one member of the board of directors of a parastatal organisation should be nominated by the National Union of Tanganyika Workers. Under a subsequent ministerial directive the management committee (formerly the board of directors) of a subsidiary was to be appointed by the minister responsible for the industry, who would appoint 40 per cent of the members from within the subsidiary, while additional members would come from outside it. This formula attributing 40 per cent of the seats (out of a total of 12 to 20) to representatives of the personnel was confirmed by the Parastatal Organisations (Modification of Management Provisions) Act, 1976, its application to specified organisations (about 150) being made effective by an order to be issued by the minister responsible for labour matters, except in the case of organisations partly financed by foreign capital (which are excluded from the scope of the Act). In public authorities, corporations and holding companies, the board of directors comprises 60 per cent of members representing the public (e.g. members of parliament and leaders of the party and its affiliates) and 40 per cent of persons from the group, civil servants from the ministry concerned with the particular industry, and personnel from the subsidiaries.

Turkey

In Turkey, under Act No. 440 of 1964 and the related regulations, one worker representative, generally designated by the majority trade union which is the bargaining agent, sits on the board of directors of large state economic undertakings in manufacturing industry, agriculture and transport. The same holds for the management committees of establishments belonging to those undertakings, if they employ a specified minimum number of workers. Under the government in power up to the autumn of 1979, and in accordance with a "social contract" signed for the public sector, a considerable broadening of this participation was under study and its scope was to be extended to all undertakings in the sector.

Venezuela

In Venezuela an Act of 11 July 1966, amended by Acts of 28 August and 23 December 1969[88] and supplemented by a decree of 27 April 1976, introduced workers' representation on the management bodies (boards of directors or similar bodies) of autonomous institutes and in public undertakings and state economic development bodies. Nominations must be made by the trade union confederation or federation, or by the largest union in the trade or occupation concerned. The workers' organisation puts forward five candidates, from among whom the government partment most directly concerned has to choose one titular and one substitute member. The only conditions required for nomination are to be of age and of Venezuelan nationality. Although at first this participation was more formal than real, since the trade union movement did not then have a clear policy on the subject, it seems that more recently participation has become quite active, in spite of its being very much on a minority basis and in spite of the rule that the worker representative may not be appointed to any executive office on the board. The 1966 Act, lacking penal provisions, had had little effect, and so the Act dated 28 August 1969 provided that all contracts and deeds of undertakings subject to the Act would be null and void if workers' representation had not been established within a prescribed period. The Act of 23 December 1969 gave the trade union organisations the right of appeal to the Supreme Court, and gave that Court the power to appoint a workers' representative on the management body. Today workers' representation is therefore found in virtually all Venezuelan public undertakings.[89]

Other Countries

In addition to Angola, Somalia, the Sudan, Tunisia, and Democratic Yemen, where the workers are represented on the boards of public undertakings, there are a number of developing countries where only some public undertakings have minority representation for their workers, or where there may be one or more persons with a trade union background on boards without there being legislation on the subject applicable to the whole of the public sector; among these countries are Ghana, Guyana, Jamaica,[90] Jordan, Malaysia, Malta, Mexico, Nigeria, Portugal,[91] Senegal, Sierra Leone and Singapore.

Notes

[1] *Employee participation and company structure in the European Community*, op. cit., p. 30.
[2] International Organisation of Employers, op. cit., pp. 28–35.

[3] ILO: *Workers' participation in decisions within undertakings, Oslo symposium*, op. cit., p. 45.

[4] *Employee participation and company structure in the European Community*, op. cit., p. 33. This same report observes nevertheless that the distinction between a supervisory board and a board of directors is often blurred in practice by the fact that a board of directors may appoint from its number an executive board, thus being left with functions similar to those of a supervisory board. See also John Crispo: *Industrial democracy in Western Europe, A North American perspective* (Toronto, McGraw Hill Ryerson, 1978), pp. 81–83. Moreover, in day-to-day management the management enjoys considerable autonomy.

[5] This sometimes raises problems of personal financial liability. Another point is that the remuneration which goes with membership, instead of being kept in its entirety by the workers' representatives, may be paid over to some fund so as to ensure that those representatives will not be better off than the workers they represent. Thus, in the Federal Republic of Germany where, depending on the undertaking, the workers' representatives on supervisory boards may draw between several hundred and several thousand Deutschmarks a year in fees, a certain percentage, fixed by the unions, must be paid over to a foundation which finances research, information and study grants in the field of participation.

[6] See in particular *Employee participation and company structure in the European Community*, op. cit., pp. 23–24, 33 and 45.

[7] Minority worker representation on the supervisory boards of companies (by two members elected by the works council) first appeared in German legislation after the First World War. Moreover, co-determination was already demanded in the previous century, particularly in 1848. Parity representation in the mines and in the iron and steel industry after the Second World War was introduced in special historical circumstances. The formula of parity co-determination finally adopted at the instigation of trade union leaders, in particular, and which was embodied in an Act in 1951, was initially tried out in a number of large iron and steel undertakings in the Ruhr by agreement in each case between the management (and the control body) and the trade union. The legislation adopted in 1952 for other industries provided for only minority representation. For additional detail on this historical background, see in particular Wilhelm Herschel: "Employee representation in the Federal Republic of Germany", in *International Labour Review*, Aug.–Sep. 1951, pp. 207–215. See also Schregle: "Co-determination in the Federal Republic of Germany: A comparative view", op. cit.

[8] ILO: *Legislative Series*, 1951—Ger. F.R. 2; 1952—Ger. F.R. 6; 1956—Ger. F.R. 3; 1972—Ger. F.R. 1; 1976—Ger. F.R. 1.

[9] For the importance of the role played by the management board, see for instance Friedrich Fürstenberg: "West German experience with industrial democracy", in Windmuller (ed.), op. cit., pp. 51–52.

[10] ILO: *Legislative Series*, 1951—Ger. F.R. 2.

[11] For further details see A. Jungbluth: "The role of the labour manager in undertakings under co-management in the Federal Republic of Germany", in *International Labour Review*, Oct. 1958, pp. 368–387.

[12] ILO: *Legislative Series*, 1952—Ger. F.R. 6.

[13] ibid., 1976—Ger. F.R. 1.

[14] For an analysis of the electoral rules adopted on 18 May 1977 and reactions to them, see *Social and Labour Bulletin* No. 3/77, pp. 209–210.

[15] See *Welt der Arbeit* (Düsseldorf, Deutscher Gewerkschaftsbund), 17 Aug. 1978. Of 2,747 seats to be filled (excluding those for executives), 86 per cent were filled by members of trade unions affiliated to the German Trade Union Confederation.

[16] On the second point the main argument was that the future occupational career of the persons representing the employer in negotiations would depend on the worker' representatives on the supervisory board.

[17] For a summary of the decision of the Constitutional Court, see *Social and Labour Bulletin*, No. 2/79, pp. 134–136.

[18] Among the principal publications the following may be cited: EMNID [Erforschung-, Meinung-, Nachrichten-, Informationsdienst]-Institut: *Wirksamkeit der erweiterten Mitbestimmung auf die Arbeitnehmerschaft* (Bielefeld, 1966, 3 vols, summary in Graf Viggo Blücher: *Integration und Mitbestimmung* (Sennestadt, 1966)); Alfred von Christman: *Wirtschaftliche Mitbestimmung im Meinungsstreit* (Cologne, Bundverlag, 1964); Fürstenberg, op. cit.; Otto Neuloh: *Der neue Betriebsstil* (Tübingen, J. Mohr, 1960); T. Pirker et al.: *Arbeiter, Management, Mitbestimmung* (Stuttgart, Ring-Verlag, 1955); O. Blume et al.: *Zwischenbilanz der Mitbestimmung* (Tübingen, J. Mohr, 1962). Reference has already been made to the important report of the Biedenkopf Commission, *Mitbestimmung im Unternehmen*.

129

[19] See for instance B. Wilpert: "Research on industrial democracy: The German case", in *Industrial Relations* (Nottingham), Spring 1975, p. 61.

[20] Schregle: "Co-determination in the Federal Republic of Germany: A comparative view", op. cit.

[21] ILO: *Legislative Series*, 1973—Aus. 2.

[22] ibid., 1962—Sp. 3. This Act was supplemented by a decree dated 15 July 1965; plans for its revision have recently been made. See also *The labour and trade union situation in Spain* (Geneva, ILO, 1969), pp. 259–262.

[23] García-Nieto, *Workers' participation in management in Spain*, op. cit.

[24] However, the French Christian Employers' Confederation expressed its support for a parity supervisory board and a right of veto for the works committee, while the Young Managers' Association (*Centre des jeunes dirigeants d'entreprise*) suggested that the managers should be elected by a works council appointed exclusively by the workers of the undertaking.

[25] See *Journal officiel de la République française*, 2–3 Jan. 1978, p. 149.

[26] For further details see *Social and Labour Bulletin*, No. 1/78, p. 16. Already in 1974, an agreement had been signed between the French Employers' Confederation and the General Confederation of Executive and Supervisory Staff committing management to make systematic arrangements, by agreement with such staff, for information and consultation, and a number of undertakings had subsequently set up committees for concertation with them.

[27] In addition, an Act passed in March 1974 imposed a state appointee on the boards of directors of banks and insurance companies.

[28] The important report of a tripartite committee on workers' co-ownership and co-determination, published in November 1978, is analysed in *Social and Labour Bulletin*, No. 1/79, pp. 21–22.

[29] See ILO: *Legislative Series*, 1972—Nor. 1, which also includes a translation of regulations dated 24 November 1972 applying the Act.

[30] Since the passing of an Act in 1977, the boards of banks must have a tripartite composition, including representatives of the shareholders, the public authorities and the employees, none of the groups holding a majority of the seats.

[31] Staff representation on the boards of insurance companies is governed by an agreement signed in August 1974.

[32] See *Arbeidsgiveren* (Oslo, Norsk Arbeidsgiverforening), 21 Aug. 1975.

[33] This survey, also based on a questionnaire, was carried out by the periodical *Økonomisk Rapport*, and the results were summarised in the *Financial Times* (London), 18 Nov. 1975, p. 15. Replies had been received from some 200 managers of big Norwegian undertakings. Norwegian employers have often stated that they are not in favour of this new type of assembly (see for instance *Arbeidsgiveren*, 1974, No. 20, pp. 443–445, and No. 22, p. 506, of which an analysis was published in French in *Documentation étrangère* (Paris, Union des industries métallurgiques et minières), Apr. 1975, p. 15).

[34] Knut Isachsen: *Aktivt Styrearbeid* (Oslo, Tanum-Norli, 1977), p. 152.

[35] ILO: *Legislative Series*, 1972—Swe. 1.

[36] This representation can be requested only if at least half of the personnel belong to a local union or unions having concluded a collective agreement with the undertaking concerned (which is generally the case in Sweden).

[37] For a summary of the report on this survey see National Swedish Industrial Board: *Board representation of employees in Sweden*, A summary of a survey (Stockholm, Liber Förlag, 1976).

[38] National Swedish Industrial Board, op. cit., p. 38.

[39] Another Act of the same date, also adopted for an experimental period of three years, allowed the Government to appoint one member and one substitute to sit on the boards of particularly big joint stock companies (up to a limit of 60, including groups of companies) employing a large number of workers or having several establishments in Sweden, or having subsidiaries abroad, or belonging to a company trading outside Sweden. The government which succeeded the social-democratic government which had been in power when the Act was passed declared that it did not intend to appoint such members. Since then an Act of 1979 has lowered the above-mentioned limit from 60 to 30 companies, and has limited its scope to companies whose object is the purchase, sale or administration of property, including real estate. Another law, also adopted on 3 June 1976, governs the participation of worker representatives on the boards of banks and insurance companies; under earlier legislation, the Government may appoint representative to sit on such a board.

[40] See in particular R. Meidner, A. Hedborg and G. Fond: *Löntagarfonder* (Stockholm, Tidens

Förlag, 1975), and idem: *Employee investment funds: An approach to collective capital formation* (London, George Allen and Unwin, 1978).

[41] See *Information Bulletin* (Geneva, International Organisation of Employers), Oct. 1976.

[42] For further details see *Social and Labour Bulletin*, No. 1/79, pp. 30–31.

[43] See Svenska Arbetsgivareföreningen (Swedish Employers' Confederation): *Comments on the proposals for employee investment funds presented by the joint LO-Social Democratic (SAP) working party on February 23, 1978* (Stockholm, mimeographed doc. No. 1449, 25 May 1978).

[44] ILO: *Legislative Series*, 1974—Lux. 1.

[45] For further details see Hak and de Jong, op. cit., and the "Green Book" published by the Commission of the European Communities, pp. 90–91.

[46] See *Onderneming* (The Hague), 29 Nov. 1974, p. 1. Between 1973 and 1978, one case of veto was referred to the Economic and Social Council (and was rejected); see "Workers lose test case on veto rights", in *European Industrial Relations Review* (London), Nov. 1978, p. 4.

[47] Department of Labour: *Worker participation*, A discussion paper (Dublin, Stationery Office, 1980). The paper also deals with other aspects of participation, such as participation in such bodies as works councils and participation at shop floor level (see *Social and Labour Bulletin*, No. 2/80, pp. 162–164).

[48] *Industrial democracy*, A report by the TUC General Council to the 1974 Trades Union Congress (London, 1974).

[49] See, for instance: *Involving people: CBI proposals for employee participation*, op. cit.

[50] Department of Trade: *Report of the committee of inquiry on industrial democracy*, op. cit.

[51] Department of Education and Science, Department of Employment, Department of Trade: *Industrial democracy*, Cmnd. 7231 (London, HM Stationery Office, 1978).

[52] *In place of Bullock* (London, Confederation of British Industry, 1977).

[53] *Social and Labour Bulletin*, No. 1/80, pp. 38–39. The same issue describes the results of two government surveys carried out in the United Kingdom with regard to company structure, participation and, in particular, worker-director schemes (pp. 29–33).

[54] TUC-Labour Party Liaison Committee: *Into the eighties*, An agreement (London, Labour Party, 1978), p. 8.

[55] *Department of Employment Gazette* (London), June 1979, p. 570.

[56] For further details see for instance Bruno Gruber: *La commission du Conseil national présente un nouvel article sur la participation* (Bern, Service de presse de la Confédération des syndicats chrétiens de la Suisse, 1978).

[57] See *Bulletin of the European Communities* (Luxembourg, Office for Official Publications of the European Communities), Supplement 4/75.

[58] See in particular *Bulletin trimestriel FGTB* (Brussels), First Quarter 1971; J. Gayetot: *La participation des travailleurs aux décisions dans l'entreprise en Belgique* (Geneva, ILO, 1974, doc. SWPDU/D 15); and "La démocratie économique: Une réforme? Quelle réforme?", in *CMB-Inform* (Brussels, Centrale des métallurgistes FGTB), Apr.–May 1978, pp. 28–34.

[59] See *Le Peuple* (Paris, CGT), 16–31 Oct. 1973, pp. 9–24; ibid., 15–31 Oct. 1974, pp. 11–19; *Cadres-informations* (Paris), June 1978, pp. 10–12; proposals put forward at a symposium on democratisation of the economy and the role of the workers held in 1977 (*Le Peuple*, 15–31 May 1977); and the action programme adopted by the 40th Congress of the CGT, part of which is devoted to democratic management of nationalised undertakings and the powers claimed for works committees (ibid., Jan 1979).

[60] See for instance *CFDT-Syndicalisme* (Paris), Nov. 1972, pp. 5–32; in relation to immediate claims in respect of participation, *CFDT Magazine* (Paris), Oct. 1977, pp. 15–16 and 29–40; and *Elargir les libertés dans l'entreprise*, Collection CFDT-Réflexion, (Paris, CFDT, 1977).

[61] See *Social and Labour Bulletin*, No. 1/74, p. 11–12, and CFTC: *Programme adopté au 39e Congrès, Versailles, 24–27 novembre 1977*, pp. 25–31.

[62] See for instance "La réforme de l'entreprise", in *Le Creuset* (Paris), 25 Jan. 1975, pp. 6–7, in which the CGC came out in favour of concertation committees for executive personnel, and of employee representation with voting rights on boards of directors or supervisory boards in the proportion of one-third, of whom half should be executives or supervisors.

[63] Commission of the European Communities, op. cit.

[64] See Commission of the European Communities, *Information note P/70*, Nov. 1975, and *Employee participation and company structure*, op. cit., pp. 42–46.

[65] See *Bulletin of the European Communities* (Brussels and Luxembourg, Office for official

publications of the European Communities), No. 2/78, and *Official Journal of the European Communities: Information and notices* (Luxembourg), 10 Apr. 1979, pp. 2–15. (This opinion and the corresponding reports and record of discussions have also been published by the European Communities in a brochure.)

[66] For further details see European Parliament: *Working documents*, 1979–80, doc. 136/79 (Luxembourg, Office for official publications of the European Communities).

[67] *Social and Labour Bulletin*, No. 2/75, p. 136.

[68] See the series of articles on participation in Japan by Tadashi A. Hanami and other authors in *Japan Labor Bulletin* (Tokyo, Japan Institute of Labor), 1 Jan., 1 Aug., and 1 Sep. 1977, and *Nikkeiren Times* (Tokyo), 26 Oct. 1978, p. 1.

[69] ILO: *Workers' participation in decisions within undertakings, Oslo symposium*, op. cit., p. 73.

[70] See for instance *Industrial Bulletin* (Bombay, Employers' Federation of India), Sep. 1978, pp. 70–71, and *Indian Worker* (New Delhi), 17 July 1978, p. 11, and ibid. 28 Aug. 1978, pp. 1 and 3.

[71] See *Worker participation in the private sector* (Kingston, Agency for Public Information, 1978), and *Social and Labour Bulletin*, No. 2/77, pp. 118–120, and ibid., No. 1/78, pp. 17–18.

[72] See ILO: *Legislative Series*, 1970—Per. 2A and 2B.

[73] ibid., 1977—Per. 1. That decree has since been amended it its turn on several points by Legislative Decree No. 22229 dated 11 July 1978 to facilitate investments and the construction of housing; see *El Peruano* (Lima), No. 11250, 16 July 1978, p. 7. On the relationship between the industrial communities and the trade unions, see Luis Pásara and Jorge Santistevan: "Industrial communities and trade unions in Peru: A preliminary analysis", in *International Labour Review*, Aug.–Sep. 1973, pp. 127–142. See also Giorgio Alberti, Jorge Santistevan and Luis Pásara: *Estado y clase: La comunidad industrial en el Peru* (Lima, Instituto de Estudios Peruanos, 1977), and William Foote Whyte and Giorgio Alberti: "The industrial community in Peru", in Windmuller (ed.), op. cit., pp. 103–112.

[74] On this point see for instance Jean Dufau: *Les entreprises publiques* (Paris, Editions de l'actualité juridique, 1973), p. 128.

[75] On this point see Yves Saint-Jours: *Les relations du travail dans le secteur public* (Paris, Librairie générale de droit et de jurisprudence, 1977), p. 406.

[76] P. Brannen, E. Batstone, D. Patchett and P. White: *The worker directors*, A sociology of participation (London, Hutchinson, 1976). For workers' representatives' views on their ten years' experience in the divisional management boards and the central board of directors, see John Bank and Ken Jones (ed.): *Worker directors speak* (London, Gower Press, 1977). It is worth noting that when the incompatibility rule was abolished 16 out of the 17 workers' representatives on the divisional boards of the British Steel Corporation were re-elected to trade union posts.

[77] See also *White Paper on nationalised industries*, Cmnd 7131 (London, HM Stationery Office, 1978) and in particular the legislation proposed therein for electricity supply in England and Wales. Two-tier arrangements providing for a supervisory board plus a board of management were rejected having regard to the role of the government departments directly concerned.

[78] See "Industrial democracy in the nationalised industries", in *Industrial Relations Review and Report* (London), July 1979, pp. 2, 8–10. On the participation system introduced in the British Leyland undertaking in the automobile industry when it passed under government control, see *Social and Labour Bulletin*, No. 1/76, pp. 25–26, and "Worker participation agreed at British Leyland", in *Industrial Relations Review and Report*, Dec. 1975, pp. 2–10.

[79] For further details see Norman Stagg: *Industrial democracy: The Post Office experiment* (London, Union of Post Office Workers, 1978), and idem: "Setback for industrial democracy: British Post Office experiment ends", in *Free Labour World* (Brussels, International Confederation of Free Trade Unions), Mar.–Apr. 1980, p. 21; see also *Social and Labour Bulletin*, No. 1/80, p. 29.

[80] ibid., No. 3/76, pp. 220–221.

[81] See Mansour Fahmi Taha: *Ishtrak el-Aamileen Fi-Al Idarah* (Cairo University Press, 1968), pp. 200, 258–259, quoted in International Centre for Public Undertakings in Developing Countries, Ljubljana: *Report on workers' participation in management in Egypt*, Report submitted to a meeting at Portoroz, Yugoslavia (Ljubljana, 1976), pp. 12–14; see also p. 11 of that report. For a more recent study, in English, see Mansour Fahmi Taha: *The functioning in practice of workers' participation in management in Egypt*, A field study (Cairo, 1979).

[82] ibid., p. 16.

[83] On these unfavourable factors see in particular C. P. Thakur and K. C. Sethi (ed.): *Industrial democracy, Some issues and experiences* (New Delhi, Shri Ram Centre for Industrial Relations and Human Resources, 1973), especially pp. 11–13, 49–66.

[84] See, for instance, Jameel Ahmed Bhutto: "Labour-management relations in public enterprises in Pakistan", in Friedrich-Ebert-Stiftung: *Labour-management relations in public enterprises in Asia*, Proceedings of the seminar in Bangkok, 23–28 January 1978, pp. 258–259.

[85] Public undertakings account for about 68 per cent of industrial production and employ about 40 per cent of the industrial manpower of the country (*L'Economiste arabe* (Beirut), Nov.–Dec. 1978, p. 18).

[86] For further details see *Social and Labour Bulletin*, No: 2/78, p. 133.

[87] ILO: *Legislative Series*, 1970—Tan. 1.

[88] ibid., 1966—Ven. 1 and 1969—Ven. 1.

[89] See in particular J. J. González: "La participación de los trabajadores en la gestión de las empresas públicas en Venezuela", in a work published by the Italo-Latin American Institute: *La participazione nel quadro dell' economia mondiale: Alcune esperienze nazionali*, Symposio internazionale, Roma, 2–6 ottobre 1978 (Rome, 1979), which also reports the recent development of workers' participation in the capital of some public undertakings (for example, the Caveguias company, a subsidiary of the national telephones company of Venezuela, in which the workers now own 40 per cent of the shares and may elect two members of the board of directors). See also O. Mantero: *El funcionamiento en la práctica de los sistemas de participatión de los trabajadores en las empresas públicas venezolanas* (Caracas, 1979).

[90] See *Worker participation in statutory boards and local government* (Kingston, Agency for Public Information, 1978), which contains (guiding principles similar to those referred to earlier in connection with the private sector in Jamaica.

[91] Under an Act dated 12 September 1979, if a public undertaking has a works council (referred to as a "workers' commission"), that council may designate or elect representatives on the undertaking's management bodies, their number being laid down in the by-laws of each undertaking; see *Diário da República* (Lisbon), 12 Sep. 1979, pp. 2275–2282.

WORKS COUNCILS AND SPECIALISED BODIES 7

In both the industrialised and the developing countries works councils or committees, or joint consultation committees, are still by far the commonest bodies met with for associating workers with decisions in undertakings.

In many countries these bodies have been set up by legislation. That is the case, for instance in Burundi, Gabon, Mauritania, Somalia, the Sudan, Swaziland, Tanzania, Tunisia, Zaire and Zambia in Africa; in Bangladesh, Burma, the Republic of Korea, Nepal, Pakistan, Sri Lanka and Thailand in Asia; in Austria, Belgium, France, the Federal Republic of Germany, Luxembourg, the Netherlands and Spain in Western Europe; and in Iraq. In some countries legal obligation is limited to public undertakings (for instance in Sri Lanka). In others, such as Bahrain, Mauritius, New Zealand, Oman and Thailand, the law merely provides for the establishment of works councils or committees in suitable cases. In Portugal the Act of 12 September 1949 on workers' commissions covers those that were already in existence or might be established subsequently, but imposed no general obligation to establish such bodies. In other countries such as Denmark and Norway they have been established by agreements between the national workers' and employers' organisations. And in some countries they have been set up, not by national agreements, but by collective agreements in particular industries or directly between the management of an undertaking and its workers represented by their trade union, or by the employer on his own initiative. Arrangements of this kind are found, for instance, in Australia, New Zealand, Japan, Canada, the United States, Ireland, the United Kingdom and Switzerland; and in some developing countries, including Cyprus, India (where there is also legislation on the subject), Indonesia, Jordan, Malaysia, the Philippines, Singapore, Jamaica and a few other Caribbean countries, Venezuela (in some public undertakings), Mauritius[1] and some English-speaking countries of Africa.

In some countries bodies of the works council type are found in a limited economic sector only, or with very limited terms of reference. That is the case for instance in Morocco (in the mines) and in Uruguay, where a 1947 Act provided for the setting up in private undertakings providing a public utility of joint councils to deal with disciplinary matters, dismissals and transfers, and questions of work organisation and safety, and where a decree of 15 February 1977 offered the possibility of setting up "joint commissions" with rather broad consultative powers including the settlement of grievances in undertakings in the private sector in general (about 20 have been set up). In Colombia, as in some other Latin American countries, collective agreements have provided for joint bodies to be set up to settle disputes over the grading of jobs. In Mexico, where there are health and safety committees and where some collective agreements provide for joint bodies to play a part in dealing with grievances, joint committees may be set up under an article of the federal Labour Act[2] and ad hoc joint committees have sometimes been appointed under a collective agreement to deal with internal work regulations; the existence of productivity committees in some undertakings is also reported.[3] In Panama the 1971 Labour Code[4] prescribes the establishment of works committees wherever 20 or more workers are employed; their main task is to settle grievances and interpret collective agreements. Several Caribbean countries and some other countries such as Cyprus and Turkey have disciplinary committees (in particular in the public sector), production committees or other similar bodies.

Reference will be made at the end of this chapter to shop stewards and other workers' representatives, who may perform some of the functions of a works council where no such council exists.

The statutory trade union committees set up in the USSR and other countries of Eastern Europe will be dealt with in the next chapter, since their role is not entirely comparable with that of works councils in market economy countries.

STATUTORY BODIES

The establishment of statutory works councils or committees is probably the most widespread and best-known means of associating workers with decisions in undertakings through machinery which can be geared in with the trade unions while remaining, in principle, distinct from them, both inside and outside the undertaking. The earliest laws of general scope on works councils date from the years 1918–20 (Austria, Czechoslovakia, Germany and Norway). After the Second Word War most countries of Western and Central Europe and, more recently, a number of countries in other regions, adopted similar laws.[5]

The following pages contain a survey of the main characteristics of works councils established by legislation in a number of countries, selected to illustrate the variety of the statutory provisions (see also the country-by-country summary in the appendix).

Composition

The different types of body are clearly associated with two schools of thought. According to one school, the purpose is to set up a body to represent the workers collectively, which, on its own initiative, deals with all the tasks within its competence, then "communicates" with the management, or "meets" the employer or general manager (in particular in Austria and the Federal Republic of Germany). The other school provides for direct co-operation with the employer and his presence at all meetings of the council, which he normally chairs (as in Belgium, France, Tunisia and Zaire, for instance); there is however no question of equality of numbers—the employer-chairman is normally the only representative of management (except in Belgium, where several representatives of the management may belong to the works council).

As regards the worker members, most systems endeavour to reconcile the advantages of unitary representation of all the workers, whether wage earners or salaried employees, with the need to share out the seats so as to have a body representative of all categories of personnel, sometimes with provision for election by several electoral colleges. It may happen—as for instance in Austria—that there are separate works councils for the two categories of personnel which, however, themselves elect a committee to deal with problems common to the two categories.

There have been changes in the representation of certain groups of workers. Special representation for young workers was provided for by law some years ago in Belgium, Luxembourg, the Netherlands (Act of 1971 on works councils)[6] and in Austria (Act of 14 December 1973 on collective labour relations). Representation of young workers was strengthened in the Federal Republic of Germany by the Act of 15 January 1972 concerning the organisation of undertakings.

Another noteworthy development has been the extension of the voting and eligibility rights of foreign workers, for example in the Federal Republic of Germany (in respect of the eligibility of foreign workers who are not nationals of member countries of the European Communities) and in France, both being countries employing large numbers of foreign workers.

In general, the legislation pays special attention to the relationship between the works councils and the trade unions—a subject which will be dealt with in greater detail later. Under most national systems, trade unions have an exclusive right to put forward candidates (as in Belgium), or priority in this respect (as in France, Tunisia and Zaire, for example). In some countries the trade unions can remove those whom they have put up as candidates, sometimes subject to the agreement of the majority of the electoral college. In practice, even where the law does not give trade unions any privilege of this kind (as in Austria and the Federal Republic of Germany) a very large majority of the members of works councils, at least in the industrialised countries, are elected from persons proposed by the representative trade unions or are active trade unionists. Direct election by secret ballot is the rule in most countries; so is proportional representation if there is more than one list of candidates.

Powers and functions

In the main, the powers of works councils may be classified under four main heads: information, consultation (giving workers' representatives the opportunity to make their views known and to propose alternative solutions), co-decision (prior agreement to, or right of veto on, certain decisions), and direct autonomous management of some of the activities of the undertaking (in particular, welfare activities). Particularly where the management does not take the necessary action, works councils may be entitled to bring their opinions or decisions to the notice of the appropriate administrative or legal authority (which may be given the power of arbitrating in the event of disputes) or of an internal arbitration body with or without the right of appeal to the ordinary authorities. This is seen by some to be a very important element in the operation of co-decision, even if it is rarely resorted to in practice.

The information to be supplied has sometimes been the subject of precise regulation—for instance in the case of a royal decree in Belgium dated 27 November 1973—as have also the standards to be observed in regard to maintaining the confidentiality of certain information. The main subjects covered are the general situation of, and the economic and financial outlook for, the undertaking, as well as technical change and employment prospects. In the past few years, in industrialised countries, there has been a trend towards including in the information to be given forecasts in relation to investments, rationalisation on the introduction of new methods or processes, cut-backs in production, and changes in the structure of the undertaking (closures, total or partial relocation, mergers, etc.), that is to say, forecasts of events which may lead to marked changes in the employment situation and in conditions of work.

In most cases this right to information is now accompanied by a right of consultation at the time when the forecasts are prepared: the employer has to indicate the measures he is thinking of taking to avoid, or to soften the impact of, unfavourable consequences for the personnel, and the works council is entitled to discuss these forecasts and proposals and to suggest alternative solutions.

Generally speaking, the competence of works councils covers three main areas of management: economic questions, staff problems and welfare activities. However, for some time now, a number of countries have imposed on employers the obligation to ask the views of the council and to seek its collaboration on certain specified points; this tends to associate the council more closely with management so that, in extreme cases, it may become an essential part of it. In the past few years there has been a very marked tendency in some West European countries—in particular in Austria, Belgium (by agreement rather than by law), the Federal Republic of Germany and the Netherlands—to extend the co-decision powers of these bodies, especially with regard to welfare and personnel questions.

Direct management of staff welfare has assumed considerable importance in some countries such as France where the other functions of works committees have generally remained more limited, at least until recently, for various reasons linked with the attitudes of many employers and those of the main workers' organisations. In the developing countries, where management of welfare activities by works councils is fairly common, it provides, on top of the services it may render in improving the living conditions of workers and their families, an opportunity for training in participation.

In some countries works councils may sign works agreements with the management, usually within the framework of agreements signed at a higher level, in particular where collective bargaining in its full sense is not usual at undertaking level, or on questions other than the major ones (such as wages) that are covered in collective agreements; this is to avoid any conflict between the activities of works councils and those of the trade unions. In practice the borderline between co-decision on a number of specified points and traditional collective bargaining is not very clearly defined, except that the former does not usually result in a formal written agreement but is merely reported in the minutes. Yet in practice it does give rise to a sort of bargaining on the basis of mutual concessions. In the opinion of some observers, this is an enlargement of the range of matters for negotiation, particularly in view of the fact that there are countries where trade union representatives now quite frequently negotiate on many points within the undertaking without concluding real collective agreements; the latter are reserved for major problems and are generally negotiated on a fixed date. The functions of works councils in regard to consultation and co-decision cannot be dissociated from the particular conditions and needs of the country concerned (level of social and economic development, general industrial relations setting, past history of the works council system, etc.).

In a number of countries, including France, the United Kingdom and the Scandinavian countries, legislation has been adopted in the past few years to improve general conditions of work and the working environment through subcommittees of works councils (or, similar bodies), through health and safety committees or through special representatives. Recent laws in Norway and Sweden even allow the health and safety representatives to halt production when it is being carried out under dangerous conditions. In some countries the committees or representatives responsible for health and safety do not depend directly on the works councils or corresponding bodies which, in the United Kingdom and the Scandinavian countries, are set up under collective agreements, not legislation. This extension of legislation to matters hitherto covered by the fringe activities of works councils may have considerable influence on those bodies.[7] Several Latin American countries without works councils nevertheless have health and safety committees; that is the case for instance in Brazil (where they are called accident prevention committees), Costa Rica, Honduras and El Salvador.

In addition, as has been noted in previous chapters, it is often the works councils which elect, or appoint from among their members, some or all of the workers' representatives on supervisory boards or boards of directors in countries where the legislation provides for such representation.

Works councils need not restrict themselves to the functions conferred upon them by law; they may take on other important functions. Thus, when conditions are favourable (for instance where there is strong support from the trade union movement, as well as the necessary material and intellectual resources), works councils may embark, on their own or with the help of others, on a whole range of social and cultural activities having to do with mutual aid, training, leisure, and so forth.

Facilities and protection afforded to members

In various countries facilities and privileges are afforded, to a greater or less degree, to workers' representation bodies or their members, as well as special protection for the latter against dismissal; these apply also to workers who are candidates and, for a certain period, to workers who have ceased to be workers' representatives.[8] The same rules as regards protection are usually also applicable to workers' representatives on supervisory boards or boards of directors, health and safety committees and other similar bodies, as well as to works, shop floor, or departmental trade union representatives. It is common for the same rules to apply to transfers.

In large undertakings the works council often has at its disposal notice boards and permanent offices, and some of its members are wholly or partly relieved of their normal duties without loss of pay.

General observations

In several countries difficulties were experienced, especially in the early stages, in setting up works councils in the undertakings covered by national legislation. This was particularly so in small undertakings employing fewer than 100 workers, where one or both of the parties might think that it was unnecessary to institutionalise their relations. The lukewarmness of some heads of undertakings, and apathy or hesitation on the part of the workers and their organisations, are often given as possible reasons for these difficulties. The amending laws passed several years ago in Belgium and France, which widened the scope and functions of works councils and increased the penalties for non-compliance with statutory provisions, were clearly aimed at overcoming this kind of difficulty. Similar measures are under study or have been proposed by trade unions in some other countries.

In the Netherlands the 1971 legislation on works councils raised the minimum number of personnel entailing the obligation to have a council from 50 to 100, since several inquiries had shown that, in most cases, works councils had not been set up in undertakings with fewer than 100 workers. Since then, however, collective bargaining in some industries such as construction and printing has covered the setting-up of works councils in undertakings employing fewer than 100 workers. In the printing industry, under a collective agreement of 27 January 1978, a works council is to be set up in any undertaking with 50 workers or more, and even in any with between 25 and 50 workers if they request it, while a labour-management meeting to discuss the general operation of the undertaking must be convened at least once a year in undertakings with fewer than 25 workers. A Bill requiring works councils with limited terms of reference to be set up in undertakings with between 35 and 100 workers has been submitted to Parliament.

No major problem has arisen in the past 30 years (as distinct from what happened previously) in countries such as Austria[9] and the Federal Republic of Germany, in spite of the considerable extension of the scope of national legislation, which now applies even to very small undertakings employing only five workers. The long tradition of works councils, their broad acceptance by employers, and the extent and quality of the technical and educational support which they receive from the trade union movement in these two countries, have no doubt contributed to this development. Nevertheless, trade unions in the Federal Republic of

Germany sometimes complain that, in some small or medium-sized undertakings, the works council has to overcome some reluctance on the part of the employer.[10]

Whatever may be the problems which arise in practice, and even though these bodies are often far from fulfulling their allotted functions, works councils set up under the law are none the less operating in a high proportion of undertakings, including the very great majority of large undertakings.

In most cases, work councils or similar bodies were set up for purposes of collaboration between the management and representatives of the workers primarily for mutual exchange of information and consultation on questions not subject to collective bargaining or which were regarded as lying within the prerogatives of management. Yet, as will be seen later, the trend over the past few years, has been towards a substantial growth of negotiation at the level of the undertaking or establishment and a reduction of management prerogatives. Some observers have even spoken of the development of "conflictual participation".

The distinction which the law sought to make in most countries between the role of works councils and collective bargaining is thus tending to become blurred, more so where the councils are broadly under trade union control and less so where an attempt is made to maintain a clear line of demarcation between trade union representation and these bodies representing all the workers, whether trade union members or not. In fact, trade unions have often shown hostility to these bodies (on which they have not always been fully represented) for fear either that works councils might encroach on trade union activities, or that the councils might be used as substitutes for genuine negotiation with only the appearance of participation.

Two trends emerge from recent experience in a number of industrialised countries. In some the co-decision powers of works councils have been extended, supplementing, at the level of the undertaking or establishment, negotiations which have generally taken place at a higher level. In some other countries there has been a revival of interest in works councils because the information that can be gleaned through them may be of great use in future collective bargaining. The major problem seems to be to find arrangements which are clearly compatible with trade union representation and activity. It has often been observed that works councils may be active in parallel with strong trade union entrenchment in undertakings, particularly if collective bargaining usually takes place at the regional or national level or at the level of the industry. Not only may most members of these councils be active trade unionists, but also trade union representatives proper may follow the proceedings of the councils very closely, as is the case for instance in the Federal Republic of

Germany. Problems of harmonising trade union representation and the works council seem to arise more in countries where collective bargaining takes place primarily at the level of the undertaking. The solution in these cases would seem to be to have one form only of trade union representation, or to have a works council to which the trade union representatives have completely free access and in which they can perform their role without difficulty.[11]

The draft statute for European companies fits in well with this development, since it foresees the formation of European works councils; a number of amendments made to this draft in 1975 are also significant in this connection.

European works councils, elected directly by secret ballot, with the trade unions and groups of workers having the opportunity to put up lists of candidates, would, in the new draft have—

(a) the right to be extensively informed (with precise rules regarding trade secrets) on such matters as finance, production and sales, employment, production and investment programmes, rationalisation plans, the introduction of new working methods and, in general, on any measure or project which might have an appreciable effect on the workers' interests;

(b) the right to participate in various decisions, with the management not being able to make decisions without the agreement of the council on rules concerning the recruitment, promotion and dismissal of workers, the implementation of vocational training, the determination of terms of remuneration and the introduction of new methods of computing remuneration, measures concerning industrial safety and health, the introduction and management of welfare facilities or general criteria for the daily times of commencement and termination of work and for preparing holiday schedules; if the works council were to refuse agreement, or not to come to a decision within an appropriate time, agreement could be given by an arbitration body provided for in the draft statute;

(c) the right to mandatory consultation before any decision is taken on the winding-up of the company, the closure or relocation of an establishment or substantial parts of it, the curtailment, extension or major alteration of the activities of the company, substantial organisational changes within the company, or the establishment or termination of long-term co-operation with other undertakings; in these cases, if workers' interest are likely to be adversely affected, the management must, before seeking the compulsory prior authorisation of the supervisory board, enter into negotiations with the works council to reach agreement on the measures to be taken on

behalf of the workers, that is to say, on a real "social plan" taking the form of a company agreement; in the absence of agreement, the above-mentioned arbitration body could decide on such measures at the request of either party; and

(d) the right to be consulted before decisions are taken on job evaluation, piece or task rates, or the introduction of any technical device intended to monitor the workers' conduct or performance.

The participation of trade union representatives in an advisory capacity in meetings of the works council has been simplified; a decision taken by the majority of members is still necessary, but the number of members who must make the request is no longer specified.

While the works council may make company agreements with the management in the areas which are subject to co-decision, the last version of the draft statute has withdrawn from this council the possibility it previously had of negotiating and signing collective agreements on conditions of work, which may only be negotiated by the trade unions represented in the undertaking, unless a European collective agreement expressly gives the council authority to make supplementary agreements.

In view of the importance of groups of companies, there have been special provisions, from the time of the first draft of the statute, for group works councils.

BODIES SET UP BY NATIONAL AGREEMENTS

Scandinavian countries

The joint bodies set up after the Second World War in three Scandinavian countries—Denmark, Norway and Sweden—in pursuance of national agreements have many common characteristics, but mention will only be made of those in Denmark and Norway, in view of the denunciation of the relevant Swedish agreement[12] in the autumn of 1976.

In Denmark, under an agreement on collaboration and collaboration committees of 2 October 1970 (ensuing on agreements signed in 1947 and 1965), a joint body must be set up in undertakings employing 50 or more persons if the employer or a majority of the personnel so request; a similar arrangement is recommended for undertakings with fewer than 50 workers. In Norway, under a co-operation agreement which forms part B of a basic agreement as renewed and amended in December 1977, a joint body must be established in any establishment employing 100 persons or more, and in smaller undertakings if one of the parties so requests and if the main organisation to which it is affiliated agrees. The agreement of

December 1977 opens up the possibility of merging works councils with the working environment councils.[13]

Composition

In Denmark an equal number of members, depending on the size of the undertaking, represent *(a)* the managerial, executive, supervisory, technical and commercial personnel not belonging to a trade union and *(b)* the remainder of the personnel. The trade union representatives in the undertaking are ex officio members of the works council. The representatives of group *(a)* are appointed by the management, while those of group *(b)* are elected by that group from among its own members. They normally serve for two years. The chairman is chosen from among management staff and the vice-chairman from among the representatives of group *(b)*. A secretary is appointed jointly.

In Norway the number of workers' representatives is laid down in the agreement, according to the size of the workforce, and the management may have a number of representatives equal to that of the workers. Besides the representatives of manual workers, there are two or three representatives of supervisors, technicians and salaried employees.

The chairman of the shop stewards' committee, as well as the vice-chairman if the undertaking employs over 400 workers, are ex officio members of the works council. As a rule members of the council serve for two years. The management representatives are appointed, while the workers elect theirs by secret ballot from among the workforce. Unless otherwise agreed the chairman is designated by the representatives of the management and of the workers alternately, while in each case the other party appoints the secretary.

Operation

The council meets at least once every two months in Denmark and once a month in Norway, except when both parties consider that an extraordinary meeting should be held. The agenda must be sent out at least three days before the meeting in Norway and at least a week before in Denmark.

In Denmark specialised subcommittees may be formed and standing subcommittees must be formed in the different departments of the undertaking, while the Norwegian agreement provides for the formation of department councils in the different divisions of undertakings employing over 200 workers if those divisions are organised as independent departments with their own management (the chief shop steward and a representative of the foremen designated by them are ex officio members).

The works councils in Denmark and Norway are generally very flexibly organised, and the parties have considerable latitude for action and initiative as well as the possibility of calling on specialists in subjects under discussion.

Competence and functions

In the past the Danish and Norwegian works councils played only a consultative role, and the subjects discussed were not usually voted on. The councils dealt mainly with matters such as output and productivity, and the management had to supply them at regular intervals with economic and financial data on the progress of the undertaking. In the past few years, however, questions of personnel policy have taken up a substantial part of their time.

In Denmark the agreement on collaboration committees lists among their duties that of participating in the taking of decisions of principle on the organisation of local conditions of work, safety and welfare, and on the undertaking's personnel policy. The parties must endeavour to come to an understanding, and an agreement so reached carries joint responsibility of the management and the workers' representatives for seeing that the agreed principles are applied in practice. It is only the principles which are discussed in the collaboration committees, not the actual decisions to be taken. However, if one of the parties claims that, in a specific instance, action has been taken contrary to the agreed principles, then the matter may be raised in the collaboration committee. The general agreement between the employers' confederation and the trade union confederation signed in October 1973, like the 1970 collaboration agreement, provided also that the employer's right to manage and to allocate work, and to employ appropriate personnel, should be exercised in accordance with the provisions of collective agreements and in collaboration with the workers and their representatives.

The Norwegian agreement states that the works councils must examine important changes in production plans and methods and plans for the expansion, reduction or reorganisation of production which have major importance for the personnel and their conditions of work. The new version of this agreement signed in 1977 imposes on employers the obligation to submit major investment proposals to the councils for comment, which means in practice before such proposals are presented to the corporate assembly in companies employing more than 200 persons. The management or the works council may delegate powers of decision in some matters to the department councils, if the subjects in question lend themselves to decision at that level. In both Denmark and Norway these bodies also concern themselves with proposals and measures for the improvement of health and safety and with vocational training measures. There are special provisions relating to the regular communication of information to the whole of the personnel.

Appeals

The agreements concluded in Denmark and Norway include a compulsory procedure for arbitration and the settlement of disputes arising in the course of their application. This procedure, which can in the last resort go as far as the intervention of a national body on which employers and workers are represented, or a national court (in Norway, the Labour Tribunal), gives these councils or committees broad legal guarantees for the proper exercise of their functions. However, the parties concerned can appeal only with the agreement of the employers' or workers' confederation concerned.

Promoting collaboration

In both countries a bipartite national body is responsible for facilitating the setting up of participation machinery in undertakings, having regard to the particular circumstances and local needs, and for promoting its development, particularly through research and training. The Norwegian Co-operation Council, for instance, is responsible for making direct contact with works councils, bringing them together in conferences and, at the request of one or other of the parties, for studying the situation in specific undertakings. These national bodies also play an important role in participation experiments at workshop level (such as the establishment of semi-autonomous work groups).

Other arrangements

Even if they already appear particularly advanced, the national agreements concluded in Denmark and Norway lay down only minimum requirements, and leave the field open for even greater participation. Recently in Denmark, "collaboration conferences" have been held, in particular in undertakings in industries hit by the slump, in order to forestall difficulties and labour unrest.[14]

Italy

The national agreement signed in Italy in 1953 and revised in 1966[15] provided for the setting up, in industrial undertakings employing more than 40 persons, of bodies composed entirely of workers' representatives (*"commissioni interne"*) to maintain contact or communication with the employer or the management, using procedures similar to those applied by works councils in Austria and the Federal Republic of Germany. These committees were composed of wage earners and salaried employees elected for two years (previously one year) under a system of proportional representation. Their duties were primarily consultative, in relation to matters such as works rules, working hours and annual holidays. Above all, they were expected to keep an eye on the application of legislation, of health and safety standards, of contracts of employment and of collective agreements, and to make initial endeavours to settle individual disputes. They could make proposals and suggestions for the improvement of working methods and welfare services.

For various reasons, due equally to the employers and the workers, these internal committees were not set up systematically, and since the end of the 1960s "factory councils" have been set up instead. These councils are a new form of staff representation which made its appearance in undertakings at that time and which often coincides with the trade union representation at undertaking level authorised by an Act of 10 May 1970 known as the "workers' bill of rights".[16]

The members of factory councils are elected individually and can be recalled at will. On the average, the "homogeneous work groups" they represent consist of between 30 and 40 workers. The councils deal with a variety of matters, including conditions of work. For communication with management, they elect an executive committee in large undertakings and a special committee in groups of undertakings. The three trade union confederations are represented on the factory councils, which have generally become the basic joint trade union bodies at the level of the undertaking. They keep in close touch with the workers' assembly provided for in the Act of 1970. It seems that of late some of these councils have lost some of their previous importance.[17]

OTHER VOLUNTARY BODIES

Among other countries the United Kingdom and the United States undoubtedly have the most experience of freely formed joint bodies in undertakings, with histories going back to the First World War and the early 1920s. In both countries the system regained popularity in the Second World War, but subsequent development has been very different.

United Kingdom

In the United Kingdom, where collective bargaining had long taken place primarily at the level of the industry, a decision of the National Joint Consultative Council set up by the Government recommended in 1947, like corresponding agreements in most industries, the establishment on a voluntary basis in undertakings of joint production committees composed of representatives of management and personnel. In the nationalised sector the principle of consultation was written into the relevant legislation. Although efforts were made to establish consultation machinery in as informal and flexible a form as possible, the various provisions nevertheless outline a certain type of body and limit the area of joint consultation at the level of the undertaking.

The joint committees are composed of representatives appointed by the management (who are often expected to represent also foremen and the higher categories of salaried employees) and representatives either elected by the workers (especially in private firms) or appointed by the trade unions (in most government undertakings).

Parity representation is the rule, but in practice representatives of the personnel are often more numerous than those of the management. Voting is seldom resorted to in coming to a decision which, in any case, would have only advisory force. Special efforts are made to avoid any overlap with subjects dealt with by collective bargaining or settled directly between the management and the union, and such matters are in fact expressly excluded from the scope of the committees.

Owing in particular to the growing role of shop stewards and of the more or less formal negotiations on an increasing number of subjects which have at the same time developed at the level of undertakings and establishments, "consultative" participation of the type just described has steadily lost ground for some years. According to a sample survey carried out a few years ago, it seemed that only about 30 per cent of undertakings in the private sector had joint consultation bodies (these were particularly undertakings in which the trade unions were least strongly entrenched), but that such bodies still existed in practically all undertakings in the public sector.[18]

United States

Where direct relations between employers and unions constitute the commonest way in which workers participate in decision-making at the level of the company or plant in the "organised" sector of the economy (i.e. where the unions are recognised as bargaining agents), consultative bodies in the United States, have always been regarded as being primarily concerned with productivity; most employers' associations and unions do not hide their scepticism as to their value, except in periods of national emergency. So it is that, as after the First World War, only a few of the 5,000-odd joint committees set up and officially recorded under the Second World War production planning programme still survived some years after the end of the latter war. In July 1945 some 3,000 were still active, but by 1948, according to a survey by the Bureau of Labor Statistics, their number had fallen to around 300.

According to a survey carried out by the United States Department of Labor—

To some degree, the relative scarcity of formalized cooperative arrangements reflects long-standing union and management attitudes as to their respective functions. As a matter of policy, management may avoid such collaboration because it is considered as, or may lead to, an encroachment on managerial prerogatives. Many employers prefer to deal with the union at arm's length, limiting joint negotiations only to those issues on which they are legally required to bargain. Similarly, unions may not wish to become too closely identified with company policies. Rank-and-file workers often tend to view such cooperation with misgivings, fearing that it may result in lack of militancy by union officials in pressing contract demands and in grievance handling.[19]

Although consultative bodies have, for instance, helped in overcoming a number of problems connected with technological development, on the whole their role has been much less important than that of collective bargaining.

At the beginning of the 1970s, with inflation, economic recession and growing foreign competition, new joint committees (generally consultative, but sometimes having powers of co-decision) were set up, in particular in the steel industry, were they were called "employment security and plant productivity committees".[20] An analysis made by the Bureau of Labor Statistics in 1974 of 1,550 major collective agreements showed that 97 contained provisions for joint committees to deal with production matters.[21] This number did not include joint committees dealing with health and safety, vocational training or industrial relations problems, nor joint committees operating in undertakings with fewer than 1,000 workers or set up under special agreements in application of the "Scanlon Plan".[22] In addition, the Federal Mediation and Conciliation Service encourages the establishment of joint committees, in particular to improve communications between bargaining periods and to reduce sources of tension.[23]

Canada

The Canada Department of Labour has given vigorous support to the growth of voluntary joint consultation and this has contributed to the establishment of joint committees, of which there were estimated to be about 2,700 in 1976.[24] Regional or national conferences, and exchanges of data on experience, have been organised by a special branch of the Department. In spite of their purely consultative character, and although they were originally set up to increase productivity, these committees have gone on to deal with the most varied topics relating to welfare, safety and health, cost reduction and anything which contributes generally to good management. However, not all the committees so set up have succeeded in their task, and they have often met with difficulties when they have approached certain important problems which, at the level of the establishment, properly belong to collective bargaining. In the past few years these bodies have been given varying names and have tended to become committees for management–union relations instead of worker-representation bodies distinct from the unions. Thus the committees now form a close link between the processes of consultation and negotiation.[25]

Australasia

Works councils have shown a marked advance in recent years in Australia and New Zealand. A body for the promotion of participation of this kind has been set up in one of the states of the Commonwealth of Australia, namely New South Wales. In New Zealand the Industrial Relations Council, a consultative body of the national employers' and workers' organisations, has declared itself against the imposition by law of this form of participation. The Industrial Relations Act, 1973,[26] merely provides that regulations may be made providing for the establishment on a voluntary basis of works committees representative of employers and workers. Management generally make efforts to exclude questions of pay from the discussions of works committees. Part of the trade union movement is still apprehensive about consultation in these bodies, for fear either that its role will be affected or that, in the absence of powers of decision, the recommendations of the committees will be ignored by top management.[27] There are also some works councils in the public sector, in particular in railway workshops and depots.

Switzerland

In Switzerland bodies of a works council type, mostly set up in accordance with collective agreements, generally bearing the title of workers' committees or personnel committees and composed exclusively of workers' representatives, are fairly active. Some recent agreements have increased their scope in relation to office workers and bank employees.

Japan

In Japan, where the basic trade union unit is the company trade union covering both wage earners and salaried employees and where, except in seafaring and a few other isolated industries, collective bargaining takes place exclusively at the level of the undertaking, there are numerous joint standing consultation bodies at that level.[28] Usually, these have been set

151

up in accordance with the collective agreement in force (in more than two-thirds of the cases, and in nine cases out of ten in companies employing more than 5,000 workers), with internal rules or with other agreements; or it may be a case of a long-standing practice going back to a management initiative. According to a survey carried out in July 1977 by the Ministry of Labour, about 70 per cent of Japanese undertakings had such a body (the proportion rose to over 80 per cent in undertakings with a trade union and fell to about 40 in those without one, while it was over 90 in undertakings with more than 5,000 workers and some 55 per cent in those employing from 100 to 200 workers).[29]

In general, the composition of these bodies is on a basis of parity, and it is the same persons who participate in collective bargaining and consultation. The trade unions—where they exist—have a monopoly of the appointment of workers' representatives on these bodies; elsewhere the representatives are elected by the personnel or sometimes chosen by the management. It is not uncommon for members of top management to attend the meetings of these bodies.

The subjects on the agenda are generally dealt with in the form of consultation of varying thoroughness, sometimes leading to co-decision, in which case approval of the workers' representatives is required. A survey carried out in 1974 produced the results given in table 1. The above-mentioned 1977 survey carried out by the Ministry of Labour showed that suspensions, dismissals and transfers gave rise to joint discussions in respectively 45, 38 and 27 per cent of the undertakings studied, while in 24, 19 and 10 per cent of them these subjects were submitted for joint consultation and agreement.

Table 1. Nature of participation in joint councils at the level of the undertaking in Japan, 1974

Subject	Percentage of joint councils discussing	Percentage of cases involving co-decision
Research and investment	68	5
Work organisation	76	17
Manpower planning	59	10
Planning and organisation in general	35	20
Education and training	42	10
Health and safety	77	12
Welfare and social activities	76	13

Source: T. Naruse: *Workers' participation in decisions within undertakings in Japan* (Geneva, ILO, mimeographed doc SWPDU/D.62), p. 2.

The kind of participation—consultation or collective bargaining or both—depends on the subjects dealt with, unless consultation is a preliminary to bargaining, as is often the case. A survey was carried out in the second half of 1975 by the Japanese Productivity Centre: 650 undertakings were surveyed and it was found that 37 per cent of the consultative bodies made a clear distinction between subjects for collective bargaining and subjects for consultation, 38 per cent started by consultation and, if no agreement was reached, then proceeded to bargaining, while 25 per cent also dealt with questions which were subject to collective bargaining.[30]

These consultative bodies often exist at at least two levels: that of the undertaking as a whole, that of the establishment and sometimes that of the workshop. Sometimes they are subdivided into councils dealing with various questions (management policy, working conditions or productivity) or they have committees of experts or technical committees (for production, sales, personnel, training etc.). In addition, workshop conferences bringing together the executive and supervisory staff and the workers or their representatives are regularly held in many undertakings to discuss work organisation, the working environment, planning or even the policy of the undertaking.[31] In this connection it should be noted that there are workshop trade union committees in Japan and that the union shop is common practice (it is provided for in over three-quarters of collective agreements).

In the public sector which, apart from the civil service, consists basically of the national railways, telegraphs and telephones and the government monopolies (mainly salt and tobacco), as well as the transport, water, gas and electricity services operated by the prefectoral or municipal authorities, there are also joint labour-management councils at the level of the undertaking which are established under collective agreements or less formal arrangements parallel with the normal collective bargaining and grievance procedures. Although these undertakings are less autonomous and trade union action in them apparently more politicised, the councils play an important role, in particular in prior consultation on rationalisation and modernisation measures involving the risk of collective redundancies. Since 1968 joint consultation bodies at workshop level have been set up on the national railways and have constantly proved active.

Although some Japanese trade unions are not, on principle, in favour of co-operating through consultation and see in it a risk of weakening their bargaining power, the most recent surveys reveal a high degree of satisfaction with the results obtained both among management (in more than 80 per cent of the undertakings surveyed in the 1977 survey of the Ministry of Labour the management thought the results had been very good, 70 per cent had no problem to report, and less than 18 per cent complained of lack of appropriate knowledge on the part of the workers)[32] and among the workers, although in a fair number of cases the latter would have liked to see an improvement in the information supplied and greater account being taken of their views in management decisions.[33]

There is some talk of legislation on participation in decision making, but the Federation of Japanese Employers' Organisations (Nikkeiren) is not in favour of recourse to legislation on this subject.

It must also be remembered that, in Japan, there are economic and social circumstances which favour a participatory style of management: traditionally, the undertaking is considered not only as a unit for the production of goods and services but also as a social community, and it is normal practice, before coming to a decision, to seek a consensus among the personnel concerned both in the undertaking and in individual workshops, with great importance being attached to communications from the workers up to the management and vice versa and to suggestions.[34] Observers have spoken of the "Oriental tradition of harmony", the word "harmony" being understood in the sense of ways of thinking and state of mind.[35]

ARRANGEMENTS IN SOME DEVELOPING COUNTRIES

Works committees or councils, or similar bodies, have been set up in quite a number of developing countries, either voluntarily or at the instigation of the authorities. It is interesting to see what arrangements have been made in some of those countries—especially in Asia, where participation has been introduced with varying degrees of success—the problems encountered and the measures taken to cope with them, in the light of the degree of development of the trade union movement and of the labour–management relations system.

It will be seen that works councils or other consultative bodies set up in developing countries have in practice had widely varying results depending on the country concerned and whether they are in the private or the public sector. It is important that their composition and activities should not be such as to provoke strong resistance either on the part of management, desirous of retaining its prerogatives, or of the unions, which are desirous of retaining their influence, especially through collective bargaining. At the same time, however, these bodies must deal with problems that are of genuine concern to the workers, who may otherwise be indifferent to their activities. This is what occurred in India, where, as will be seen below, the workers could not see the point of machinery that did not produce decisions on which their representatives had any real influence.

The question has sometimes been asked whether in developing countries the establishment of works councils or similar consultative bodies should not be an intermediate step in the introduction of participation—and a means of training both management and labour—when trade unions are not yet well developed or find it difficult to induce management to bargain collectively. It should also be said that a number of problems that arise at work can be settled through consultation without necessarily being the subject of collective bargaining in the strict sense in every case.

Jamaica

In Jamaica, in accordance with recommendations of an advisory committee on worker participation, consideration has been given to the establishment in all public or private undertakings employing 40 persons or more of works councils with extensive powers of co-decision, and of consultative councils at the level of the various departments of large undertakings.[36] The guiding principles for the private and public sectors[37] stress that works councils should be set up by agreement and suited to the characteristics of each undertaking with the help both of an internal promotion committee and of the workers' participation unit set up in the Ministry of Labour. These guiding principles indicate that labour and management should have equal representation on works councils, which should form a multi-level structure in large undertakings. There should be consultation before any decision is taken concerning, for example, expansion of the undertaking, organisational changes, internal communication, training, and safety and welfare measures. It is recommended that the chief trade union representative in the undertaking should be an ex officio member, and that the chairmanship should alternate twice a year between a representative of management and a worker representative. Also attention is drawn to the importance of the adoption of rules on frequency of meetings and on preparation of the agenda and of reports on meetings and the action taken on decisions.

India

In India joint consultative bodies had been established in some undertakings before the Second World War. After national independence the Industrial Disputes Act, 1947, provided for the establishment in undertakings employing 100 persons or more of joint committees "to promote measures for securing and preserving amity and good relations between the employer and workmen, and, to that end, to comment on matters of their common interest or concern" and to endeavour to resolve differences on such matters.[38]

155

This legislation led to the establishment of only a few of these committees, since their limited consultative role aroused little interest and the idea of extending it to bargaining led to reservations on the part both of the employers and the trade unions. There were fewer than 3,000 of these committees in 1967, though about double that number should have been set up.[39] Since then, most have gradually disappeared or ceased to play a significant role.

After the relative failure of this attempt, "joint management councils" with worker members appointed by the trade union or trade unions represented in the undertaking were formed on the initiative of the Government from 1958 onwards, in both the private and the public sector, under local agreements conforming to a model agreement. These councils, which in spite of their name were in practice akin to works councils, had consultative powers on such matters as the introduction of new production methods and the closure or retrenchment of undertakings. They had the right to receive information and to make suggestions on the economic situation of the undertaking, work organisation and methods, long-term expansion plans, the balance sheet and other subjects to be mutually agreed. They had direct responsibility (exercised in practice more often than the above-mentioned rights, and sometimes involving the setting-up of special committees) in regard to working hours and holidays, safety and health, welfare and vocational training. Questions subject to bargaining, such as wages, fringe benefits and individual grievances, were excluded from their competence, but this exclusion was sometimes ignored.

These councils scarcely seem to have fulfilled the hopes placed in them. In 1975, only 80 of them were active, 49 in the private sector and 31 in the public sector.[40] Various reasons have been suggested for this, such as the tenseness of industrial relations, the reservations of some managers who had delegated only junior executives without powers of decision to sit on these councils, the reservations of trade unions which complained that only questions of minor importance were discussed, fears of the erosion of union powers, inter-union rivalries, mistrust among workers' representatives of the information given them on the economic and financial situation of the undertaking, attempts by the workers' representatives to use the councils for pushing claims although these were outside the competence of the councils, and the fact that many of the workers are still illiterate or semi-literate. Because of the lack of practical results, people lost interest in this machinery.

The experiment is continuing, although it has taken a different turn since 1975. On 30 October of that year the central Government published general directives[41] on the establishment of a workers' participation system in industry at shopfloor and plant level. The system was intended for all public, private or co-operative undertakings in the mining and manufacturing sectors employing 500 workers or more (this figure has been lowered in several states). The system is flexible, since the ways in which participation is put into practice remain to be defined by the management, taking account both of the directives and of local circumstances. The establishment of shop councils is recommended at the level of each workshop or branch, as well as a joint council for the establishment.

Management and workers appoint their representatives from members of the workforce of the workshop or branch concerned. The chairman is appointed by the management. A shop council meets at least once a month. Its decisions are taken by unanimous agreement rather than by vote, and they must be implemented within one month (unless the council decides otherwise). Questions on which it has not been possible to reach agreement are referred by one or other side to the joint council for the establishment. The shop councils are concerned especially with the following subjects: improving productivity and profitability; reviewing absenteeism and proposing ways of reducing it; maintaining discipline; improving conditions of work and devising effective safety measures; making recommendations on health and welfare; and maintaining a dialogue betwen the management and workers.

A joint council must be set up for each establishment employing above a given number of workers. It is chaired by the head of the establishment and must meet at least once a quarter. As with the shop councils, its decisions must be reached by unanimous agreement and must be applied within a month unless previously decided otherwise. The joint establishment councils have the following functions: to improve the productivity and profitability of the establishment as a whole; to find solutions to questions which could not be settled by the shop councils and to settle those concerning several workshops or branches; to ensure that there are suitable training facilities; to fix working time-tables and holiday schedules; to set up a system of rewards for suggestions; and to recommend the health, safety and welfare measures which seem necessary at the level of the different units and of the establishment as a whole.

The directives do not lay down any uniform rules for the selection of members of shop councils or establishment councils. It is up to the management, in consultation with the workers and their unions, to determine appropriate representation systems. Each workshop or branch must also devise a system of communication between management and workers, particularly on production matters. The new system, launched during a state of emergency, seems to have aroused some interest and to have been quite widely applied since in the middle of 1977 it was estimated that about 2,000 undertakings had applied it; besides, all the main trade unions finally showed themselves in favour of it.[42] Encouraged by these results, the Government launched in January 1977 a comparable system for commerce and services in contact with the public such as hospitals, post and telegraph offices, railway ticket offices, banks, road transport undertakings, and electricity supply services employing at least 100 workers. One of the aims was to seek improvement in their operation and of the services rendered to the public.

In accordance with a recommendation of a tripartite labour conference held in May 1977 the Government that came to power in that year set up a Committee on Workers' Participation in Management and Equity[43] with a view to preparing a more advanced programme of participation at the different levels of management of industrial undertakings including, if appropriate, that of the board of directors, having regard at the same time to the interests of the national economy, of effective management and of the workers.

Malaysia

In Malaysia joint consultative bodies, to which workers' representatives are elected by the personnel and which are responsible primarily for examining grievances and suggestions, have been set up particularly in the two main sectors of economic activity—the plantations and the tin mines—at different levels in the undertaking. A code of conduct signed in February 1975 by the Minister of Labour and Manpower, the Malaysian Employers' Federation and the Malaysian Trades Union Congress recommended that such bodies should be more widely established at the level of workshops or units, since that should permit discussion of a great number of problems linked with the working situation. Joint consultative bodies have also been encouraged by the Ministry of Labour and Manpower in undertakings where the workers are not unionised, in order to facilitate labour relations.

Singapore

In Singapore joint bodies of a works council type were set up from about 1965 onwards at the suggestion of the National Productivity Office, but without much success. This result was mainly due to a fear of encroachment on their prerogatives, among both employers and trade unions, in spite of the precautions taken in defining the terms of reference of the new bodies. Other reasons have also been put forward: a lack of information among workers about the activity of the councils, lack of briefing of elected representatives, and passive attitude of management, which in many cases confined itself to replying to a steadily declining number of questions without activating the work of the councils.[44]

By 1974, of the 16 bodies set up, most were scarcely still in operation.

Recently, the Productivity Office, with the help of a national industrial relations commission set up under its auspices, the National Trade Union Congress and the Singapore Employers' Federation, has directed its attention to the establishment of productivity committees and a model text has been prepared for their constitution. This document, underlines their purely consultative role; but if a recommendation cannot be complied with, both management and unions are expected to give their reasons.

The Trade Union Congress has provided appropriate training for trade union leaders with a view to their effective participation in these bodies. It was also laid down that these bodies should contribute to the introduction of arrangements which would guarantee workers a fair share in productivity gains; in April 1978 a national tripartite conference was held to discuss problems arising in this connection and to give a new impulse to this form of participation.

Sri Lanka

In Sri Lanka, since about 1965, joint consultative bodies have been set up on a voluntary basis in a number of undertakings in the private sector, and on a compulsory basis in the civil service and public undertakings since a somewhat later date (although such bodies had, in fact, been set up in the public sector on a smaller scale as early as 1956). The intention was to provide more scope for joint decision-making in order to improve day-to-day operation and productivity, reduce waste, avoid corruption and generally improve the efficiency of management.

The joint consultative bodies in the private sector, whose members were elected among all categories of personnel below executives, are no longer very active, but attempts were made a few years ago to revive them by underlining the distinction between their functions and collective bargaining and by recommending that workers' representatives should be appointed by the trade union recognised in the undertaking, where there is such a union. The decline of these bodies was due, it has been stated, to lack of interest in them on the part of the workers, to strained labour relations and to the multiplicity of trade unions.

A survey carried out in 1974 by the National Institute of Management among 150 of the 210 employee councils then existing in the public sector showed that the majority or workers questioned wished to have greater powers and representation on management bodies (the possibility of such representation was provided for in a new Act of May 1979, which left the details to be laid down in regulations).[45] A report published on termination of this survey mentioned the constraints hanging over the managements of undertakings in this sector as a result of administrative and financial regulations which hardly made real participation any easier, the centralisation at ministerial level of important decisions which left little autonomy to the boards of directors of public undertakings, and the lack of confidence of much of management in the ability of employees to participate in management decisions.[46] Moreover, some persons with government responsibilities have in recent years stressed the politicisation and inter-union rivalries within the employee councils.[47] A national conference held in January 1975 adopted a number of resolutions to improve the working of these consultative bodies and the information supplied to employee representatives.[48]

An Act passed in May 1979 after extensive consultation provided for the establishment of employees' councils in all public undertakings of types to be determined by the Minister.[49] The members of these councils are to be elected by secret ballot for a term of two years from among permanent employees of the undertaking below the executive level. The number of members varies from three if there are no more than 50 eligible workers up to 18 if there are more than 1,000. These councils are to publish quarterly reports on their activities. They may be dissolved or, at the request of at least half of the eligible workers or at least two-thirds of the council concerned, some of their members may be removed by the Labour Commissioner for serious failure in carrying out their duties. The councils are to hold meetings once a month with the head of the undertaking, who may appoint not more than five representatives for that purpose.

The principal tasks of the councils are to keep an eye on the application of labour legislation, to make recommendations to the employer in regard, in particular, to health and safety, to promote effective workers' participation in the affairs of their undertaking, and to promote productivity and the mutual co-operation of employer and employees in achieving industrial peace and the common welfare in a spirit of mutual confidence. They examine labour disputes with a view to finding a settlement, which then has mandatory force. They are consulted on hours of work and intervals, the place and time for the payment of wages, preparation of the annual leave schedule, vocational training, social and welfare measures, discipline, and questions involving transfers and dismissals. The councils must be told about production methods and the financial situation in addition to any of the above subjects which are submitted for consultation.

Thailand

In Thailand an Act of 14 February 1975[50] gave the right to the workers of establishments employing at least 50 persons to ask the management to set up a consultative body to cover welfare problems, internal rules, grievances and disputes in general in the establishment. Such bodies have been set up in some large public undertakings such as the railways. If more than half the employees are trade union members, the trade union has the right to appoint all the members of such a body. It was left to a code of conduct to clarify the relationship between these bodies, the management and the trade unions. In some cases management was opposed to these bodies on the ground that they might encroach on its prerogatives. The unions either were exposed to rivalries among themselves or, not feeling strong enough, feared that their development would be hampered by these bodies and their bargaining power diminished.[51]

FORMAL PERSONNEL OR UNION REPRESENTATION

The next chapter deals with collective bargaining in market economy countries, as major form of participation through the unions. Trade union representatives or branches in the undertaking, briefly described below, are generally associated with such bargaining, although their varied activities are similar in some respects to those of works committees or councils and kindred or more specialised bodies when there are none in the country as a whole, or at any rate none in small undertakings. These activities are also similar to those of the official personnel representatives to be found in France and most French-speaking parts of Africa; though not trade union representatives in the strict sense, these personnel representatives are generally elected from among candidates nominated by the unions, and in fact generally act in both capacities. It will be seen that in some countries there is a tendency to broaden the functions of trade union representatives or branches in the undertaking, and even to hand over to them all or part of the functions of the joint bodies described in earlier parts of the present chapter. This tendency is often related to trade union reservations about, or opposition to, the grant of participatory functions to personnel bodies or representatives that are not offshoots of the unions themselves.

In France official personnel representatives were first appointed in 1936, initially under collective agreements and later under statutory provisions although some such appointments had been recorded earlier, especially during the First World War. They are elected in somewhat the same way as members of works committees, candidates being nominated in the first instance by the representative trade unions. Personnel representatives are mainly responsible for dealing with grievances, but in undertakings with fewer than 50 workers, where there is no works committee, they also perform some of the functions of such a body, including the running of welfare and suggestions schemes. The unions tried for many years to obtain official recognition of trade union representatives and branches in undertakings, and did not succeed until an Act was adopted in 1968. The branches are mainly engaged in such union activities as the collection of membership dues, the posting up of notices, the distribution of documents or the organisation of meetings of their members. One and the same person is often a trade union representative, a personnel representative and a member of the works committee.

In the Federal Republic of Germany there is a rather different system. In undertakings the trade unions have delegates[52] who, in practice, are also their elected representatives on works councils and who keep the rank-and-file workers informed of the activities and decisions of that council. Although the protection and facilities afforded to these persons are covered in collective agreements, the employers' organisations are opposed to the institutionalisation of this form of worker representation in undertakings.

In Belgium a model collective agreement signed in 1971 conferred new rights on trade union delegations in the undertaking, in particular the right to prior information on changes which might affect employment or agreed or customary terms or conditions of employment and remuneration.

In Italy, as already noted, an Act dated 20 May 1970 known as "the workers' bill of rights" introduced trade union representation at the level of the undertaking, which generally coincides in practice with representation through the factory councils.

In the Netherlands trade union sections have been formed in various undertakings with, among other purposes, those of lending support to the activities of works councils in regard to workers' grievances and electing delegations to negotiate with the employer on the application in the undertaking of collective agreements for the sector concerned.

In the United Kingdom shop stewards and their committees have become increasingly influential in recent years, as will be mentioned in the next chapter. They also play an important role in such countries as Australia, New Zealand, Jamaica and the Philippines.

In the Nordic countries the role of trade union representatives has been laid down in national agreements signed between the national employers' and workers' confederations.

In Sweden an Act respecting the status of trade union representatives at workplaces was adopted on 21 May 1974.[53]

In Finland the committees of a works council type set up under an Act of 1949[54] are due to go out of existence as a result of an Act of 1978 on "co-operation in the undertaking" which gives trade union representatives a pivotal role and extends their rights to information, consultation and negotiation.[55] Under that Act, which is applicable to undertakings employing 30 workers or more, the employer has to supply worker representatives at specified intervals with information on the economic situation of the undertaking, its programmes and future plans, and to submit to them at least once a year a plan relating to the personnel. He must consult the personnel or their representatives before taking any decisions which will bring about important changes in the activity of the undertaking which are likely to have repercussions on the workers, such as substantial changes in the organisation of work or production, closure or relocation of the undertaking or of a department, rationalisation, layoffs, etc. Consultation must also take place on the principles to be followed in recruitment or the use of outside manpower (in the latter case, negotiations may be demanded), on internal information and on the training budget. The employer is required to seek agreement on internal rules. In the event of failure to agree, the worker representatives have the final say, within the budgetary limits fixed by the undertaking, on matters concerning welfare facilities. Before taking a decision liable to affect a specific worker, the employer is required to examine the matter with him, either party being able to insist on the attendance of the appropriate workshop trade union representative. Decisions affecting a group or groups of workers are examined jointly by the employer and representatives of the group or groups in question. The workers may agree to a delegation within the undertaking comprising the competent workshop trade union representatives of the different groups of workers and a representative of non-union personnel, and the Act provides that, in order to fulfil the prescribed functions, undertakings must form a delegation or committee consisting one-third of representatives of the management and two-thirds of representatives of the personnel. However, the new statutory provisions only lay down general rules; details of the practical operation of the system have to be worked out through agreements, at the level either of the undertaking or of the employers' and workers' confederations. In an emergency the employer may take immediate remedial action without following the consultation procedure.

In many countries in French-speaking Africa, in particular the United Republic of Cameroon, the Central African Republic, Chad, Guinea, the Ivory Coast, Mali (in the private sector, since public undertakings, as described earlier, have a system of participation in management), Morocco, the Niger, Rwanda, Senegal, Togo and the Upper Volta, the personnel representatives provided for in legislation are responsible for the basic aspects of participation in the undertaking alongside their responsibilities in connection with collective bargaining. They are elected by the workers, most frequently from lists submitted by the trade unions. Their main duties are to intervene in the case of grievances, to keep an eye on the application of legislation and collective agreements, informing the labour inspectorate of any infringements, to transmit their own suggestions and those of the workers to the management, and sometimes to manage welfare schemes. In practice they therefore play a role similar, at least to some extent, to that of works committees or councils. In many respects they are comparable with their counterparts in France.

Many English-speaking African countries have shop stewards whose duties, though primarily related to grievances, lead them to concern themselves generally with all manner of problems affecting the personnel, including collective bargaining.

In some African countries personnel representatives or works committees have given way in recent years to trade union representation in the undertaking. For instance, in Algeria, under the provisions of the code for the socialist management of undertakings applicable to the private sector, the officers of the trade union branch in the undertaking or unit have among their tasks, in addition to the negotiation of agreements for the undertaking or unit, those of proposing any measure conducive to the improvement of productivity, of commenting on the investment programme and the annual balance sheet, of presenting workers' grievances to the employer, of guiding and monitoring training, of appointing workers' representatives on health, safety and discipline committees, and of managing welfare schemes.

In the Congo, several years ago, the "basic trade union", that is, the undertaking branch of the sectoral union, took over from the personnel representatives provided for by law in 1964.

In Tanzania, where, as has been seen, works councils still survive, the role of workers' committees established under earlier legislation has been taken over by trade union branches in undertakings.

In Zaire the personnel representatives in the undertaking provided for in a 1964 ordinance as confirmed by the Labour Code, who form the "workers' delegation" are called "trade union delegates" or "workers' delegates" according to whether they are elected in the first round (in which the trade unions have a monopoly in putting up candidates) or in the second round (which takes place if the number of votes recorded is not more than half the number of registered electors).

Notes

[1] In Mauritius the Act concerning labour relations promulgated on 24 December 1973 provided for the possibility of prescribing the establishment of works councils by a ministerial order where an enquiry had shown that such a measure was appropriate.

² ILO: *Legislative Series*, 1969—Mex. 1 (Art. 392).

³ For further details see A. Muñoz Ledo: *Participación y corresponsibilidad* (Mexico City, IEPES/PRI, 1976; mimeographed), which reports (p. 6) that Point No. 17 of the government's plan for 1976–82 drawn up by the Institutional Revolutionary Party advocated the establishment of technical works committees to play the role of bipartite consultative bodies.

⁴ ILO: *Legislative Series*, 1971—Pan. 1.

⁵ The first law on the subject dates back to 1890; it covered certain types of undertaking in the Kingdom of Prussia. This measure was adopted after much discussion and lengthy experimentation with different forms of participation. The main foundation on which works councils were built was that of the sickness insurance committees which existed at the level of the undertaking. Once a council existed (their establishment was optional), its views on factory rules had to be obtained. See G. Erdmann: *Die Entwicklung der deutschen Sozialgesetzgebung* (Göttingen, Musterschmidt-Verlag, 1957) and H. J. Teuteberg: *Geschichte der industriellen Mitbestimmung in Deutschland* (Tübingen, J. C. B. Mohr, 1961). As early as 1848 a Bill prepared for the Frankfurt-on-Main Assembly provided for the setting-up of factory councils, and although the Bill was rejected several employers spontaneously set up such councils in their undertakings.

⁶ ILO: *Legislative Series*, 1971—Neth. 1.

⁷ See B. Gustavsen: "A legislative approach to job reform in Norway", in *International Labour Review*, May–June 1977, pp. 263–276.

⁸ In this connection see ILO: *Protection and facilities afforded to workers' representatives in the undertaking*, Report VIII (1), International Labour Conference, 54th Session, Geneva, 1970. The discussion on this subject led to the adoption of the Workers' Representatives Convention and Recommendation, 1971.

⁹ See G. M. J. Kummer: "Works councils in Austria", in *International Labour Review*, Feb. 1960, pp. 110–124.

¹⁰ Schregle: "Co-determination in the Federal Republic of Germany . . . ", op. cit., pp. 86–87.

¹¹ On these various aspects, see ILO: *Workers' participation in decisions within undertakings, Oslo symposium*, op. cit., pp. 50–52, and Schregle: "Workers' participation in decisions within undertakings", op. cit., pp. 7–10.

¹² The Swedish agreement, between the Employers' Confederation (SAF) and the Trade Union Confederation (LO), was cancelled in 1976 after the adoption of the Act of 10 June 1976 on co-determination (see p. 172), which considerably altered the arrangements for participation in decisions at the level of the undertaking and opened up new avenues for collective bargaining at that level. In the opinion of the LO, this made a new agreement necessary; hence its cancellation of other co-operation agreements in force, including the agreement on rationalisation measures (which left considerable room for consultation with trade union representatives and works councils) and the agreement signed in 1975 on economic information (which provided for the establishment of a small joint committee to analyse the economic information supplied by the management or for appointment by the works council of an adviser, either from the personnel of the undertaking or, at the expense of the employer, from among outside specialists). For more details on this arrangement, which was aimed at improving the information of worker representatives on works councils and of those sitting on boards of directors, see *Social and Labour Bulletin*, No. 2/75, pp. 146–148. It should be noted that in the private sector, in the absence for the time being of new agreements, many of the existing works councils continued to function.

¹³ On the Act of 4 February 1977 concerning the working environment see Gustavsen, op. cit., pp. 266–267. In particular, Gustavsen analyses Section 12, which provides that account shall be taken, in the planning of work and design of jobs, of the need to provide opportunities for individual workers to take their own decisions and assume responsibility for what they do; an attempt is to be made to design jobs in such a way as to provide variety and opportunities of contact with other persons, to establish a relationship between individual tasks, and to enable the workers to keep informed of production requirements and results; workers and their representatives are to be kept informed of work planning and control systems; they are to be given the necessary training to understand the systems adopted and shall have the right to take part in their design. Other sections provide for more active participation of the workers in dealing with problems relating to the working environment. See ILO: *Legislative Series*, 1977—Nor. 1.

¹⁴ See, for instance, "Denmark—co-operation at the workplace", in *European Industrial Relations Review* (London), Sep. 1978, p. 20. For the Danish Act on the working environment see ILO: *Legislative Series*, 1975—Den. 1 and, for its amendment on 1 May 1978 providing for the setting-up of health and safety services and medical services in undertakings particularly exposed to occupational hazards, see *Social and Labour Bulletin*, No. 2/78, p. 83.

¹⁵ For an English translation of this agreement see ILO: *Basic agreements and joint statements*

on labour-management relations, Labour-Management Relations Series, No. 38 (Geneva, 1971), pp. 95–103.

[16] ILO: *Legislative Series*, 1970—It. 2.

[17] See for instance M. Baldassari: "Consigli di fabbrica: Crisi di ruolo e possibilità di crescita", in *Rassegna sindacale* (Rome, CGIL), 22 Mar. 1979, pp. 18–19. As regards the recent interest in production conferences, particularly in certain political circles, see Wedderburn et al., op. cit., pp. 66–68.

[18] See Clarke: *Workers' participation in management in Great Britain*, op. cit., pp. 7–8, and R. O. Clarke, D. J. Fatchett and B. C. Roberts: *Workers' participation in management in Britain* (London, Heinemann Educational Books, 1972).

[19] See United States Department of Labor, Bureau of Labor Statistics: *Major collective bargaining agreements: Management rights and union-management co-operation*, Bulletin No. 1425–5 (Washington, Government Printing Office, 1966), p. 25.

[20] See Harry Douty: *Labour-management productivity committees in American industry* (Washington, National Commission on Productivity and Work Quality, 1975); Edgar Weinberg: "Labour-management cooperation: A report on recent initiatives", in *Monthly Labor Review* (Washington, US Department of Labor), Apr. 1976, pp. 13–22; Charlotte Gold: *Employer-employee committees and worker participation* (Ithaca, New York State School of Industrial and Labour Relations, Cornell University, 1976); and I. W. Abel: *Employment security and plant productivity committees* (Washington, National Center for Productivity and Quality of Working Life, 1974), which reports the existence at the end of 1974 of some 250 of these committees, often with subcommittees, meeting as a rule at least once a month, and a productivity increase of 10.8 per cent in the steel industry in the same year.

[21] United States Department of Labor, Bureau of Labor Statistics: *Characteristics of major collective bargaining agreements*, Bulletin No. 1888 (Washington, Government Printing Office, 1974).

[22] Kind of suggestions scheme that provides for the sharing between the company and the personnel of gains achieved through increased productivity, generally in the form of monthly bonuses, with a network of joint committees in the company to monitor the suggestions and the resulting gains. See Fred G. Lesieur (ed.): *The Scanlon Plan: A frontier in labor-management cooperation* (Cambridge, Massachusetts, MIT Press, 1958); and Fred G. Lesieur and Elbridge S. Puckett: "The Scanlon Plan has proved itself", in *Harvard Business Review* (Cambridge, Massachusetts), Sep.–Oct. 1969, pp. 109–118. In 1975 it was estimated that from 300 to 500 companies in the United States were applying the Scanlon Plan.

[23] Weinberg, op. cit., p. 19.

[24] 1976 estimate quoted by Weinberg, op. cit., p. 14.

[25] ILO: *Workers' participation in decisions within undertakings, Oslo symposium*, op. cit., pp. 51 and 71.

[26] Section 223 *(a)*. See ILO: *Legislative Series*, 1973—NZ 1.

[27] See Stanley Williams: "New Zealand industrial relations: Retrospect and prospect", in ILO: *Industrial relations in Asia*, op. cit., pp. 169–170.

[28] For a historical account of these joint management-personnel bodies from the 1920s onwards see Tadashi Mitsufuji and Toshio Ishikawa: "Workers' participation in Japan", in *ILLS Bulletin* (Geneva, International Institute for Labour Studies), June 1970, pp. 201–222.

[29] Survey carried out in some 5,000 private undertakings employing 100 or more permanent workers in a variety of activities including mining, construction, manufacturing industries, wholesale and retail trade, banks, insurance companies, property agencies, transport and communications, water, gas and electricity supply, heating and the services sector in general. The results were published in *Kampô Shiryo* (Tokyo), 4 May 1978. See also *Rosei Jiho* (Tokyo), 12 May 1978, and *Shukan Rodo* (Tokyo), 17 and 24 Apr. 1978. Summaries in *Social and Labour Bulletin*, No. 4/78, pp. 339–341.

[30] See *Social and Labour Bulletin*, No. 4/76, pp. 319–320.

[31] For further details see Naruse, op. cit., p. 3.

[32] See also Kazutoshi Koshiro: "Labour management relations in public enterprises in Japan", in Friedrich-Ebert-Stiftung, op. cit., pp. 195–196.

[33] See *Social and Labour Bulletin*, No. 4/76, pp. 319–321, and the above-mentioned publications (note 29) dealing with the 1977 Ministry of Labour survey.

[34] For an account of an agreement signed in July 1978 in a large Japanese electrical appliance factory which provided for consultative bodies at different levels from workshop up to top management, see *Social and Labour Bulletin*, No. 1/79, pp. 27–28.

[35] In this connection, see Robert J. Ballon, S.J.: "The dynamics of the nation state: Japan's

industrial society", in the report published by the Japanese Institute of Labour on the Asian Conference on Labour Relations held in Tokyo in 1965 entitled *Changing patterns of industrial relations* (Tokyo, 1966), p. 45.

[36] See *Social and Labour Bulletin*, No. 2/77, pp. 118–120, and No. 1/78, pp. 17–18.

[37] See *Worker participation in the private sector*, op. cit., and *Worker participation in statutory boards and local government* (Kingston, Agency for Public Information, 1978).

[38] ILO: *Legislative Series*, 1947—Ind. 1 and 1965—Ind. 1.

[39] See M. S. Krishnan: *Workers' participation in decisions within undertakings in India* (Geneva, ILO, 1974; mimeographed doc. SWPDU/D.23), p. 2.

[40] Figures quoted by C. S. Krishnaswami: "India, industrial relations: Retrospect and prospect", in ILO: *Industrial relations in Asia*, Labour-Management Relations Series, No. 52 (Geneva, 1976), p. 84. In this connection it may be mentioned that the Tata factories at Jamshedpur have had joint councils at three levels for a long time: at the base, councils in each of the different departments of this industrial group, at the intermediate level a works council and joint councils for medical questions and matters affecting the local community and, at the summit, a joint consultative management council. See for instance A. D. Singh (ed.): *Man management in Tata Steel* and *Working together: Closer association of employees with management in Tata Steel* (Jamshedpur, Tata Iron and Steel Co., 1974 and 1973 respectively).

[41] Ministry of Labour: *Scheme for workers' participation in industry at shop floor and plant level*, Resolution No. S. 61011(4)/75-Dk.I(B), 30 Oct. 1975.

[42] For one of the first studies published on the working of these works and shop councils see Susan M. Leberman and Robert L. Leberman: "Two case studies on workers' participation in management", in *Indian Journal of Industrial Relations* (Delhi), Apr. 1978, pp. 467–510.

[43] See *Gazette of India*, Extraordinary, Part I, Section 1, 23 Sep. 1977.

[44] See K. Mok: *Works councils in Singapore* (Geneva, ILO, 1974, mimeographed doc. No. SWPDU/D.31), pp. 4–5. For details on the composition and terms of reference of these bodies, contained in a code of practice concerning productivity adopted in 1965 with a charter for industrial progress, see ILO: *Basic agreements and joint statements on labour-management relations*, op. cit., p. 166.

[45] See L. K. B. Godamunne and K. L. Chandratillaka: *Workers' participation in management: Experience in Sri Lanka* (Colombo, National Institute of Management, 1975).

[46] Ibid., pp. 19–20.

[47] D. P. A. Weerasinghe, Assistant Commissioner of Labour: "Labour-management relations in public enterprises in Sri Lanka", in Friedrich-Ebert-Stiftung, op. cit., pp. 363 and 369.

[48] See Godamunne and Chandratillaka, op. cit., pp. 44 et seq.

[49] See Supplement to Part II, *Gazette of the Democratic Socialist Republic of Sri Lanka* (Colombo), 8 June 1979. It is stressed in this Act that its provisions supplement, and do not in any way derogate from, existing legislation on employers, workers and trade unions.

[50] ILO: *Legislative Series*, 1975—Thai. 1.

[51] See Sovrat Swongram: "Thailand: Industrial relations, retrospect and prospect", in idem: *Industrial relations in Asia*, op. cit., p. 280.

[52] See for instance Douglas Miller: "Trade union workplace representation in the Federal Republic of Germany: An analysis of the post-war *Vertrauensleute* policy of the German Metalworkers' Union (1952–1977)", in *British Journal of Industrial Relations* (London), Nov. 1978, pp. 335–354.

[53] ILO: *Legislative Series*, 1974—Swe. 3.

[54] ibid., 1949—Fin. 2.

[55] ibid., 1978—Fin. 3.

PARTICIPATION THROUGH TRADE UNIONS AND COLLECTIVE BARGAINING IN MARKET ECONOMY COUNTRIES

8

When there is no special participation machinery of the types described in the previous chapters, the workers may still be in a position to exert a marked influence on decision-making in the undertaking either directly or through their trade unions. Many of the early social reformers and workers' leaders, particularly in the United Kingdom and the United States, thought that to achieve "industrial democracy" it was essential to organise this influence through official recognition of the trade unions active in undertakings. Direct relations between management and unions remain an important form of participation in a number of countries, particularly those based on a market economy.

Furthermore, in recent years, in several industrialised countries where collective bargaining traditionally took place at the level of the industry or at the national level, particularly in Western Europe, there has been a noticeable development of negotiations at the level of the undertaking or establishment, either with a view to the conclusion of agreements at that level as a matter of established practice, or on the occasion of labour disputes, which tended to become more frequent for instance in France, Italy and the United Kingdom in the latter half of the 1960s and in the first half of the following decade.

Various factors have been pointed out to explain this trend. They include the following:

(a) the desire to have formal agreements confirming the wages which can actually be secured in the individual undertaking;

(b) the desire to have some control over the immediate working conditions in the undertaking (e.g. work pace, hours, safety and health);

(c) examples of terms obtained and claims put forward elsewhere, which come to the workers' knowledge through the mass media; and

(d) the growing militancy and higher educational levels of the workers,

169

especially the younger ones, and their desire not only in general for greater participation in decision-making, but also not to have their problems regulated exclusively by central trade union bodies, which in their opinion are too sensitive to economic constraints and too remote from the realities of the undertakings in which the workers are employed.

Moreover, technological development and rationalisation (which has in some cases taken the form of mergers, relocations, etc.) have given added importance to claims in respect of employment and income guarantees, training and retraining. Also, a difficult economic situation sometimes prompts what amount to negotiations on workforce reductions with a view to avoiding or phasing dismissals or attenuating their effects (criteria of hardship to be applied, maximum use of voluntary departures including early retirement, in some cases with special redundancy payments, and provision of alternative employment where possible).

A complete description of such participation arrangements arising from trade union action cannot be given in this publication, since that would involve setting out the main elements of the different national industrial relations systems. The following paragraphs will therefore be limited to outlining the main characteristics (collective bargaining has recently been the subject of analysis and in-depth discussion in a number of publications of the International Labour Office).[1]

Collective bargaining is undoubtedly a form of participation, even an advanced form, since it implies not only informing and consulting the workers but negotiating with them on matters which would otherwise be the subject of unilateral decisions. In a number of countries collective bargaining is the most important—or even the only—form of participation in decision-making in the undertaking. The part which it plays in these countries as an instrument of participation is clearly more decisive where collective bargaining is strongly entrenched, where it covers an appreciable proportion of the labour force and where it takes place mainly or exclusively at the level of the undertaking or establishment. In addition, as will be seen in the following pages, in some countries collective bargaining covers so many important subjects that it represents a particularly extensive form of participation.

The prime example of a country where collective bargaining has all the above characteristics and where it is generally the only form of participation in the decisions of the undertaking is that of the United States.[2] The unions have great influence in the sector of the economy in which they are recognised as bargaining agents. That sector employs barely a third of the labour force, but covers most of the large industries; collective agreements signed in that so-called "organised" sector have a considerable indirect influence on conditions of employment in the "non-organised" sector. Collective bargaining covers a very broad range of subjects, so that virtually all decisions which may have repercussions on terms of employment and conditions of work are the product of agreement between the two sides. Procedures for dealing with grievances, which are included in almost all collective agreements, also give the workers considerable influence over their terms and conditions of employment. A French author, writing on the steel industry in the United States, has observed that for the worker the joint grievance procedure constitutes a guarantee of maximum justice and genuine industrial democracy. He considers that through this procedure, and the strength of the union which is a party to it, the workers are guaranteed a sort of power of co-management as regards their conditions of work.[3]

The basic reason why United States employers and unions prefer collective bargaining to other forms of participation is that, in their opinion, it has the advantage of being a relationship which marks a very clear distinction between the respective functions of management and the unions, while other forms of participation assume a relationship which, in itself, limits the possibilities of genuine trade union action and sometimes blurs the distinction between management's functions and those of the unions to such an extent that in their view there is actual incompatibility with collective bargaining.

Another argument frequently put forward in the United States in favour of collective bargaining is that it is a very flexible instrument which, without the need for a highly developed institutional and procedural framework, permits the settlement of a great number of questions in whatever way is most appropriate in the current circumstances.

Collective bargaining as a method of workers' participation in decisions within the undertaking also plays a very important part in countries other than the United States. This is for instance the case in Canada, where the industrial relations system bears many similarities with that of the United States. At a congress held in April 1977 at Laval University, Quebec, a Canadian writer stated: "There is no doubt that through the continuing contacts which it presupposes between the workers' representatives and management in the interpretation of the collective agreement as regards the rights of the workers, the union and the management, the day-to-day application of such an agreement constitutes the fullest form of participation in our system."[4]

In some Western European countries there is a marked trend towards the development of bargaining at the level of the undertaking. A few particularly characteristic examples may be cited as illustrations of this trend.

In the industrial relations system of the United Kingdom, as has been mentioned earlier, a very important role is now played by shop stewards. In 1971 their number was estimated by the Trades Union Congress to be about 200,000, that is, on average of one for every 50 to 60 union members, while at about the same period the number of full-time trade union officials was barely 3,000. There is no statutory provision for shop stewards, who may either be elected by the workers or appointed by the trade unions. They are usually formed into committees, and initiate more or less formal negotiations with the management and represent workers in grievance procedures. In practice, shop stewards exert a great influence on an ever-growing number of management decisions.

In Sweden, where the bulk of collective bargaining used to take place at the national level and where works councils set up under agreement between the employers' and workers' confederations used to play an important participatory role, an Act of 10 June 1976 respecting co-determination at work[5] opened a very wide door for negotiation at the level of the undertaking. It is apparent from this Act that practically every problem which arises at the workplace can now be the subject of negotiation, including work allocation which, up to then, was strictly a management prerogative. The employer is even under an obligation to negotiate before introducing any important change such as a change in activities or the reorganisation of production methods. Only pressing reasons may allow him to introduce an important change before the completion of negotiation on the subject. The new Act also introduces a particularly far-reaching right to information, for instance on production, the financial situation of the undertaking, and the general principles of personnel policy. It also provides that if the meaning of a collective agreement is in dispute, the interpretation of the trade union representatives shall prevail (except in matters of remuneration) until the Labour Court has issued a ruling on the subject.

For the public sector a national agreement under the 1976 Act was signed in March 1979.[6] Negotiations on a similar agreement in the private sector have not yet been successfully completed. The employers' confederation stresses that if co-determination is to work appropriately in each undertaking, it must be based on a direct influence of workers on their work and must be part of the organisation of the undertaking without adding new special bodies.[7]

Collective bargaining also constitutes the main form of workers' participation in decision-making in most of the countries in English-speaking Africa, as well as in the Americas, Asia, the Caribbean and Oceania.

In a number of countries the importance of collective bargaining as an instrument of workers' participation is that much greater because, except on a very small scale, there is practically no participation machinery of the works council type. It is clear, however, that in countries where works councils are more common, there is nothing to prevent collective bargaining from also playing a considerable parallel role; indeed, that is the case in most of the industrialised countries of Western Europe and in a number of developing countries.

The growing interest in the idea of workers' participation in decisions in the undertaking has had repercussions in the past few years on collective bargaining itself, allowing it to carry out its role as an instrument of participation much better than in the past.

The first of these repercussions relates to the level at which collective bargaining takes place. In many countries, especially industrialised ones where collective bargaining was traditionally carried on at the level of the industry, bargaining at undertaking level is growing steadily, often in a very informal manner, without, however, superseding bargaining at industry level. This development, clearly facilitating much closer association of employers and workers in the taking of decisions on the matters with which they are concerned, is evident in particular in countries such as Australia, the Federal Republic of Germany,[8] Italy, the Netherlands and the United Kingdom. Some of the factors which are generally put forward to explain this development have already been mentioned.

There has also been an increase in the number of subjects on which negotiation takes place. Originally, collective bargaining concerned only a small number of subjects, among which wage rates generally took pride of place. Subsequently, a growing number of subjects have progressively been withdrawn from management prerogatives to be covered in agreements negotiated with the parties concerned. For quite a time now, collective agreements have come to deal more and more frequently with new subjects such as subcontracting, supplementary unemployment benefits (even guaranteed annual incomes) and resettlement retraining. More recently, clauses have appeared on matters such as work organisation at shopfloor level, personnel policy and investment policy. For example, in Italy over the past few years company collective agreements have included clauses not only on hours of work, work pace and workloads, health and safety problems and job classification, but also on the limitation of subcontracting and homeworking, on transfers within the undertaking, and generally on the employment aspects of all reorganisation and rationalisation measures. Clauses concerning investment became much more frequent from 1976 on, giving the trade unions not only a right to information and consultation on investments but in practice a right to genuine negotiation on the subject.[9] In addition, the trade unions have tended in their negotiations to put pressure on undertakings to assist the local authorities (communes and provinces)

173

with public works and social services (transport, schools, housing, child-care facilities, hospitals, etc.).

This trend towards a widening of the subjects negotiated is not confined to the industrialised countries: it can be observed, with the growing strength of the trade unions and the rising educational levels of their officers and members, in a number of developing countries in Africa, Asia, Latin America and the Caribbean, where collective bargaining, which had traditionally taken place at the level of the undertaking, has become more wide-ranging both in content and in the number of undertakings covered. In contrast with the shift of collective bargaining in the industrialised countries, particularly in Western Europe, from the industry down to the undertaking or establishment, in most of the developing countries collective bargaining started in the undertaking and is at present tending to move up to the level of the industry or to multi-industry agreements.

Also, collective bargaining has been used increasingly to regulate relations between the signatory parties of agreements. Clauses with this in mind have often been designed to increase workers' participation in the taking of decisions in the undertaking, for example through various consultation or grievance procedures.

In many countries, too, collective agreements have, for some time now, afforded the trade unions a considerable role in the examination of grievances and in some other areas such as the recruitment of casual personnel, the drafting and amendment of works rules and safety and health measures, the joint management of social security funds, the management of co-operatives set up under a collective agreement, and the granting of loans to workers.

In some countries, particularly industrialised ones, there has been a marked trend towards involving the rank and file in the process of collective bargaining. This trend, which gives a new dimension to collective bargaining as an instrument of participation, has led to increasingly extensive consultation procedures, both at the stage of the drafting of claims and that of the ratification of collective agreements. For example, in the negotiations during the autumn of 1969 in Italy, before the signature of the collective agreement for the metal and mechanical engineering trades, the trade unions, in the process of drafting their claims, organised between 2,000 and 3,000 meetings for the 1.5 million workers concerned. Employers' organisations, and even more so workers' organisations, have tended to resort to ratification procedures of increasing complexity, not only in industrialised countries such as Canada, the Federal Republic of Germany, Italy and the United States but also in a number of developing countries.

The last point to be noted is that there has also been a noteworthy increase in the effectiveness of collective bargaining as a participation system in recent years as a result of its development and intensification in the public sector in many countries.

Notes

[1] See for instance *Promotion of collective bargaining*, Report V(1), International Labour Conference, 66th Session, 1980; *Background paper* and *Report* of a tripartite advisory meeting on collective bargaining, Geneva, 10–19 May 1976 (mimeographed docs. TCMB/76/1 and TCMB/76/D.6); Efren Córdova: "A comparative view of collective bargaining in industrialised countries", in *International Labour Review*, July-Aug. 1978, pp. 423–439; *Collective bargaining in industrialised countries: Recent trends and problems, Vienna symposium (November 1977)*, Labour-Management Relations Series, No. 56 (Geneva, 1978); *Collective bargaining in industrialised market economies* (Geneva, 1973); ILO/FES: *Collective bargaining and labour arbitration in the ASEAN region* (Bangkok, Friedrich-Ebert-Stiftung, 1977); *La negociación colectiva en América Latina* (Geneva, 1978); *Industrial relations in Asia*, op. cit.; *Labour relations in the Caribbean Region*, Labour-Management Relations Series, No. 43 (Geneva, 1974); and *Industrial relations and personnel management in English-speaking Africa*, Labour-Management Relations Series, No. 40 (Geneva, 1972).

[2] Among other publications, see Adolf F. Sturmthal: "Workers' participation in management: A review of United States experience", in *IILS Bulletin*, June 1969, pp. 149–186, which also deals with a number of problems encountered in practice; Donald E. Cullen: "Recent trends in collective bargaining in the United States", in *International Labour Review*, June 1972, pp. 507–530; and Windmuller: "Industrial democracy and industrial relations", op. cit., pp. 22–31.

[3] A. Benhamou-Hirtz: *Les relations collectives dans la sidérurgie américaine*, Cahiers de la Fondation nationale des sciences politiques (Paris, Armand Colin, 1966), pp. 393–394.

[4] Gilles Laflamme: "Peut-on concilier négociation collective et participation à la gestion?", in L. Bélanger, J. Boivin, G. Dussault and A. Larocque (ed.): *Participation et négociation collective* (Quebec, Presses de l'Université Laval, 1977), p. 82.

[5] ILO: *Legislative Series*, 1976—Swe. 1 and Ake Bouvin: "New Swedish legislation on democracy at the workplace", in *International Labour Review*, Mar.–Apr. 1977, pp. 131–143.

[6] See *Social and Labour Bulletin*, No. 2/79, pp. 141–142.

[7] In January 1979 a national agreement was signed by the banking employers' organisation and the bank employees' union which provides in particular for close contacts between the personnel representatives and management representatives at various levels for participation in the decision-making process, particularly on personnel policy and work organisation, with, if necessary, jointly agreed recourse to outside experts (see ibid., p. 142). More recently, an agreement has been signed in the insurance sector.

[8] As regards negotiations carried out in the Federal Republic of Germany by works councils, although under the law they are not entitled to sign agreements on pay and other conditions of employment which are usually determined by collective agreements between the unions and the employers, see Schregle: "Co-determination in the Federal Republic of Germany", op. cit., and idem: "Labour relations in Western Europe: Some topical issues", in *International Labour Review*, Jan. 1974, particularly pp. 6–9.

[9] See in particular *Contrattazione* (Rome, CISL), New Series, May–June 1977, pp. 23–24. An agreement signed in 1974 in the Fiat automobile company contained a clause by which the company undertook to invest capital in southern Italy, a region with a long history of underemployment. In the same year clauses of this kind were included in "development agreements" signed in several large undertakings with state financial participation, such as Alfa Romeo, Montedison and Montefibre.

PARTICIPATION THROUGH TRADE UNIONS IN SOME CENTRALLY PLANNED ECONOMIES

9

Direct relations between the management of undertakings and trade union branches at factory level traditionally constitute the main channel of workers' participation in the centrally planned systems of the USSR and other countries of Central and Eastern Europe belonging to the Council of Mutual Economic Assistance.

Mention has already been made of the trend, in Yugoslavia and Poland, towards making participation an integral part of management within a framework of decentralisation of planning systems, through the medium of workers' councils or similar bodies and, increasingly in Yugoslavia, of workers' assemblies. In those two countries trade union bodies continue to play an important role in the undertaking. In other countries, such as the USSR, Bulgaria, Czechoslovakia, the German Democratic Republic, Hungary and Romania, workers' participation is largely based on direct relations between the trade union and the management, particularly since the economic reform which took place in the second half of the 1960s. That reform increased the autonomy of undertakings, in each of which a fund built up by the retention of a proportion of the profits when the undertaking's targets are fulfilled or over-fulfilled allows the material motivation of the undertaking and each of its workers to be strengthened.[1] Planning was also made more flexible through greater decentralisation and there was a further broadening or workers' participation in the management of production and in decision-making: in particular, factory or establishment trade union committees were given a more important role.

COMMON FEATURES

The systems prevailing in these countries have common features, the main one being the existence of a single trade union movement at all levels. All the manual and non-manual workers of an undertaking (including the technicians, the engineers and the management personnel) are members, in accordance with the principle of "one undertaking, one organisation".[2] This trade union unity, which is the result of historical revolutionary changes in these countries, is reflected in national legislation, which has progressively entrusted various administrative functions to the unions in fields directly affecting workers' interests such as social security, labour inspection, health services, welfare, leisure and cultural activities. At the level of the undertaking, the trade union bodies have been progressively merged with the works councils which existed under earlier legislation (for instance in Czechoslovakia); they have thus been given responsibility for a great variety of functions relating to economic and social matters and personnel problems; these functions, based on collaboration and co-determination, have been added to their trade union activities proper as defined in their by-laws by national trade union congresses.

Another common characteristic concerns the direct links between the trade union movement and the party (the Communist Party or Workers' Party, according to the country) based on their common ideology; these links, which also have a historical origin, are mentioned in the by-laws of the unions and in the Constitution and legislation of each country. The close relationship is reflected in undertakings at the level of the executive bodies of the two organisations, both of which are supposed to represent the workers' interests, in different but closely connected fields.

The next few pages describe the participation machinery established in the USSR. Except in Yugoslavia and to some extent in Poland (see Chapter 5), a similar system is to be found in the other countries of Eastern Europe and in Mongolia.[3]

USSR

In the USSR up to 1929 there was tripartite machinery for party-union-management co-operation in industry. Then, with the introduction of centralised planning (the first five-year plan), it was superseded by a system of undivided responsibility: under this system, the manager of each undertaking had sole authority in all management fields and he was responsible, through a single chain of command, to the relevant ministry or other government department. More or less important functions were left in the hands of the trade unions or other workers' bodies in the undertaking, but the unions were not to intervene in decisions taken by the manager in his own field or competence, namely economic and production matters. The main responsibility of the trade unions was to initiate a competitive attitude to work and to apply methods aimed at full participation by the workers in achieving the targets assigned to the undertaking by the plan. Wages and conditions of employment were laid down with great precision in laws adopted in connection with the national plan in collaboration with the Central Council of Trade Unions, and this arrangement left very little scope for adjustment at the level of the undertaking. From 1935 to 1947, no collective agreements were negotiated.[4]

Although it is possible to trace earlier measures, the origin of current developments in the field under study seems to lie in the decisions taken by the 20th Congress of the Communist Party of the USSR, which drew attention to the need to adapt planning and economic management methods, including the machinery for workers' participation, to the new conditions then prevailing. Various measures strengthened the power of trade union committees and prepared the way for the establishment of joint labour-management bodies in undertakings.[6] Powers of co-decision were conceded to trade union committees in most personnel matters, including dismissal; subsequently these bodies were gradually associated with the drafting of the undertaking's annual and long-term plans.

Collective agreements are signed by the factory or establishment trade union committee with the management after consultation of the workers and approval by their general meetings, and following the general recommendations of the government departments concerned and the central trade union bodies. Such agreements have now assumed considerable importance. In May 1979 there were some 150,000 collective agreements in force in the USSR. The procedure for drawing them up was made more flexible by abolition in 1971 for the formality of official confirmation of agreements. They deal with fulfilment of state economic plans, the application of scientific and technical progress, the improvement of skills, work organisation, productivity and the system of remuneration (though not with wage rates, which are supposed to be the national minimum rates determined by the authorities jointly with the trade unions at the corresponding level). Particular emphasis is placed on the development of forms of collective remuneration and of financial incentives in the shape of bonuses or allowances paid from the special fund established in each undertaking for that purpose.

Collective agreements aim at ensuring workers' active participation in production management and in the improvement of working conditions, housing and welfare in general, including socio-cultural activities. They specify the mutual obligations of the management, the trade union committee and the workers in these various respects, including disciplinary matters and health and safety. If there are differences between the management and the trade union committee at the time of negotiation, the parties appeal to higher economic and trade union bodies. Within the framework of social planning (which will be referred to later), it has been possible for some years to sign collective agreements of five years' duration corresponding to undertakings' five-year economic targets, although this is not yet the general practice.[6]

The regulations respecting the rights of factory, works or local trade union committees approved by a decree of 27 September 1971[7] entrust to some 712,000 elected committees of this type[8] (having from 7 to 21 members according to the size of the undertaking) the role of representing the interests of the workforce in all matters concerning production and living and working conditions, and in general in their relations with the management and local state bodies.

The trade union committee must be consulted on the appointment of senior executives. After consulting the management of the undertaking, it decides on the use of the financial incentives fund and of the fund for socio-cultural needs such as kindergartens and holiday camps, leisure, convalescence and rest centres, libraries, sports facilities and housing for the personnel.

The trade union committee has a right of co-decision on work rules and output norms. It may take part in the adoption of reduced output norms for newly recruited young workers and consider in conjunction with the youth organisation such questions as the protection of young workers. The factory trade union committee plays a part not only in setting output norms and production targets in general but also in deciding on the manning of work teams. The above-mentioned regulations also provide that overtime requires the committee's approval; staff grading by skill must be carried out with its agreement and, in conjunction with the management, it may determine what piecework or hourly system of remuneration shall be used. Under Section 2 of the 1971 regulations the trade union committee is required to ensure the participation of manual and non-manual workers in management through workers' assemblies and standing production committees.

Workers' assemblies constitute a major form of workers' participation in management. They regularly examine all aspects of the workers' life, study ways of improving production and raising labour productivity, approve the draft development plans of the undertaking before they are submitted to the appropriate government department, and monitor the implementation of production plans and collective agreements. Reports are submitted to them by the management and by trade union officials. The management must examine their proposals and criticisms and must give an account of action taken on them. In large undertakings general meetings take the form of conferences attended by delegates elected by the workers to represent them.

The rights and obligations of standing production conferences functioning under the auspices of the trade union committee, which were laid down in the 1958 regulations,[9] were the subject of new rules adopted by the Council of Ministers and the Central Council of Trade Unions in 1973. They exist in establishments employing at least from 100 to 300 workers, depending on the industry; when the number of workers is less, production matters are discussed at the workers' assemblies. The standing production committees are bodies elected for one year. Between 60 and 70 per cent of the total number of members are manual workers, and there are also non-manual workers, and representatives of the trade union committee, of the party, of the youth organisation, of technical and learned societies and of the society of inventors and rationalisers.[10] There were about 140,000 of these committees in 1980. In 1977 more than 5 million proposals were made, and it was possible to apply 89 per cent of them. The committees meet at least once or twice a quarter at the level of the undertaking and at least once a month at the level of the workshop. They concern themselves with training, and examine all aspects relating to the improvement of production, of production organisation and planning, and of labour discipline. The new regulations require the management to apply the decisions and recommendations of the committees, subject in the event of disagreement to appeal to higher trade union and economic bodies.

The factory or establishment trade union committee has considerable powers of supervision; it can apply to the appropriate authorities for the penalisation, or even the dismissal, of the general manager and other senior managers if they do not observe the provisions of the collective agreement or of labour legislation, or if they have a bureaucratic outlook or are indifferent to the workers' needs.[11] Where prior consultation of the committee is required, a decision taken without such consultation constitutes a serious breach of the law. The trade union committee may suspend production in any unit where the safety rules are not being observed.[12]

Any disputes between a worker and the management are usually submitted to the undertaking's joint labour disputes commission. If this commission fails to obtain agreement on the case under dispute, the trade union committee is entitled to take a decision itself, subject to appeal to a tribunal. The latter may also, on its own initiative or at the request of the public prosecutor, annul any decision of the disputes commission that is contrary to labour legislation. The workers also have the right to apply directly to the public prosecutor.

The trade union committee is assisted by various subcommittees concerned, for instance, with production, training, wages and work norms, young workers, and health and safety. Each is chaired by a member of the trade union committee.

Teams of workers known as "brigades", in respect of which regulations were issued on 15 December 1975,[13] elect a council from among their members by show of hands to take care of matters of direct interest to them, such as the preparation of production programmes, work organisation, or the engagement of new members. The management must take account of their views. For some time now the brigades have tended to become self-managing wherever possible in various respects including the distribution of wages and bonuses among their members.[14]

At the 16th congress of the trade unions the attention of the unions was drawn to a number of problems, and they were asked to step up their activities[15] through the various means open to them such as workers' assemblies and the standing production committees, particularly in order to reduce absenteeism and to improve working conditions and accident prevention.

A new factor of growing importance in Eastern Europe, particularly in the USSR, is social planning; this has spread progressively since 1971 to individual undertakings, many of which already have a social planning service. Short-term social measures are included in the collective agreement; long-term social development plans with mandatory force containing major social measures to be taken at the level of the undertaking are laid down jointly by the management and the trade union committee after a period of consultation. These measures relate to such matters as the elimination of arduous tasks, in particular through mechanisation and automation, to the prevention of accidents, to raising the workers' standard of general and technical education and to increasing their participation in the management of production. This social planning, which is becoming an integral part of the planning of the undertaking, linking up with the economic targets established for it in the five-year plans, foreshadows the probable content of future collective agreements in the undertaking.

As already indicated, in most countries of Eastern Europe the machinery of participation is similar to that established in the USSR. Accordingly the following pages deal with the specifically national features of participation in Bulgaria, Czechoslovakia, the German Democratic Republic, Hungary and Romania.

Bulgaria

In Bulgaria economic committees set up by government decision in 1964 (under the name, at that time, of production committees) still exist, and perform important functions side by side with the trade unions. These functions were specified in provisions adopted by the Council of Ministers in November 1970, and are to be included in the new Labour Code under preparation. Apart from the manager of the undertaking, who acts as chairman with a casting vote, half of the members of an economic committee are representatives of the management and half of the personnel, making a total varying from 11 to 21 members. The representatives of the personnel are elected for two years on the occasion of a workers' general meeting (or at a meeting of delegates where the workforce exceeds 300 persons); at least half of them must be manual or non-manual workers directly engaged in production work. These economic committees, in agreement with the trade union organisations, lay down the labour aspects of the undertaking's economic plan. They approve the distribution of work among different workshops and units, as well as the undertaking's balance sheet. Any differences of opinion which may arise between this committee, the trade union and the manager of the undertaking are submitted for arbitration to administrative and trade union bodies at a higher level.

Nowadays it is generally the trade union which drafts socio-economic plans, which are discussed in the trade union committee before being submitted to the undertaking's economic committee.

The workers' general meeting (or the meeting of their delegates in large undertakings), convened by the economic committee and the trade union committee, adopts the works rules, the draft plan and the collective agreement for the undertaking, which is then signed by the manager of the undertaking and the chairman of the trade union committee. The meeting examines the pay system, the periodic activity reports of the economic committee, the balance sheet and various measures affecting the activities of the undertaking, especially those designed to improve the working and living conditions of the personnel. Workers' general meetings also take place at the level of the undertaking's departments and workshops.

In 1974 the Council of Ministers and the Central Council of Trade Unions jointly adopted a decision on relations between the manager and the trade union in the undertaking. The decision stresses the need for close co-ordination between the five-year plans and the collective agreements. Nowadays the collective agreements in most large undertakings are signed for five years. Under the new draft Labour Code, a collective agreement is concluded in an undertaking to supplement labour legislation, and may be for either one or five years, according to whether the undertaking's plan to which it corresponds is itself for one or five years. With the consent of the Central Council of Trade Unions and the ministry concerned, a collective agreement may be signed for a department or even a section of an undertaking if the unit concerned has its own accounting facilities, even if it is not a legal entity.

Production conferences are held monthly. Proposals and criticisms put forward on those occasions are recorded in a special register and information must be given at the following meeting on the measures

183

planned to implement them, or the reasons why it has not been possible to take them into account. Section and workshop production conferences also discuss the draft collective agreement.

It has been observed on occasion that if the economic committee plays a predominant part in decisions on the various activities of the undertaking, this complicates the tasks of the management and may give the workers the impression that the trade union has only an advisory role. Conversely, if the trade union plays a predominant part, it is the economic committee which may seem to have no more than an advisory role.

In a state economic organisation comprising several undertakings, the workers' right to participation is exercised through the organisation's economic council. The members of this council are the general and other managers of the state economic organisation, the managers and trade union committee chairmen of the affiliated undertakings, a representative of the central trade union committee for the industry concerned, the heads of the legal and accountancy departments and possibly other persons such as representatives of youth organisations; and representatives of various bodies such as government departments and territorial people's councils are invited to some of the meetings. The council meets at least once every half-year, approves the principal tasks of affiliated undertakings, examines the management's activity reports from the point of view of what is known as "social supervision", adopts the organisation's plan and balance sheet, lays down the technical policy to be followed, and deals with a number of questions with regard to such matters as remuneration and distribution of the funds available.

The body which directs a state economic organisation is the organisation's executive bureau, which consists of from seven to 15 members elected by the economic council. Various councils and committees are set up under the executive bureau to deal with matters bearing on the development of the organisation.

In order to improve workers' participation in management, each state economic organisation has a council of trade union committee chairmen from all the units belonging to the organisation. This council co-ordinates the activities of the constituent trade union organisations, organises competition between their workers and drafts agreements on social policy within the economic organisation, which are then signed by the general manager and the central trade union committee for the industry concerned.

Czechoslovakia

In Czechoslovakia the trade union committee in the undertaking has the power of decision on a number of questions relating to occupational safety and sickness insurance. It has the power of co-decision with management in certain fields specified in the Labour Code, in particular in respect of approval of the undertaking's collective agreement, the introduction or amendment of pay systems, the endowment and use of funds for cultural and social purposes, the publication or amendment of work regulations and improvement of the working environment and of welfare services. Under this power of co-decision the committee may insist that a subject shall be submitted for its prior consent, or that a measure shall be taken only in agreement with it. In that case at least half of its members must be present, and the decision must be taken by simple majority.

The trade union committee must also be consulted in relation to certain questions in respect of which the final decision belongs to the management; that is the case for instance with the preparation and implementation of the undertaking's economic plans, the long-term planning of the undertaking's development, its investments, rationalisation (including the closure of a factory or a workshop, or a halt to production), improvement of productivity, and the principles of raising pay in parallel with this improvement and that of quality, and with the savings made. The committee also has monitoring powers with regard to the application of legislation and other rules in force.

There are also other trade union bodies such as the workshop committees, the sector committees and the sector representatives. The trade union committee of an undertaking may delegate to workshop committees powers of co-operation with regard, for example, to the preparation of plans for the workplace and supervision of their executions; the conclusion of collective agreements and supervision of their application; improvement of health and safety; and action to facilitate the employment of women, young persons and the disabled; it may also delegate to them powers of co-decision with regard to the transfer of a worker from one workplace to another for longer than one month, and the introduction or amendment of output norms.

In 1972 the eighth congress of the trade unions addressed itself to the problem of absenteeism and the lack of dynamism of a certain number of workers.[16]

Since 1974 government agencies and the national trade union authorities have shifted their attention to long-term (15-year) economic and social planning, while the management and trade union committees of undertakings prepare their own economic and social development plans on an annual, quarterly or monthly basis, or even for periods of ten days. Collective agreements are co-ordinated with the annual plan, and special importance is attached to social welfare planning.[17]

In 1976 directives were issued by the government and the Central

Council of Trade Unions on the signature, content and monitoring of collective agreements.[18]

German Democratic Republic

In the German Democratic Republic Article 21 of the Constitution guarantees the right to participation and a chapter of the new labour Code[19] entitled "Management of undertakings and workers' participation" is specially devoted to it.

Joint directives of the Council of Ministers and the federal executive of the confederation of trade unions were issued in 1971 regarding the signing of annual collective agreements for individual undertakings (plans for the advancement of women workers and young workers must be annexed to such agreements).[20] Collective agreements may even be signed at the level of departments of large undertakings. Since the beginning of 1975 unions and management have prepared five-year economic and social development plans for undertakings, and it is intended to extend the duration of such collective agreements to five years. Plans for the introduction of new techniques and for the installation of modern equipment now form an integral part of an undertaking's economic and social plan.

Another directive, whose principles have been incorporated in the Labour Code, dealt with labour-management collaboration in the planning of rationalisation measures. When these measures entail the transfer of workers, the latter have to be informed, in close collaboration with the trade union committee of the establishment, of their future responsibilities, of the skills needed and of their future conditions of employment. Agreements concerning changes in their pay (which must not be to their disadvantage) and conditions of employment have to be arrived at with the workers and teams of workers at least three months in advance in cases where they are to take on new tasks.

There are also various "social working groups", generally set up on a provisional basis to facilitate certain administrative and managerial tasks. "Workers' and peasants' supervisory committees" are elected at workers' general meetings to operate in undertakings.

From the time of the economic reform up to the beginning of the 1970s, management was in the hands of a single person, who had the assistance of a basically advisory and supervisory body—the economic committee—which was not a trade union body but which contained a minority of representatives elected by the personnel and a majority of appointed or ex officio members. As in other Eastern European countries, this body was abolished in 1973 and its functions were taken over by the trade union or the standing production committee or council.

Generally speaking, the trade union committees in establishments see that the management informs the workers at monthly intervals of the fulfilment of plan targets and of targets for the coming month. However, it has been observed that, in their everyday activities, the trade union bodies often face bureaucratic tendencies, and that they apply themselves to defending the workers against any violation of rights guaranteed to them by legislation.[21]

Hungary

In Hungary for a long time the trade union committee in the undertaking in practice performed the functions of the workers' assembly, though it determined its attitude only after exchanges of views and discussions with the workers, in particular at the time of production meetings or trade union meetings, and made use of their proposals and criticisms; however, in workshops and small factories, a meeting of trade union members basically took care of participation.

Production committees similar to the economic committees mentioned in the preceding pages stopped functioning in 1968.

In April 1973 the Central Council of Trade Unions defined the role of the trade unions in participation, and stressed the importance of trade union general meetings and production committees.

In confirmation of the development which has taken place in recent years, the Council of Ministers and the Presidium of the National Council of Trade Unions jointly adopted on 7 May 1977 a decree concerning democracy in the undertaking.[22]

The system is based on participation meetings or bodies at various levels as determined by the internal rules of the undertaking in accordance with its particular characteristics and local conditions so that they may function regularly and effectively. All major questions affecting the operation of the undertaking and the interests of the workers must be discussed at these meetings, which must as a rule be held outside working hours.

Direct participation of the workers implies consultations at the levels of work teams ("brigades"), workshop, and section or department[23]. It is indirect at the level of a large undertaking as a whole or its different establishments, where it normally operates through meetings of representatives elected by groups of workers in conjunction with the trade union council or trade union committee of the undertaking. (In large undertakings the trade union body is called a "trade union council", the "trade union committee" being the executive body of this council; elsewhere, the trade union body bears the name of "trade union committee".) In small undertakings participation is direct, and is exercised through the workers' general meeting. A consultative meeting of brigade foremen with the manager and the trade union bodies must take place at least once a year.

The undertaking's trade union council or committee, in joint meetings with the workers' representatives, must decide on its attitude to the broad principles for utilisation of the wage fund and other funds of the undertaking, in particular those for social and cultural needs; it must also decide on the preparation, signature, implementation and amendment of collective agreements, and on the undertaking's social plan; comment on the undertaking's annual and long-term plans; and evaluate the work of the manager of the undertaking and his immediate subordinates.

The trade union council or committee (which, it must be stressed, comprises a majority of production workers) may veto measures contrary to rules in force or to collective or other agreements. This right has assumed special importance for some years. The management may take decisions affecting the workers' conditions (for example, on output norms, hours of work and pay) only with the agreement of the trade union council or committee. If no agreement is reached the matter remains in suspense until new arrangements are made, if necessary through higher or regional agencies of government departments or the trade unions. In practice the management itself may give up a measure on which the trade union committee lets it be known that it will use its right of veto.[24]

From 1973 on, undertakings drew up five-year plans, and since then collective agreements of five years' duration have been signed in all undertakings. They are drafted within work brigades, production committees and trade union meetings. Generally, there is a review of the existing agreement each year to check whether its provisions have been respected and ascertain what provisions the workers would like to see changed, in particular as regards the distribution of profits. Special committees composed in particular of the undertaking's lawyers, planners and trade unionists take part in this review. The draft put forward by such a committee is then examined by the management and by the trade union council or committee before being put to the workers for discussion. Thus there is an annual revision of certain parts only of a collective agreement rather than negotiation of an entirely new one.

The decree of 7 May 1977 was followed by an Act concerning the management of state undertakings, which came into force on 1 January 1978. The Act recalls that the manager is still personally responsible for the running of the undertaking from a social as well as an economic point of view. It stresses that he and the other members of the management must rely on the workers' representative bodies and encourage them to participate in coming to decisions and in monitoring the application of decisions.[25]

Before adoption of the decree and the Act referred to above, major surveys had been carried out, including some by trade unions, to examine how participation was working in practice and how the workers in fact saw it, the aim being to find out the best ways of developing and improving the system.

For instance, early in the 1970s a survey was carried out by the Institute of Legal and Administrative Sciences bearing on 14 undertakings in different industries and analysing some 5,000 questionnaires completed by workers, as well as a number of interviews with workers and executives.[26] To the question: "Do you consider that life in your undertaking is democratic?", 37 per cent of the workers answered that, on the surface it seemed that the workers were consulted but that in fact decisions were made without taking account of their opinions; 10 per cent that they had the opportunity to express their opinions but did not dare to do so; and 10 per cent that so long as things went well in the undertaking, nobody was interested in expressing an opinion. However, 73 per cent of the workers thought that they could give advice, 28 per cent even on questions not directly concerning their own work. Interviews with executive, supervisory and technical staff showed that some managers thought that their scope for decision was limited (by long-term plans, etc.). To the question: "What do you think is the reason why, in many undertakings, many of the workers do not take part in discussions on draft collective agreements?", the replies of the workers were distributed as follows: "Because they were satisfied with the draft", 17 per cent; "Because they did not attribute much importance to collective agreements", 12 per cent; "They didn't ask our opinion", 19 per cent; "Giving your opinion is useless because in any case no account will be taken of it", 34 per cent; "Don't know", 14 per cent; no answer, 4 per cent.

Other surveys have shown that the information supplied by the management was regarded as incomplete, too abstract, containing too many data or statistics which were difficult to understand and insufficiently analysed, or else devoid of interest.[27] Sometimes too, a number of workers considered that it was useless to discuss things with people who did not have any power of decision over the matters at issue.

According to the results of a survey carried out in 1974 in three factories of a Hungarian undertaking manufacturing railway equipment and rolling stock[28] the fields which, in the workers' view, lent themselves best to participation were those where decisions (a) concerned the workshop or the factory, (b) directly affected their own situation in the workshop or factory, and (c) once taken, allowed them the opportunity intervene, such as decisions on work organisation, working conditions and wages. They felt they had less opportunity of participation in, or even showed ignorance of, decisions at higher echelons of the undertaking, for instance concerning production, personnel policy and the introduction of new techniques, as well as fields such as recruitment, which they saw as clearly a management responsibility. With regard to the respective contributions of the trade union committee and the party in the advancement of their interests, the results were the following: on the services of the party, 46.6 per cent of the workers were "entirely satisfied"; 34.6 per cent were "on the whole satisfied"; and 12.9 per cent "more or less satisfied"; on trade union action, the corresponding percentages were: 20.3, 34.9 and 33.1.[29]

The party and the Central Council of Trade Unions tended to take the view that there was no real need for new bodies in the participation structure, but that the operation of the existing bodies should conform better to the objectives sought. That is the line which was followed in the above-mentioned decree of 7 May 1977 which laid down that management should *(a)* see that workers were informed clearly and in good time of any subjects which they would be asked to discuss, so that they might be fully prepared to do so, and be informed of the various possible solutions; *(b)* make certain that the executives who had the relevant information and power of decision would participate in the various meetings concerning their fields of competency; *(c)* identify the reasons why workers hesitated to give their opinions and do everything possible to encourage them to change their attitude[30]; *(d)* see that action was taken on the conclusions reached, suggestions made and comments expressed at the meetings and say what, if anything, could not be done and why; *(e)* and prepare minutes of these consultations, and give a written reply within a fortnight when special consideration had to be given to the questions raised.

Under the same decree government departments and other supervisory bodies must keep track of developments and assist in the promotion of democracy in undertakings; see that middle management and supervisors had more scope and that they received appropriate training on democracy in the undertaking; and require managers to submit periodic reports on the development of democracy in their undertakings, and to publicise successful achievements and organise exchanges of views. The evaluation of members of management should take into account what they had done to develop democracy in their undertakings and the appreciation of their work by the personnel. All training courses were to cover the theoretical and practical aspects of democracy in the undertaking.

Romania

In Romania a national conference of the Communist Party decided in December 1967 on a change-over from management by a single manager to the collective management of undertakings, and collective management bodies were introduced by a decision of the Council of Ministers on 3 April 1968. An Act dated 28 October 1971 made formal provision for workers' assemblies, and, at the same time, introduced collective management bodies for units or establishments. Today the collective management bodies are governed by an Act dated 6 July 1978 on the organisation and management of state socialist entities,[31] which states that the workers' assembly is the supreme body in collective management, and exercises supervision over the management bodies of the unit.

The workers' assembly (or the meeting of workers' representatives in large undertakings[32]) takes place at least twice a year.[33] The assembly discusses and approves the undertaking's five-year and annual plans, and its programmes to raise labour productivity, lower production costs, and improve the workers' working and living conditions. It approves collective agreements, and analyses and approves the annual reports of the undertaking or establishment and of the collective management bodies. It distributes the profit-sharing fund. The assemblies elect the workers' representatives on the collective management bodies, and may also decide on the removal of those whose work on those bodies leaves something to be desired. Also present at assembly meetings are the members of the workers' councils described in the next paragraph, and representatives of party and other mass organisation bodies higher up in the hierarchy.

In 1971 the undertaking's workers' council superseded the management committee, which was akin to the economic committees mentioned earlier. The workers' council has considerable powers. It meets at least once a month, and consists in principle of from 15 to 35 members, including from seven to 17 workers' representatives elected for a two-year term (at least three-quarters of them must be manual workers or foremen working directly on production). Other members are the secretary of the party branch in the undertaking, who takes the chair, the manager of the undertaking (senior vice-chairman), the chairman of the trade union committee (vice-chairman), the secretary of the youth organisation (vice-chairman), the chairman of the undertaking's women's committee (who is also a vice-chairman in undertakings employing many women workers), executives holding posts of responsibility, and specialists and scientists. The workers' council is responsible for adopting appropriate measures on work organisation and vocational training; it appoints senior executives, including section and branch heads, and may amend or terminate their contracts of employment. The council is responsible for drafting the undertaking's five-year and annual plans in accordance with guidelines of the group of undertakings concerned, and watches over the correct application of labour legislation and collective agreements, of the pay system and of health and safety standards. It also keeps an eye on implementation of the production plan and improvement of the workers' working and living conditions, and draws up the programme of measures to increase productivity. It is now under an obligation to draw up a budget of income and expenditure for the undertaking and to approve the balance sheet. It drafts the collective agreement with the trade union committee. The workers' council is assisted in its work by specialised committees.

The executive of the workers' council, with from five to 11 members, meets at least every ten days; it is chaired by the manager of the undertaking and consists of several senior executives and specialists appointed by the workers' council from among its members. The secretary of the party branch, the chairman of the trade union committee, the secretary of the youth organisation and the chairman of the women's committee also attend these meetings when certain problems are discussed. The duty of the executive is in particular to organise execution of the tasks laid down in the plan. It approves staff transfers and applies disciplinary sanctions in respect of senior executives. It takes all appropriate measures in regard to health and safety and the improvement of working conditions, and also deals with cultural and welfare activities for the workers.

The manager assumes the day-by-day management of the undertaking, puts the decisions of the workers' council and its executive into effect and monitors the application of those decisions.

In addition, there are in each undertaking a "technico-economic council" and a "council for workers' supervision of economic and social activity"; the latter has the right to make proposals to the management bodies of the undertaking (in the first instance to the workers' council) for action to improve the undertaking's operations in general and in particular sectors.

At the level of each department, office, section or workshop, the staff forms a "work group" or "work collective" within which there is very active participation. Any recruitment must be brought to the knowledge of the work group in the sector where the new recruit is going to work. A promotion to a managerial post may be made only in favour of the candidate who has obtained the best recommendation as regards performance of service obligations and respect for order and discipline at the workplace from the group to which the candidate belongs. The work group is under an obligation to make a firm stand against any shortcomings and, if necessary, to insist on the imposition of penalties, which may go as far as the termination of the employment of workers who infringe order and discipline and do not do their work. At the request of a work group for the application of a disciplinary sanction, the collective management body is under an obligation to take the necessary action and to inform the group of its decision.[34] However, an important role is played by the "workers' judicial councils" in undertakings.[35]

The Act of 6 July 1978 also specified in detail the participation structure to be set up at the level of groups of undertakings. They too have their workers' councils, which include, among other members, the managers and workers' delegates of attached undertakings, again with an executive, and assemblies held at least once a year, which play a role comparable with that of workers' assemblies in undertakings; these assemblies are attended by members of the management, of the over-all workers' council, and of the workers' councils of attached undertakings or of their executives, as well as other workers' representatives.

An Act dated 26 December 1978[36] specified the rules concerning the formation, planning, distribution and payment of the profits of undertakings.[37]

A survey of undertakings carried out by the Bucarest Institute of Philosophy in 1971 had revealed, side by side with the many positive aspects of participation, a number of weaknesses in practice, for example in regard to supervision of the application of collective agreements. Thus, in 20 reports of general meetings, while there were 55 critical observations by the management on the work of the personnel, there was only one suggestion of a critical nature made by a worker concerning management methods in the undertaking; this state of affairs gave the impression that monitoring of the activities of management was perhaps not always very highly developed.[38] Two-thirds of the suggestions submitted by workers at the general meeting reappeared later, which probably reflected a lack of supervision over action taken on suggestions.[39] As regards participation in assemblies, a little less than a third of the workers questioned replied that they had regularly attended meetings in the previous two years; a third replied that their attendance had been occasional; and a little more than a third said that they had never gone, or only rarely, having been on night shift.[40]

In the following years various experiments were made with the object of increasing participation in practice. The preamble to the 1978 legislation referred to above lays emphasis on "raising the level of workers' self-management" and "consolidating the economic and financial self-management" of undertakings. Various provisions have also increased the responsibilities of undertakings, particularly as regards raising productivity and quality, and more efficient use of production capacity, raw materials and energy; total output is no longer the main index in the planning system and use is made of the concept of value added or "net output".[41]

POSSIBLE EFFECTS OF ECONOMIC CONCENTRATION

It is possible that the recent trend towards mergers of industrial undertakings in Eastern Europe may raise problems of adjustment of the existing participation machinery. For example, in Hungary undertaking trade union councils have already been set up in the large merged undertakings and, as mentioned, the Romanian management bodies of associated undertakings have collective management bodies similar to those of individual undertakings and establishments.

We have also seen that, in Bulgaria, the chairmen of trade union committees from affiliated undertakings are members of the economic councils of state economic organisations and that, in addition, they form a council which co-ordinates the activities of the basic trade union organisations and prepares agreements on social policy within the said economic organisations. In the USSR a new industrial structure was introduced in 1973. Since then, undertakings, especially those of small size, have been merged into giant groups to improve the efficiency of their management. This required a corresponding reorganisation of the trade union structure, with the establishment for each group of a trade union committee which is thus at a higher level than the trade union committee of the constituent factories and establishments. A group trade union committee consists of from 21 to 65 members (depending on the number of unions represented) elected by secret ballot at the trade union general meeting (or delegate conference) of the group for a term of two or three years. The committee may elect a presidium, consisting of the chairman and vice-chairmen and additional members up to a total of between seven and 15 persons. In principle the committee has the same rights in relation to the management of the group as the trade union committees at lower levels have in relation to the management of the factories and establishments that make up the group. It is still too early in general for there to have been an appreciation of the effect of this concentration of important decisions on actual participation by the workers at the level of undertakings and establishments.

Notes

[1] This reform provides an incentive for undertakings to raise their targets continually, since the bonus obtained from the material incentives fund is of the order of 100 per cent in the case of fulfilment of targets which show an increase over the previous year's plan, while it is only 40 per cent in the case of over-fulfilment of targets already existing in an earlier year.

[2] In some cases certain categories of workers employed in a given undertaking belong to another trade union; in the USSR this is so in the case of works medical officers, for example.

³ The systems have a legal foundation in the provisions of labour codes adopted in recent years or now in course of adoption. See in particular for the USSR the Act of 15 July 1970 to approve fundamental principles governing the labour legislation of the USSR and the Union Republics (ILO: *Legislative Series*, 1970—USSR 1), particularly Section 97; Act of 9 December 1971 to approve the Labour Code of the RSFSR (ibid., 1971—USSR 1) and amendment (ibid., 1974—USSR 2); for Czechoslovakia, consolidated text of the Labour Code as published, ibid., 1975—Cz. 2; for the German Democratic Republic, Labour Code of 16 June 1977 (ibid., 1977—Ger. D.R. 1); for Romania, Act (Labour Code) dated 23 November 1972 (ibid., 1972—Rom. 1). In Hungary a special paragraph concerning participation was added to the Labour Code on 1 January 1978. In addition a number of recent provisions, most of which have been published in the ILO *Legislative Series*, relate to collective agreements—this applies in particular to the German Democratic Republic and Hungary.

⁴ See A. S. Pachvov (ed.): *Sovetskoe trudovoe pravo* (Moscow, Juridishkaya Literatura, 1976), p. 165.

⁵ See "Participation of workers in management in the Soviet Union: Trade union committees and permanent production conferences", in *Industry and Labour* (Geneva, ILO), 1 Oct. 1958, pp. 252–257; see also order of the Council of Ministers and of the Central Council of Trade Unions of the USSR dated 9 July 1958 to approve regulations respecting standing production conferences for industrial undertakings, construction sites, state farms, machine and tractor stations and technical repair centres (ILO: *Legislative Series*, 1958—USSR 2); ukase dated 15 July 1958 of the Presidium of the Supreme Soviet of the USSR to approve regulations respecting the rights of factory, works and local trade union committees (ibid., 1958—USSR 3); resolution of the Central Committee dated 17 December 1957 (*Trud*, No. 297, 19 Dec. 1957); resolution of the Central Council of Trade Unions of the USSR concerning the tasks of Soviet trade unions in relation with the decisions of the Plenum of the Central Committee of the Communist Party of the USSR (ibid., No. 10, 12 Jan. 1958).

⁶ For the regulations in force on collective agreements, see ILO: *Legislative Series*, 1977—USSR 1.

⁷ ibid., 1971—USSR 2.

⁸ Figure for June 1978.

⁹ ILO: *Legislative Series*, 1958—USSR 2.

¹⁰ In 1978 these societies had more than 18 million manual and non-manual worker members (*Trud*, 20 July 1978, p. 2).

¹¹ See *Les syndicats soviétiques et la participation des travailleurs à la prise de décisions*, mimeographed document submitted to an international trade union round table on the trade unions and workers' participation in decision making, Sarajevo, 10–11 May 1971, p. 4.

¹² According to official information given in *Trud*, 20 July 1978, p. 2, this occurred in 3,500 cases in 1977.

¹³ See *Sbornik zakonodatel' nikh aktov o trude* (Moscow, Jurizdat, 1977), pp. 65–68.

¹⁴ For further details see *Social and Labour Bulletin*, No. 3/78, pp. 227–229.

¹⁵ See L. I. Brezhnev: *The trade unions: An influential force of Soviet society*, speech at the 16th congress of the trade unions of the USSR, March 21, 1977 (Moscow, Novosti Press Agency, 1977).

¹⁶ See *Hlavní dokumenty VIII. Všeodborového sjazdu* (Prague, Prace, 1972), particularly pp. 9 and 67–69, as quoted in "La participation en Tchécoslovaquie", in *Annales de l'économie publique, sociale et coopérative* (Liège, Centre international de recherches et d'information sur l'économie collective), Apr.–June 1978, p. 163.

¹⁷ For further details on social welfare planning and the development of welfare activities in general, see Vladimir Tesar: "Social welfare programmes in Czechoslovak entreprises", in *International Labour Review*, July–Aug. 1978, pp. 441–451.

¹⁸ See *Sbírka Zákonů*, 30 Sep. 1976, No. 25, item No. 103, pp. 564–569.

¹⁹ ILO: *Legislative Series*, 1977—Ger. D.R. 1.

²⁰ ibid., 1971—Ger. D.R. 1.

²¹ See Reinhard Sommer: *Some aspects regarding the involvement of the working class and its trade unions in planning and managing national economy in the German Democratic Republic* (Geneva, ILO, 1974; mimeographed doc. No. SWPDU/D64), p. 6.

²² See *Magyar Közlöni*, No. 36, 7 May 1977, pp. 529–531.

²³ It had already been possible for several years for a workshop meeting to be convened at any moment and on any subject by the management, the trade union or the workers themselves. These meetings give the workers the opportunity to express themselves and to make proposals on questions relating to production, wages, health and safety, and welfare facilities.

[24] For examples of the application of this right of veto see László Gál: "Le droit de veto et son application", in *Revue syndicale hongroise* (Budapest), No. 12, 1975, pp. 8–9, which states: "Although positive co-operation with those who manage the economy may be considered a general feature of society, we cannot help noticing that particular persons and groups do make mistakes—whether because they are ill informed, because of faulty interpretation of local or central provisions, or because they start from a false conception of individual or group interests. Arbitrary actions and bureaucratic administration are occasionally encountered."

[25] For a more detailed analysis of the Act see *Social and Labour Bulletin*, No. 2/78, pp. 122–123.

[26] See Gabriella Garancsy: "A vállalati demokrácia egyes munkajogikérdései (Egy vizsgálat tapasztalatai)", in *Allam és Jogtudomány* (Budapest), No. 1/1975, pp. 12–57.

[27] See for example Artúr Kiss: *Hogyan fejlödik a szocialista demokrácia?* (Budapest, Kossuth Könyvkiadó, 1975), pp. 148–149.

[28] See L. Héthy and Cs. Makó: *Az automatizáció és a munkástudat* (Budapest, Institute of Sociological Research and of Scientific Research on Work Safety, 1975), pp. 96–97, and idem: "Workers' direct participation in decisions in Hungarian factories", in *International Labour Review*, July–Aug. 1977, pp. 9–21.

[29] Héthy and Makó: "Workers' direct participation in decisions in Hungarian factories", op. cit., p. 15.

[30] Already in 1975, at the 11th congress of the party, support of, and protection for workers who criticised the management was one of the factors mentioned as leading to improved participation (see *Az. MSZMP XI. Kongresszusának jegyzökönyve*, op. cit., p. 468).

[31] Act published in *Buletinul Official* (Bucarest), Part I, 12 July 1978, No. 56 (see in particular pp. 14 et seq.).

[32] These meetings of workers' representatives are preceded by workers' meetings in individual departments, workshops, building sites or establishments, at which workers elect their representatives by show of hands. A recent article spoke of a general meeting of some 300 delegates in an undertaking employing over 8,000 persons which had been preceded by 11 department meetings (I. Poenaru: "Penser plus économiquement", in *Les syndicats de Roumanie* (Bucarest), No. 4/1978, p. 8).

[33] In units where activities are seasonal, general meetings are organised at the beginning and end of work campaigns.

[34] These provisions are contained in the Labour Code (ILO: *Legislative Series*, 1972—Rom. 1), sections 65, 75 (2) and 10 (2), and in Act No. 12 of 1971 concerning conditions of employment and promotion in socialist state entities (*Buletinul Oficial*, Part I, 21 Oct. 1971), sections 16 and 12.

[35] See "Magistrats sans robe", in *Les syndicats de Roumanie* (Bucarest), No. 49 (2), 1973, pp. 16–17.

[36] See *Buletinul Oficial*, Part I, 27 Dec. 1978, No. 114, pp. 1 et seq.

[37] For adaptations of this participation system to agriculture, see *Scintia* (Bucarest), 3 Feb. 1979, pp. 1 et seq.

[38] See Maria Popescu: *Conducere, participare, constiintă* (Bucarest, Academia de Stiinte Sociale Si Politice a Republicii Socialiste România, Editura Academiei Republicii Socialiste România, 1973), pp. 116–117.

[39] ibid., p. 124.

[40] ibid., p. 128.

[41] See also "Les assemblées générales de travailleurs: L'autodirection ouvrière en action", in *Actualités roumaines* (Bucarest), 25 July 1978, p. 2; Ioan Poenaru: "Un nouveau mécanisme économique en Roumanie", in *Les syndicats de Roumanie*, No. 2/1978, pp. 4 et seq.; G. Cretoiu: "Improvement is imperative", in *Romania Today* (Bucarest), No. 4/1978, pp. 2–4; and Constantin Enache: "Workers' self-management, a topical issue", ibid., pp. 11–12.

SUMMARY AND CONCLUDING REMARKS

DIVERSITY, SIMILARITIES AND COMPLEMENTARITY

10

The main impression left by this general survey of institutional machinery for workers' participation in decisions within undertakings is that of considerable diversity, which reflects the diversity of conditions in which the machinery was introduced, developed and continues to evolve—historical, political and cultural conditions, stage of social and economic development, degree and type of industrialisation and so forth.

The diverse forms of machinery can be classified into several main types of system:

(a) self-management or related systems such as producers' co-operatives;

(b) parity or minority representation of workers on boards of directors, supervisory boards or other management bodies, both in the private and the public sector;

(c) works councils or committees, and similar or specialised institutions for representing the workers;

(d) collective bargaining, as it is conducted in market economy countries; and

(e) the operation of trade unions, through the influence they exert on management or by virtue of their own powers, in some centrally planned economy countries, in particular those of Eastern Europe.

Yet in spite of this diversity, the participation machinery set up in many countries tends to have the same objective and a sort of complementary character: an attempt is made to associate the workers and their representatives in certain kinds of decisions, thereby avoiding whenever possible a situation in which those decisions would be taken unilaterally; and there is a certain complementarity in the sense that, for a given type of decision, in the same country and sometimes even in the same undertaking, resort may be had to a series of different kinds of participation arrangements that can complement each other or be linked together in a logical sequence, as when the communication of information is followed by consultation in a works council, leading finally to collective bargaining proper.

MAIN TRENDS

The fundamental importance of collective bargaining in many countries has been highlighted in this study, and it has been shown that in practice, negotiations are also conducted on works councils whenever it is a matter of co-decision, or even of extensive consultation on problems which are important for the workers. Even compromises reached between shareholders' representatives and workers' representatives on boards of directors (or supervisory boards) where such dual representation exists are often in fact the outcome of bargaining. Thus, job security safeguards may be adopted in some countries in the course of negotiation of a collective agreement in the undertaking, while in other countries they may be agreed upon at a meeting of the supervisory board, though even in that case the decision is likely to have been preceded by active negotiation.

Collective bargaining proper is increasing at the levels of the undertaking and of the establishment in many market economy countries and is covering a much greater number of subjects—including working conditions and the organisation of the undertaking, welfare, and employment and income security—than in the past, when bargaining usually centred on questions of wages and fringe benefits, grading, hours of work and holidays.

In the centrally planned economies of Eastern Europe, along with a strengthening of the powers of trade union committees, there has been a development and enrichment of collective agreements in the past ten years or so (after the economic reforms), culminating in social planning at the level of the undertaking. In Yugoslavia, in view of the special character of its self-management system, it can be considered that the self-management agreements and social compacts, which have assumed great importance, give rise to very frequent negotiations.

The development of other machinery for participation in many countries has generally not slowed down the development of collective bargaining—rather the opposite: collective bargaining remains a fundamental element of workers' participation in decisions in undertakings, whether looked at from the usual point of view of the conclusion of collective agreements or in the broader sense of informal discussions and reciprocal concessions on boards of directors or supervisory boards with seats for workers' representatives or on works councils and similar bodies.

Works councils and kindred bodies were originally set up chiefly to deal with matters of common interest other than those reserved for collective bargaining, and such bodies continue to raise problems in a number of countries. In some developing countries they have aroused little enthusiasm and are virtually dormant, where they still exist at all. The workers have lost interest in bodies which in law or in fact have no powers of decision on matters except on some minor welfare questions. The trade unions fear that the councils will be used to undermine them, and employers fear that under the influence of workers' representatives, particularly trade union representatives, they may become militant bodies attacking management prerogatives. However, there is now some movement away from the idea of participation seen as collaboration between workers' and management representatives on non-controversial subjects towards the idea of participation in dealing with conflict situations, most often involving bargaining in the broad sense of the term, whether formal or informal.

In some industrialised countries, particularly in Western Europe, where trade unions are strongly entrenched in undertakings, works councils have acquired powers of co-decision on a number of important matters of personnel policy and other welfare questions, more often through legislation than by collective agreement. In most countries where this development has taken place, the trade unions are in fact duly represented on these bodies. Membership may be restricted to trade union representatives; the trade unions alone may have the right to nominate candidates (at any rate for the first round); the chairman of the trade union branch in the undertaking and other trade union representatives may be members of the council ex officio; the elected workers representatives may in practice be active trade unionists, irrespective of whether the workforce in general is unionised or not.

The strengthening of the role of works councils by increasing their rights of co-decision and signing more agreements within them has been particularly marked in those countries where, traditionally, collective agreements in the strict sense were signed not at the level of the undertaking but at that of the industry, or regionally or nationally, or even for all occupations; it is current practice today in some of those countries for agreements made in works councils to supplement national industrial agreements.

In some countries works councils have also become valuable sources of information and useful bodies for consultation, capable of supplementing and strengthening collective bargaining and occasionally of being specifically linked with it. In various quarters there is emphasis on the possibility of supplementing traditional collective bargaining by other forms of participation, such as participation in works councils and workers' representation on management bodies. This trend is particularly evident where collective bargaining customarily takes place at levels other than that of the undertaking.

One of the main problems is whether participation should extend to the earlier stages of forecasting and of the basic decisions which are customarily taken at the highest level in the undertaking. Serious objections are often raised in employers' circles in the private sector to the development of participation at these stages. Even in public undertakings, far-reaching participation in management has in fact remained the exception in many countries, whether industrialised or developing. According to the particular country, important decisions are the responsibility of government departments and planning bodies, or of the central management bodies of groups of undertakings, although active consultation may take place in certain countries with senior trade union bodies and with the workers or their representatives in individual undertakings. Even under systems which more or less fit the description of "self-management", the authorities retain major powers of decision and still appoint the general managers of undertakings and, in some cases, their principal assistants. However, there has been a strengthening of the role of workers' assemblies and a decentralisation of participation machinery, often down to the level of the workshop or work team.

However that may be, it is probable that the scope of participation will increasingly extend beyond welfare activities and services and questions of personnel policy; that it will penetrate to the roots of the decision-making process in the field of forecasting; and that it will cover economic, financial, commercial, technical or organisational decisions which may affect employment and working conditions. Hence the claims put forward and the discussions arising in different parts of the world in connection with the representation of workers on the management bodies of undertakings. As we have seen, such representation may raise issues of principle for the trade unions, not to mention the practical difficulties to which it may give rise in some developing countries (such as the relatively low level of education of the workers and even of their representatives).

The repercussions of participation on efficiency continues to give rise to concern. The effect of current economic difficulties on labour-management relations and participation is hard to assess. It is nevertheless probable that a number of factors—such as the search for employment and income security in the industrialised market economy countries, adjustment to technological progress and reforms in the international economic order, the achievement of higher production targets in the centrally planned economies, people's participation in development in the developing countries, increasingly broad access to education, the development of more critical and open attitudes, and general concern with improving the quality of working life—will continue to give rise to an expansion of workers' participation in decisions within undertakings in its different forms in the course of the coming years.

According to the report on an international management seminar on workers' participation held under the auspices of the Organisation for Economic Co-operation and Development in 1975, it was clear that, for a complex of reasons concerned with social and economic changes, widespread pressures would continue to be experienced for more extensive workers' and trade union participation. Such pressures might be expected to take the form of a variety of changes, according to the nature of the industrial relations system and social institutions of the particular country. Amongst the changes would be changed structures for the enterprise itself—and worker representation on its directing organisation; strengthened works councils; changes in the structure and content of collective bargaining; more participative styles of management; and greater participation in the planning and carrying out of jobs.[1]

A growing number of writers are indeed tending to advocate the establishment of an integrated network of participation bodies to correspond to the various processes and levels of decision, since a single type of institutional machinery can no longer, on its own, meet the whole range of participation needs.[2] In addition, it seems that the practical application of participation in its different forms benefits from clear recognition of the existence not only of common interests, but also of divergent interests which must be satisfied as fully as possible, always bearing in mind that in the medium and long terms the parties are in many respects interdependent in the undertaking.

Throughout this study we have seen that there is virtually no participation system which does not give rise to problems, and it is unanimously agreed that, in this field as in many others, there are no ready-made solutions. Participation institutions are complex and always come into existence and develop against a specific historical, political, economic, social and cultural background which is never quite the same elsewhere.

Notes

[1] See *Workers' participation*, Final report on an international management seminar convened by the OECD, Versailles, 5th–8th March 1975, International Seminars 1975–1 (Paris, Organisation for Economic Co-operation and Development, 1976), p. 7. In the same connection see: *Policies for life at work* (Paris, Organisation for Economic Co-operation and Development, 1977). The above-mentioned final report also referred (pp. 57–58) to remarks made by certain participants on the shortcomings of collective bargaining as the sole form of workers' participation, such as that it was not continuous in character.

[2] This is the point of view put forward by Walker, op. cit., p. 20.

201

APPENDIX

MAIN CHARACTERISTICS OF WORKS COUNCILS AND
SIMILAR BODIES ESTABLISHED BY
LAW IN VARIOUS COUNTRIES

AUSTRIA

Body

Works councils.

Basic legislation

Federal Act of 28 March 1947 (*Legislative Series (LS)* 1947—Aus. 2) as amended in 1948, 1954, 1962, 1965 (*LS* 1965—Aus.2) and 1971 (*LS* 1971—Aus. 2), and repealed and superseded by a Federal Act of 14 December 1973 concerning collective labour relations (*LS* 1973—Aus. 2), as amended in 1975 and 1976; and ordinance of 24 June 1974.

Undertakings covered

Undertakings permanently employing at least 5 persons.

Composition

Workers (wage earners and salaried employees) only are represented. There are separate councils for wage earners and salaried employees if each of these categories comprises at least 5 workers. Subjects of common interest are dealt with in a committee on which members of the two councils sit and vote jointly; if the workers so decide by ballot, there may be a common works council.

There is a central works council when the undertaking comprises several establishments.

Number of workers' representatives

No. of wage earners/salaried employees	No. of representatives
5-9	1
10-19	2
20-50	3
51-100	4
>100	1 additional representative for every 100 workers or fraction thereof
⩾1 000	1 additional representative for every 400 workers or fraction thereof.

Representatives of the workers' and employers' organisations may be invited to take part in the proceedings.

Method of election of workers' representatives

All wage earners and salaried employees aged 18 years or over (including homeworkers regularly working for the undertaking) have the right to vote.

Lists of candidates may be put up only by groups of wage earners or salaried employees; however, lists may bear the name of a particular organisation and may include trade union representatives from outside the undertaking up to a proportion of one-quarter.

Election is by direct secret ballot and seats are allotted under proportional representation.

Term of office

Three years.

Powers

General principles

The powers of the works council are consultative and cover all sectors of management of the undertaking: economic problems, personnel questions and welfare matters.

The council meets every quarter (every month if it so wishes) with the employer (in the presence on occasion of representatives of the organisations competent to sign collective agreements, whenever the matters involved may have appreciable repercussions for the personnel) to obtain information on all matters affecting the interests of the personnel and on general management policies, including investment plans and the financial position of the undertaking. It must be notified in advance of recruitments and promotions, and may demand to be consulted on these subjects. The council monitors the application of labour legislation and of collective and other relevant agreements; it participates in all inspections of the plant and may participate in inspections relating to on-the-job training.

In special fields

The council's special rights (co-determi-

205

nation or right of veto) include the determination of wage, job and piece rates and output and other bonuses when such matters are not governed by collective agreements; permanent transfers involving pay reductions or less advantageous conditions of employment; holiday rosters; working hours; the adoption and application of disciplinary rules; and dismissals (when it has not expressly approved them, it may in some cases challenge them before the conciliation board, particularly if it considers them socially unjustifiable).

It must be consulted on changes such as reduction of activity, relocation of an establishment, mergers, or changes in equipment or work organisation; if agreement cannot be reached on measures to avoid or soften the impact of unfavourable consequences for the personnel, the question is settled by an arbitration committee. It may participate in the planning and carrying out of on-the-job training and retraining programmes.

The council may sign company agreements on a number of subjects such as training, hours of work, measures to prevent or lessen the unfavourable effects of certain changes (reduction of activity, relocation, mergers, etc.) for the personnel, health, safety and work humanisation measures and periods of notice and grounds for dismissal. In the event of deadlock, most of these matters can be settled by an arbitration committee.

Other key features

The legislation provides for general meetings of the personnel and of the wage earner and salaried employee groups at least once every six months (these may be attended by the employer on his representative and by representatives of the workers' and employers' organisations concerned) and, if necessary, for sectional meetings.

A council of young workers' representatives is set up when the undertaking regularly employs at least 5 persons under the age of 18.

The works council collects contributions, after the agreement of general meetings of the personnel or group, from all the workers (subject to a maximum of 0.5 per cent of gross wages) to cover its expenses and to finance the welfare services. It may also set up and manage provident schemes.

The central works council or (when there is only one establishment) the works council of the undertaking appoints from among its members the workers' representatives on supervisory boards of joint stock and limited liability companies.

In undertakings employing more than 400 workers, if the council believes that the management is acting contrary to the general interest and not taking any notice of the council's views, it may lodge a protest with the competent authority under a special procedure; in the case of closure proposals, this protest entails a stay of execution for four weeks.

BELGIUM

Body

Works council.

Basic legislation

Act dated 20 September 1948 (*LS* 1948—Bel. 8), as amended in 1953, 1954, 1963, 1967 (*LS* 1967—Bel. 1) and 1971 (*LS* 1971—Bel. 1); order of the Regent dated 13 June 1949 (*LS* 1949—Bel. 7), as amended several times; royal order dated 18 February 1971, as amended in 1975 and 1976; and royal order dated 11 October 1978, made under an Act dated 5 August 1978.

Undertakings covered

Since the royal order of 11 October 1978, undertakings employing an average of at least 100 persons.

Composition

Wage earners and salaried employees are represented in proportion to their respective numerical strength.

The head of the undertaking is chairman. He may appoint one or two representatives, but their total number must not exceed that of the workers' representatives; since the royal order of 11 October 1978 his representatives must be in a position, on the basis of the management functions which they perform, to commit the employer.

The assistance of experts, either from the undertaking or from outside, may be obtained.

Number of workers' representatives

Number of workers	Number of representatives
<100	4
101-500	6
501-1 000	8
1 001-2 000	10
2 001-3 000	12
3 001-4 000	14
4 001-5 000	16
5 001-6 000	18
6 001-8 000	20
>8 000	22

When the undertaking employs not fewer than 25 persons under the age of 21, those young workers are represented, depending on their number and the total numerical strength of the workforce, by from one to three representatives.

Method of election of workers' representatives

The council is elected by all the workers of the undertaking by proportional representation.

Only "representative workers' organisations" may put up lists of candidates, which must give each category of the workforce—wage earners and salaried employees—representation proportionate to its numerical strength.

Term of office

Four years.

Powers

General principles

The council, which meets at least once a month, may present its views and submit suggestions or objections on such matters as training activities, measures which might affect work organisation or the organisation of the undertaking, conditions of work, and productivity.

The employer is required to supply the council with information, in particular on personnel policy (including the rules for recruitment and selection), productivity, the economic and financial position of the undertaking and operating results, plans and prospects, including those for the structure and development of employment in the undertaking.

In special fields

The special powers of the council include the determination of the general principles to be followed in cases of recruitment and dismissal; the drafting and amendment of works rules, including those relating to the dates of annual holidays and work rosters; the management of the undertaking's welfare schemes and supervision of all general provisions relating to welfare, skills and vocational training.

Other key features

Safety and health are normally dealt with by a special committee which has a legal status comparable with that of the council. Grievances and trade union matters are dealt with by trade union representatives (elected under special rules).

The provisions on application of the works council system were markedly strengthened in 1967. The rights to information and of consultation and co-determination were widened through collective agreements, consolidated in 1972, the consolidated text being amended in 1974 and extended by royal orders of 1972 and 1974; the rules to be followed in regard to information were spelt out in detail in a royal order dated 27 November 1973.

BURUNDI

Body

Works council.

Basic legislation

Labour Code dated 2 June 1966 and ministerial ordinance dated 24 November 1970.

Undertakings covered

Any establishment employing at least 30 workers.

Composition

The employer and representatives of the personnel.

Number of workers' representatives

Number of workers	Number of representatives
30-50	3
51-200	4
201-500	5
501-1 000	6
>1 000	1 additional representative for every 500 additional workers.

Method of election of workers' representatives

The workers' representatives are elected by a secret ballot of the entire workforce.

A second poll is organised if the number of votes recorded in the first ballot is less than half the number of registered voters.

Lists may be submitted through trade unions that have obtained prior ministerial authorisation in this connection.

Term of office

One year.

Powers

The council, which meets at least once a quarter, has the task of ensuring permanent contact between the employer and his personnel, affording the latter an opportunity to submit their wishes and individual or collective grievances concerning conditions of work and protection of the worker, the application of collective agreements, occupational grading and wage rates and to pass on to the employer any useful suggestions for improvement of work organisation and productivity, or of the application of rules relating to health, safety and social security.

FRANCE

Body

Works committee.

Basic legislation

Ordinance dated 22 February 1945, as amended in 1946, 1947, 1951, 1954, 1958, 1959, 1966 (*LS* 1966—Fr. 1), 1969, 1971 and 1972.

Other slight changes in the works committees are the result of provisions which do not amend the basic texts, such as an Act of 1973 on the improvement of conditions of work and an Act of 1975 on collective dismissals.

Undertakings covered

All undertakings employing not fewer than 50 workers.

Composition

Representatives of the workers only, divided (unless otherwise agreed) into two or three electoral colleges as follows: *(a)* wage earners and subordinate salaried employees; *(b)* department chiefs, supervisors, engineers, and administrative, commercial or technical staff; and *(c)* in undertakings where there are no fewer than 25 department chiefs, engineers, and administrative, commercial or technical staff, those persons form a college of their own.

The employer is chairman.

If the undertaking includes establishments employing not fewer than 50 workers, establishment committees and a central works committee are set up, with the latter consisting of 1 or 2 full and substitute members from each establishment committee up to a maximum strength of 15 full members in all. It meets at least twice a year.

Number of workers' representatives

Number of workers	Number of representatives
50-75	3
76-100	4
101-500	5
501-1 000	6
1 001-2 000	7
2 001-4 000	8
4 001-7 000	9
7 001-10 000	10
>10 000	11

Under the legislation of 1966 the committees may be enlarged by way of collective agreements.

One representative, who must be employed in the undertaking, may be designated by each trade union "recognised as being representative" to attend meetings in an advisory capacity.

A workers' representative may be recalled by the trade union which nominated him if the recall is approved by secret ballot by the majority of the electoral college to which he belongs.

Method of election of workers' representatives

The committee is elected by all the workers, under proportional representation. Only "the most representative trade unions for each category of personnel" may put up lists of candidates.

However, if the number of votes cast is less than half the number of registered voters, a second ballot takes place and the electors may then vote for lists other than those submitted by the above-mentioned trade unions.

Term of office

Two years.

Powers

General principles

The committee, which meets at least once a month, co-operates with the management on improvement of the personnel's terms of employment and working and living conditions; all rules relating to these matters are referred to it for its opinion.

The committee manages the undertaking's welfare schemes itself or supervises their management.

It must be consulted on all matters concerning the organisation, management and general progress of the undertaking, and it must receive quarterly and annual reports on production, financial results, investments and plans for the following financial year, wages, conditions of work and the employment situation in the undertaking. The committee must be informed of proposed changes in equipment and production or operational methods and of their effect on working conditions and employment, and it must be consulted in advance on those subjects.

The head of the undertaking must make a reasoned report on the action taken on the recommendations and wishes of the committee.

In special fields

The opinion of the committee must be sought whenever works rules are being drawn up, and before any reduction of the workforce, in which event it must be consulted on the ways in which it is proposed to carry out the reduction (phasing, resettlement measures, etc.).

It is to be consulted on general problems relating to training, on any changes in working hours or annual holiday schedules and before the introduction of new working methods or changes in work pace and productivity standards. Jointly with the personnel representatives, the works committee appoints the worker representatives on the health and safety committee and, in undertakings employing more than 300 workers, it sets up committees on training, on the employment and conditions of work of women and young persons, on housing assistance and on improvement of working conditions.

Under an Act and decree of 1977, in undertakings employing over 300 workers, the employer must submit for the opinion of the works committee, as a basis for action programmes, an annual "social report" concerning in particular the employment situation, absenteeism, pay, working conditions, health and safety, welfare activities, training and labour-management relations (this report is also communicated to the trade union representatives in the undertaking). The committee's agreement is required for the appointment of the works doctor.

Other key features

The workers in all undertakings elect, in addition to the works committees, personnel representatives who deal primarily with grievances and who assume some of the functions of a works council where none exists.

Under an Act of 1968 each representative trade union may form a trade union section within the undertaking and may appoint one or more trade union representatives, according to the numbers employed, to represent it in dealings with the employer. Specialised committees may be set up; they may include experts from the undertaking. The works councils of joint stock companies may have recourse to the help of a chartered accountant, paid by the firm, and 2 to 4 of their members attend meetings of the board of directors or of the supervisory board in an advisory capacity (1 representative of wage earners and salaried employees and 1 of staff management and supervisors, or one of each of the two latter categories if there are three electoral colleges in the undertaking).

GABON

Body

Standing joint economic and social committee.

Basic legislation

Ordinance and decree dated 10 April 1976; sections 200–209 of the Labour Code of 1 June 1978 (*LS* 1978—Gab. 1).

Undertakings covered

All agricultural, forestry, mining, industrial or commercial undertakings employing at least 50 workers (extension to undertakings with fewer than 50 workers and to public services, in particular those of an industrial or commercial character, being possible by decree of the head of state).

Composition

Representatives of the wage earners and salaried employees, representatives of supervisory, executive and technical staff and heads of department, and 3 to 7 representatives of the shareholders.
The head of the undertaking is chairman. Sections of the committee may be set up by ministerial order in any branch of the undertaking employing at least 25 workers.

Number of workers' representatives

| | Number of representatives of— | |
Number of workers	Wage and salary earners	Supervisory, executive and technical staff and department heads
50-100	4	1
101-500	6	2
501-1 000	8	3
1 001-2 000	10	4
>2 000	12	4

Duly accredited members of the party and the labour inspector may attend all meetings of the committee as observers.

Method of election of workers' representatives

The members representing the wage earners and salaried employees are appointed half by the personnel representatives and half by officers of the party committee. The representatives of the supervisory, executive and technical staff and of department heads are elected specially.

Term of office

One year.

Powers

General principles

The committee, which meets at least once a month, must be kept informed of matters relating to the management, the financial position and the general progress of the undertaking; at least once a year the head of the undertaking must present an over-all statement on the situation of the undertaking and on its operations and his plans for the coming financial year.
The balance sheet and any other documents submitted to the shareholders' general meeting are submitted to the committee by the management, and the committee may make any comment that is called for.

In special fields

The committee gives its opinion on all measures concerning productivity, work organisation (including the introduction of innovations and new machinery), conditions of work (but not questions relating to wages), health and safety, the efficient use of human resources, and discipline. It participates, together with the appropriate government department, in the planning of training programmes. It supervises, or is itself responsible for, the management of welfare schemes.

Other key features

The committee may set up such subcommittees as it deems necessary.

FEDERAL REPUBLIC OF GERMANY

Body

Works council.

Basic legislation

Works Constitution Act dated 11 October 1952 (*LS* 1952—Ger. F.R. 6), repealed and superseded, except for certain provisions, by the Works Organisation Act of 15 January 1972 (*LS* 1972—Ger. F.R. 1), as supplemented in 1974, and order dated 16 January 1972 on application of that Act.

Undertakings covered

All undertakings employing at least 5 workers of whom at least 3 are eligible to stand as candidates.

Composition

Only workers are represented on the council; there is separate representation for wage earners and salaried employees (proportional to their numerical strengths) when the council consists of at least 3 members.

When an undertaking has several establishments, each of the latter has its own council, and a central works council is set up for the undertaking as a whole. In the case of a combine, there is provision for the possibility of having a works council for the combine.

Number of workers' representatives

Number of workers entitled to vote	Number of representatives
5-20	1
21-50	3
51-150	5
151-300	7
301-600	9
601-1 000	11
1 001-2 000	15
2 001-3 000	19
3 001-4 000	23
4 001-5 000	27
5 001-7 000	29
7 001-9 000	31
> 9 000	2 additional representatives for every additional 3,000 workers or fraction thereof.

If either the wage earners or the salaried employees are in a minority in relation to the other group, the minority group has at least the following number of representatives:

Number of persons in the group	Number of representatives
50	1
51-200	2
201-600	3
601-1 000	4
1 001-3 000	5
3 001-5 000	6
5 001-9 000	7
9 001-15 000	8
> 15 000	9

At the request of a quarter of the members of the works council or of the majority of one of the groups represented on it, an officer of a trade union represented on the works council may attend its meetings in an advisory capacity.

Since the passing of an Act on 29 April 1974 a representative of severely disabled workers elected by them in any establishment employing at least 5 such workers participates in the meetings of the council.

Method of election of workers' representatives

The council is elected by all permanently employed workers by direct secret ballot, with the wage earners and the salaried employees forming separate electoral colleges (unless they agree to a joint election). Lists of candidates are put up by groups of at least 10 per cent of the workers (100 signatures are enough in the case of large undertakings). The seats are allocated by proportional representation.

Term of office

Three years.

Powers

General principles

The employer and the council collaborate in good faith within the framework of the collective agreements in force and in co-operation with the trade unions and employers' organisations represented in the undertaking. They must abstain from any measure that might hamper the operation of the undertaking; they may not have recourse to strikes or lockouts.

The employer and the works council meet at least once a month for an exchange of views and to settle any disputes; they may conclude undertaking agreements, except on wages and other conditions of employment determined, or normally determined, by collective agreement (unless the latter expressly provides for supplementary undertaking agreements).

The council monitors the application of laws, regulations, and collective agreements (including undertaking agreements). It receives grievance complaints from the workers and approaches the employer with a view to their settlement.

In special fields

The council receives prior information and is consulted, in particular, on engagements, promotions, transfers, individual and collective dismissals (in specified cases it is entitled to object to them on certain grounds, and in the event of a dispute its opinion is communicated to the tribunal or other authority); it receives prior information and is consulted on the construction and transformation of premises, installations, processes and workplaces. The council has a right of co-determination, in particular in regard to directives concerning selection of personnel for engagements, transfers and dismissals, and on hours of work and rest and holiday periods, disciplinary matters, determination of the principles to govern selection and remuneration, piece rates, bonuses and other methods of payment by results, the adoption of new remuneration methods, vocational training, and the organisation and management of welfare services. The council has the right of co-determination when major changes are contemplated which would lead to unfavourable repercussions for the personnel (such changes must be the subject of a compromise and a "social plan"). The council assists the competent authorities in action relating to safety, health and occupational accidents.

Other key features

There is provision for the intervention and arbitration of tribunals or ad hoc mediation bodies in all cases where application of the Act is jeopardised either through the fault of one or other party or through disagreement on points of law or fact (for matters of economic policy, in particular investments, only conciliation is provided for, the final decision being reserved for the employer).

The council appoints 2 out of any 5

workers' representatives on the supervisory boards of the large steel and mining undertakings which operate the parity co-determination system under the Act of 1951.

In establishments employing at least 5 workers under the age of 18, young workers' representatives are elected by those workers by direct secret ballot for a term of 2 years. Those representatives take part in the works council's discussions, and vote, on matters directly concerning young workers. They may submit relevant proposals to the council. Young workers' representatives for the entire undertaking are also provided for in undertakings consisting of several establishments.

In principle, the council reports on its activities every quarter to a general meeting of the personnel to which the employer is invited; representatives of the trade unions represented in the establishment may attend this meeting in an advisory capacity and the employer may be accompanied by a representative from his employers' association.

Separate meetings by sectors may be organised, if necessary. Each year, the employer or his representative must report to a general meeting of the personnel on the situation of the undertaking and on personnel matters.

In establishments with more than 20 workers, safety representatives are appointed by the employer in consultation with the works council.

Body

Economic committee.

Basic legislation

As for works council.

Undertakings covered

Undertakings employing over 100 workers.

Composition

The committee consists of 3 to 7 members who must belong to the undertaking, and of whom 1 at least is a member of the works council; its members are appointed by the works council and may include senior executives. By a majority decision the economic committee may delegate its duties to a committee of the works council.

Powers

The economic committee must receive information from the employer each month on production methods and plans, the financial situation of the undertaking, production and sales. It must be informed of investment plans, structural changes and any project appreciably affecting the interests of the personnel. It reports to the works council and, with the latter, is consulted by the employer regarding the information on the situation and prospects of the undertaking which he must supply every quarter to all members of the personnel.

IRAQ

Body

Joint work organisation committee.

Basic legislation

Labour Law (No. 1 of 1958), as amended in 1961 (*LS* 1961—Iraq 1) and superseded by Chapter X of the Labour Code of 1970 (*LS* 1970—Iraq 1).

Undertakings covered

All undertakings employing more than 30 workers.

Composition

Equal numbers of representatives of the employer and of the personnel.

Number of workers' representatives

Number of workers	Number of representatives
31-99	2
$\geqslant 100$	3

Method of election of workers' representatives

In the (rare) event of there being no trade union committee in the undertaking, the workers' representatives are elected directly by the workers from among members of the personnel; otherwise the trade union appoints these representatives on the joint committee.

Every effort must be made to ensure that all sections of the undertaking are represented.

In a public undertaking or group of public undertakings with a board of directors the representatives of the management must be members of the board; one must be a workers' representative on the board, who chairs the joint committee with a casting vote. In other cases management and workers' representatives alternate in the chair each month, as in undertakings that are privately or semi-privately owned.

Term of office

Two years.

Powers

General principles

The committee, which meets at least twice a week, must strive to obtain maximum collaboration between the management (or employer) and the personnel in the interest of the workers and of the undertaking. The committee represents the personnel in all matters pending between the workers and the employer.

It monitors conditions of work and strives to organise industrial relations in the best way possible and to settle disputes.

The decisions of the committee, which generally take the form of proposals or recommendations, are taken by simple majority. In the event of a dispute, decisions voted unanimously are binding on the parties, subject to the possibility of appeal to the labour court.

In special fields

The committee examines the undertaking's production plans and issues directives for their successful implementation; organises periodical discussions between the management and the personnel with a view to improving production and gathering suggestions; and examines works rules and working conditions in order to seek their improvement.

Other key features

A committee of 5 members has special responsibility for training matters.

LUXEMBOURG

Body
Joint works committee.

Basic legislation
Act dated 6 May 1974 (*LS* 1974—Lux. 1).

Undertakings covered
Craft, industrial and commercial undertakings in the private sector employing at least 150 workers.

Composition
The committee has an equal number of members representing the employer and the personnel.
The employer chairs the committee.
Advisers appointed by the nationally most representative employers' and workers' organisations, whether they belong to the personnel of the undertaking or not, may take part in the meetings of the committee in an advisory capacity whenever an absolute majority of one of the various categories of members so requests; the number of such advisers may not exceed half that of the members of the committee in the particular category.

Number of workers' representatives

Number of workers	Number of representatives
< 500	3
500-1 000	4
1 001-1 500	6
1 501-5 000	7
>5 000	8

Method of election of workers' members
The workers' members are elected by the one or more groups of personnel representatives (there may be separate groups of representatives of wage earners and salaried employees), by separate ballots if necessary, with proportional representation and according to the respective proportions of wage earners and salaried employees in the undertaking (if one of these categories forms at least 10 per cent of the total personnel, it must have at least 1 member on the committee).

Term of office
Four years.

Powers

General principles
The head of the undertaking must inform and consult the committee before taking any important decision on the introduction or changing of equipment, working methods or production processes. He must inform and consult it at least once a year on manpower requirements and on training measures. The committee must be informed and consulted, in principle beforehand, on any economic or financial decision which could decisively influence the structure of the undertaking and the level of employment (for instance on the volume and trend of production, investment policy, plans for closure or relocation of the undertaking, the restriction or extension of its operations, mergers or changes in its organisation); the possible repercussions on employment, and on terms of employment and conditions of work, must be examined, as well as social measures being taken or contemplated, such as retraining and resettlement.
The committee must be informed and consulted in writing at least twice a year on the economic and financial progress of the undertaking (the head of the undertaking presents the committee with an over-all report, also containing specific information on wage and investment trends and, in joint stock companies, the annual balance sheet and all other documents submitted to the shareholders' general meeting).

In special fields
The committee, which meets at least four times a year, has a power of co-decision on the introduction or alteration of health and safety measures, the establishment or amendment of the general principles governing the selection of workers for employment by the undertaking and their assessment, promotion, transfer or dismissal, as well as the adoption or amendment of works and shop rules.
In the event of disagreement, recourse to the official conciliation and arbitration procedure is possible.
The committee supervises the management

of welfare schemes, including those relating to housing.

Other key features

A note by the head of the undertaking in the minutes of a meeting of the committee that some item of information supplied is confidential may be challenged by appeal to the director of the Labour Inspection Service, whose decision is final.

In addition to joint works committees, there are elected personnel representatives (of wage earners and salaried employees respectively (they include representatives of young workers), who are mainly responsible for dealing with grievances and welfare activities, and who are consulted on works rules.

There are also safety representatives.

The head of the undertaking or the board of directors is required to make a reasoned report to the committee on the action taken on its decisions.

MAURITANIA

Body

Works advisory committee.

Basic legislation

Act dated 11 July 1974 (*LS* 1974—Mau. 2).

Undertakings covered

Undertakings normally employing more than 250 workers.

Composition

Representatives of the personnel.
The head of the undertaking is chairman. When the undertaking has establishments employing more than 250 workers and located more than 50 km away, establishments committees are set up under the same rules and there is a central committee for the undertaking.

The committee may constitute subcommittees to examine special problems.

Number of workers' representatives

Number of workers	Number of representatives of wage earners and salaried employees
250-500	3
500-1 000	4
>1 000	5

A higher number of members may be provided for by agreement.

One representative of engineers and executive staff.

One representative of supervisory staff.

When there is a trade union branch in the undertaking with a trade union representative recognised under a collective agreement, he is a member of the committee ex officio.

Experts and technicians of the undertaking not belonging to the committee may be called upon by the chairman to take part in some of its meetings at the request or with the consent of the committee.

Method of election of workers' representatives

The workers' representatives are elected by the personnel (which is divided into three electoral colleges—wage earners and salaried employees, supervisory staff and engineers and executive staff) under a system of proportional representation.

Lists of candidates are put forward by the national executives of the workers' organisations.

If, on the first ballot, the number of voters is less than half of the number of persons entitled to vote, a second ballot is held, with lists which may be amended by the said national executives.

Term of office

Two years.

Powers

General principles

The committee, which meets at least once a quarter, has strictly advisory powers. It co-operates with the management in improving the working and living conditions of the personnel and in improving the productivity and progress of the undertaking; it may submit any suggestions in this connection.

In special fields

Once a year the committee receives from the head of the undertaking a report on the welfare services, sports, cultural and educational activities and vocational training, with statistical information on the results obtained, the benefits provided, the numbers and categories of beneficiaries and an indication of the management's plans.

Plans, decisions and rules relating to the above-mentioned fields and to housing for the personnel are referred to the committee for its opinion.

Other key features

There are also personnel representatives who may simultaneously be members of the committee.

NETHERLANDS

Body

Works council.

Basic legislation

Act dated 4 May 1950 (*LS* 1950—Neth. 2), repealed and superseded by an Act dated 28 January 1971 (*LS* 1971—Neth. 1), supplemented by an Act dated 23 August 1974 on financing the training of council members and amended in 1976 (in respect of groups of undertakings), and subsequently by an Act dated 5 July 1979 (*LS* 1979—Neth. 1).

Undertakings covered

Undertakings employing at least 100 workers (subject to ministerial approval, the tripartite Economic and Social Council may set the minimum at less than 100 for certain industries).

Composition

Each list of candidates (see under "Method of election") must be made up in such a manner that, as far as possible, all categories of workers are represented.

When an undertaking has separate sections, these sections may each have a works council.

Merging of works councils within an undertaking or a number of undertakings is possible. In a group of undertakings the employer may set up a group works council, and must do so if so requested by the majority of the works councils in the group.

Exemptions from the obligation to set up a works council are possible.

Number of workers' representatives

Number of workers	Number of representatives
25-50	3
50-100	5
100-200	7
200-400	9
400-600	11
600-1 000	13
1 000-2 000	15
> 2000	2 additional representatives for every additional 1000 workers (maximum 25 representatives)

Members of the supervisory board, managers or experts may be requested to attend in order to discuss a specific subject at meetings of the council or its committees. Standing committees may be set up for matters relating to certain categories of personnel or for specific subjects, as well as committees responsible for preparing reports for later study; these committees may include other workers employed in the undertaking.

Method of election of workers' representatives

The council is elected by all the workers. A list of candidates may be submitted by any trade union having members in the undertaking after consulting those members on the composition of the proposed list, or by one-third or more of the workers who are not members of a trade union submitting a list (30 signatures suffice).

The standing orders of the council may provide for separate lists for different categories of personnel.

Term of office

Two years.

The standing orders may specify a term of 3 years and may limit re-eligibility.

The employer or the council may make a reasoned request to the industry committee concerned (see under "Other key features") to suspend an elected member of the council for a specified period after giving the member the possibility of being heard.

Powers

General principles

Meetings between the management and the works council may be convened by either party at two weeks' notice. Such meetings must take place at least six times a year to discuss questions on which consultation is considered by one or other side to be desirable, or on which consultation is prescribed by law. The direction of the undertaking's affairs in general must be discussed at least twice a year.

The opinion of the works council, which was already required in respect of important decisions such as a major change in the organisation of the undertaking, total or partial closure or relocation, considerable reduction or expansion of activity, merger or association, is henceforth also required for major investments or loans, collective recruitment and the setting-up of new undertakings.

The council must be given a statement of the reasons for, and probable consequences of, decisions submitted for consultation. In addition to information for joint meetings or on matters submitted for co-decision or consultation, the employer must supply twice a year a report on the operations and results of the undertaking, including its investments in the Netherlands and abroad; the annual accounts; long-term plans and any financial estimates relating to them, as well as internal manpower forecasts.

In special fields

As before, the consent of the works council must be obtained for all decisions relating to the drafting or amendment of works rules, and to the establishment or modification of pensions schemes, profit-sharing or savings plans, hours of work and all arrangements relating to working hours and holidays, and to health and safety.

For a number of measures which hitherto only required consultation, co-decision is now compulsory: that is the case, in particular, of the establishment or modification of systems of remuneration or evaluation, measures concerning young workers or the welfare facilities provided by the undertaking, questions concerning shopfloor consultation, grievance procedures, measures concerning training and recruitment, and dismissal and promotion policies.

The head of the undertaking must supply a summary of the reasons for the decision contemplated and of its probable consequences for the personnel.

Compulsory co-decision does not apply in cases in which the subject has already been covered in a collective agreement.

Other key features

Like the general meeting of shareholders, the works council may nominate candidates (other than employees of the undertaking and trade union representatives) for appointment to the supervisory board, and has a right of veto when new members are co-opted to serve on that board.

As far as possible, the council must ensure consultation of the personnel on the subject of work and the delegation of responsibilities.

Application of the legislation on works councils is the responsibility of the tripartite Economic and Social Council and the joint industry committees set up by that Council for various groups or categories of undertakings. Those committees provide mediation in the event of a dispute before it goes to the local court for decision.

If the works council fails to agree on a matter subject to co-decision, an appeal lies to the industry committee, the minister, the local court and the court of appeal.

When the employer rejects the decision of the works council, as a whole or partially, he must inform the council of his reasons and may not implement his decision before one month has elapsed. For decisions subject to consultation, the works council has the possibility of appealing to a special chamber of the Amsterdam court. However, the time-limit and the possibility of appeal are not applicable in the case of compulsory consultation on the appointment or removal of a manager.

PAKISTAN

Body

Works council.

Basic legislation

Industrial Relations Ordinance, 1969 (*LS* 1969—Pak. 2), as amended in relation to works councils on various occasions, in particular in 1970, 1972, 1973 (*LS* 1973—Pak. 1, codified text) and 1977.

Undertakings covered

Undertakings or establishments employing at least 50 workers.

Composition

Representatives of the employer and an at least equal number of workers' representatives.

Method of appointment of workers' representatives

The trade union recognised as bargaining agent in the undertaking or establishment appoints the workers' representatives on the council; in the absence of such a trade union, those representatives are chosen from among the personnel.

Powers

General principles

The council is responsible for all action likely to promote and maintain good relations between the employer and the workers.

In special fields

The council must facilitate the settlement of disputes by negotiation; promote employment security, occupational safety and health, good conditions of work and job satisfaction; encourage vocational training; and examine any other question of common interest with a view to improving industrial relations.

Other key features

If the employer or the bargaining agent notices that a labour dispute has arisen or is about to arise, that party's written observations may be submitted to the council, with a copy to the other party, so that the council may attempt to settle the dispute within 10 days or some other jointly agreed period, before any notice of strike or lockout is given which would set in motion the procedure of conciliation, and possibly later of arbitration.

SPAIN

Body

Works committee.

Basic legislation

Decree of 18 August 1947 (*LS* 1947—Sp. 3), supplemented by decrees of 11 September 1953 and 24 June 1963, and superseded by the transitional provisions of a royal decree of 6 December 1977 and subsequently by sections 63 ff. of a "workers' charter" embodied in an Act of 10 March 1980.

Undertakings covered

Every establishment in which 50 or more workers are permanently employed.
In some circumstances a joint works committee may be set up for several establishments of which none has as many as 50 permanent workers.
A central works committee, of not more than 12 members appointed by the works committees in individual establishments, may be established by collective agreement.

Composition

Only the workers are represented on the committee.

Number of workers' representatives

Number of workers	Number of representatives
50-100	5
101-250	9
251-500	13
501-750	17
751-1 000	21
> 1 000	2 additional representatives for every 1 000 workers or fraction thereof, with a maximum of 75 representatives

Method of election of workers' representatives

Normally there are two electoral colleges, one consisting of administrative and technical staff and the other of unskilled and semi-skilled workers. A third college may be established by collective agreement.
Candidates may be nominated by the trade unions, or by groups consisting of three times as many workers as there are seats to be filled; the workers making a nomination must be employed in the same establishment and belong to the same electoral college as their candidate. Members are

elected by a personal, direct and secret ballot of all the workers.

In establishments with more than 250 workers, there is proportional representation.

Temporary or casual workers are eligible for election where they account for not less than 20 per cent of the workforce.

In certain circumstances members may be recalled by a majority vote in a meeting of the workers who elected them.

Term of office

Two years.

Powers

General principles

The committee, which must meet at least once every two months, ensures the collective representation of the interests of all the workers in the undertaking or establishment.

The committee is informed of general economic trends, the production and sales of the undertaking, the production programme and the probable employment trend. Each quarter it must receive statistics of absences from work and their causes and of occupational accidents and diseases, as well as any periodic or special reports on the working environment and preventive measures. It must examine the balance sheet.

The committee monitors the application of collective agreements and of statutory and other provisions in force, and institutes appropriate proceedings before the employer and the competent bodies or courts. It monitors safety and health conditions. It co-operates in increasing productivity.

The committee has priority in the negotiation of collective agreements at the level of the undertaking.

In special fields

The committee makes a preliminary report before the employer takes any action concerning regrading of posts, individual or collective dismissal, total or partial closure, transfer of plant, reduction of hours of work, training plans, work organisation and control, time and method study, incentive schemes and job evaluation.

The committee must be informed of penalties imposed for any very serious shortcomings.

It participates in the management of welfare services.

Other key features

In undertakings or establishments with more than 10 but fewer than 50 workers, 1 to 3 personnel representatives are elected, in particular to put forward grievances (if the workers so request, the minimum number of workers for the election of a personnel representative may be reduced to 6).

The workers of an undertaking or establishment are entitled to hold meetings, which are convened by the personnel representatives, the works committee or one-third of the workforce.

Before the adoption of the Act of 10 March 1980 a national collective agreement on collective bargaining signed in January of that year had already recognised most of the above-mentioned powers of works committees, as well as certain other rights such as that of consultation in relation to overtime.

TANZANIA

Body

Workers' council.

Basic legislation

Presidential circular dated 10 February 1970 (*LS* 1970—Tan. 1).

Undertakings covered

Public undertakings employing more than 10 workers.

Composition

The manager or general manager of the undertaking; all department or section chiefs; the chairman and members of the branch of the workers' organisation set up in the undertaking; a certain number of specially elected workers' representatives; and in case of need and in agreement between the management and the workers' organisation, one or more co-opted members not belonging to the undertaking.

Number of workers' representatives

The number of workers' representatives specially elected to the works' council is proportional to the number of workers employed in the various departments or sections in accordance with a complicated formula as a result of which the workers' representatives, including the workers' committee members (see below), are in the majority, though without exceeding three-quarters of the total number of members of the works' council, excluding any co-opted members.

The national executive of the workers' organisation is entitled to be represented at meetings of the works' council.

Powers

General principles

The council, which meets at least every six months, advises the board of directors or management committee, which is the body empowered to determine the policy to be followed by the undertaking.

The council must receive and examine the balance sheet.

In special fields

The council gives its opinion on the measures to be taken in the undertaking in regard to government wages and incomes policy, planning, organisation of work and of the undertaking, the quality and volume of production, marketing, workers' education and other matters affecting productivity.

Other key features

The council elects, from among its members representing the workers, one-third at most of the members of the executive committee, which includes also the manager or general manager (who is chairman) and the department and section heads of the undertaking.

The main functions of the executive committee are the following: to examine forecasts and programmes relating to the improvement of productivity, workers' education and marketing and the increase of exports; to give its opinion on the execution of the undertaking's general policy as proposed by the council and approved by the board of directors or management committee; to give its opinion in general on the management of current activities in the industry concerned; and to advise the manager or general manager of the undertaking.

Body

Workers' committee.

Basic legislation

Security of Employment Act, 1964 (*LS* 1964—Tan. 2), as amended on 4 April 1975.

Powers

General principles

The committee, which meets at least once a month, facilitates good relations between the personnel and the employer.

It holds consultations with the latter in matters of discipline, works rules, in cases of reduction of the workforce and, at least every three months, on the improvement of productivity.

In special fields

The committee delegates one of its members to accompany official inspections of the undertaking.

It checks pay sheets and other documents relating to the personnel, and may report any infringement of the law or of the collective agreement to the competent authority.

It advises the employer on occupational safety and welfare.

Note

The functions of the workers' committee have now been taken over by the branch of the workers' organisation in the undertaking.

TUNISIA

Body

Works committee.

Basic legislation

Act dated 14 December 1960 (*LS* 1960—Tun. 2) and decree issued thereunder on 13 January 1962 (*LS* 1962—Tun. 1), both abrogated and superseded by Labour Code of 1966 (*LS* 1966—Tun. 1).

Undertakings covered

Undertakings normally employing at least 50 workers (including homeworkers), if the trade union or the employer submits a request to a tripartite commission, chaired by the labour inspector, which gives its ruling in the light of the undertaking's economic, labour and financial situation; this decision must be approved by the Minister of Social Affairs.

Composition

Elected representatives of the workers. The employer is chairman.
When the undertaking comprises several establishments, establishment committees follow the same rules and elect delegates to the central committee for the undertaking.

Number of workers' representatives

The composition of the committees was to be laid down in detail in regulations issued under the Labour Code of 1966.
In practice, and on the basis of earlier legislation:

Number of workers	Number of representatives
50-100	3
101-500	5
> 500	7

Method of election of workers' representatives

The method of election is to be specified in regulations to be issued under the Labour Code of 1966.
Members are elected from lists put forward by the trade union or, in its absence, by the personnel themselves.

Term of office

Two years.

Powers

General principles

The committee, which meets once a month, co-operates with the management in improving collective working conditions and the living and educational standards of the personnel.
It monitors health and safety. It is associated with the management of the undertaking's welfare schemes.
It considers any suggestions aimed at raising productivity, and it must be consulted on the drafting of works rules and on all questions concerning the organisation of the undertaking "so as to be associated progressively with its management and development".

In special fields

The committee examines individual and collective grievances.
It proposes rewards for workers who have distinguished themselves by their merit or their initiative, and penalties for those who have not applied themselves to producing normal output.

Other key features

Special rules may be laid down for undertakings in the public sector.
In undertakings with 20 to 50 workers, and in those employing a greater number but without a committee, the workers elect personnel representatives who have comparable powers.
In addition, there are trade union representatives.
Under the national model collective agreement of 1973 (LS 1973—Tun. 1), joint consultative boards with 3 workers' representatives are elected in establishments with more than 20 workers by a ballot with proportional representation as for works committees. These boards function as disciplinary boards; they study all personnel-related problems (training, promotions, transfers, welfare facilities, etc.). In the absence of a works committee, they give an opinion on individual or collective claims put forward by the trade union or the personnel.
There are also health and safety committees.

ZAIRE

Body

Workers' representative committee.

Basic legislation

Ordinance dated 1 May 1964 (LS 1964—Congo(Leo.) 2), and subsequently sections 249 – 260 of the Labour Code of 1967 (LS 1967—Congo(Kin.) 1) as amended, and Ministerial Order dated 11 August 1970.

Undertakings covered

Undertakings employing at least 20 workers.

Composition

The committee consists exclusively of representatives elected by all the workers who are sometimes divided into separate electoral colleges.

The employer or his representative is chairman.

The employer or his representative may be accompanied by managerial staff or specialists from the undertaking who attend the meetings in an advisory capacity.

Number of workers' representatives

Number of workers	Number of representatives
20-99	3
100-499	5
500-1 000	9
> 1 000	9 + 1 for every additional 1 000 workers or fraction thereof

These are minimum figures which may be raised by a collective agreement.

Method of election of workers' representatives

The representatives are elected under a system of proportional representation.

For the first ballot, only legally registered trade unions whose activities cover the undertaking may put up lists of candidates; if the number of votes properly recorded on that occasion is not higher than half the number of persons entitled to vote, all electors, in addition to the above-mentioned trade unions, may put up lists for the second ballot.

According to whether representatives have been elected on the first or second ballot, they are called respectively "trade union representatives" or "personnel representatives".

Term of office

Three years.

Powers

General principles

The committee, which meets at least every three months, has consultative powers covering all conditions of work.

It also meets with the employer to examine grievances and to negotiate on conditions of work.

The employer is required to supply the committee, at least every six months, with information on the progress of the undertaking and its financial situation, and on future prospects and development programmes.

In special fields

The employer is required to consult the committee with regard to hours of work, the general principles governing recruitment, dismissal and transfer, pay and bonus systems, and works rules and sometimes shop rules.

The committee participates in the management of all the undertaking's welfare schemes, and is associated with the preparation and implementation of collective training programmes. It concerns itself with measures designed to ensure occupational health and safety.

Other key features

The workers' representative committee combines the functions of personnel representatives (or shop stewards) and those which normally fall to works councils.

An agreement between the National Union of Workers of Zaire and the National Association of Zaire Undertakings dated 23 August 1977 laid stress on improving communication on labour matters in undertakings, on the presentation of claims by the trade union representatives, and generally on negotiation within the undertaking.

The health and safety committees are now governed by a departmental order dated 23 January 1978; those of mining undertakings remain covered by a departmental order dated 15 November 1973. An Act dated 29 December 1977 makes special provision for the setting-up of such committees in establishments where there are occupational health or safety hazards.

ZAMBIA

Body

Works council.

▶asic legislation

Part VII of the Industrial Relations Act, 1971 (*LS* 1971—Zam. 2), which came into force in May 1976.

Undertakings covered

Undertakings employing at least 100 workers.

Composition

One-third of the council must consist of members appointed by the management and two-thirds of members elected by the workers.

The President of the Republic may grant total or partial exemptions from the provisions of the Act to individual undertakings or to specified categories of undertakings.

Number of workers' representatives

Not less than 2 workers' representatives, nor more than 10.

Method of election of workers' representatives

Initially, in each undertaking subject to the Act, a joint working party including 4 workers' representatives appointed by the trade union, or in the absence of a union by the personnel, explains the statutory provisions relating to works councils, determines the number of members of which the works council shall consist in the particular undertaking having regard to the total number of workers, receives nominations and organises the elections, which must take place by secret ballot. When the first election is completed, this working party is dissolved.

When the workers of an undertaking are represented by a trade union, the latter must approve the nominations made by the workers; the reasons for any refusal to approve a nomination must be stated, and an appeal against such a refusal may be made to the Industrial Relations Court.

Term of office

Two years.

Powers

General principles

The main objectives of the council, which must meet at regular intervals not exceeding 1 month, are to promote the effective participation of the workers in the affairs of the undertaking and to secure the mutual co-operation of the workers, the management and the trade union in the interests of industrial peace, improved working conditions and efficiency and productivity.

The council has the right to be informed immediately in writing of all decisions of the board of directors or the management concerning investment policy, financial control and the distribution of profits, economic planning, job evaluation, wages policy and the appointment of senior managers.

It has the right to be consulted on health and welfare programmes, including medical facilities, canteens, housing and pensions schemes. It must be consulted beforehand on the appointment or removal of the manager responsible for personnel matters and labour relations.

In special fields

Approval of the council (which must not be unreasonably withheld) is required for any decision of the management on a matter of policy in the field of personnel management and industrial relations, including any decision relating to recruitment and the determination of the wages to be paid to newly engaged workers, transfers to another undertaking owned by the same employer, disciplinary rules, redundancy, incentives and bonuses, and safety. In the event of refusal of approval, and after communication in writing of the reasons, the matter is referred to a board of review consisting of 1 management representative, 1 representative of the works council and 1 member appointed by agreement between the two parties or, failing that, by an appropriate official, with the possibility of appeal to the Industrial Relations Court.

Other key features

The council must inform the management of any infringement of the provisions of the law, of collective agreements or of the works rules that may come to its notice; if an end is not put to this infringement, it must notify the trade union representing the workers in the undertaking, which must

thereupon negotiate an agreement on the measures to be taken; in the absence of such a trade union or such an agreement, the council or the trade union, as the case may be, refers the matter to the Industrial Relations Court.
The council submits an annual report on its activities to a general meeting of the personnel.
Its powers of co-decision as set out above may be suspended by order of the President of the Republic or, for a fixed period, with the written approval of the Minister of Labour.

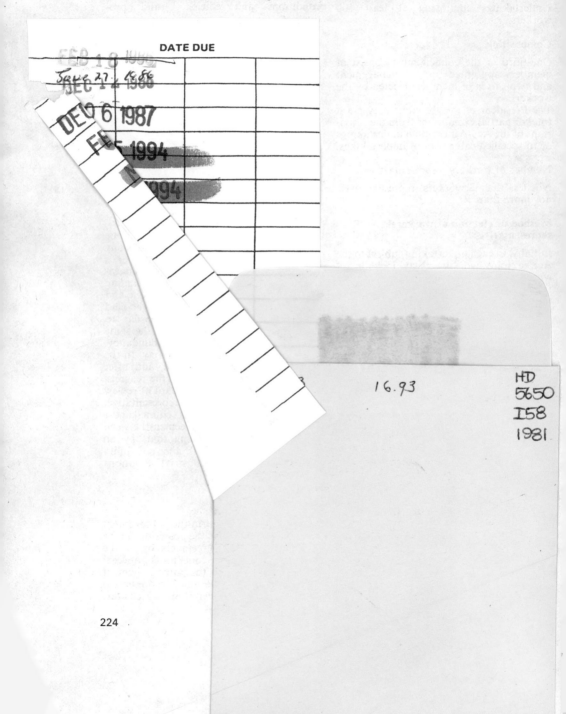